BUDDHIST MISSIONARIES IN THE
ERA OF GLOBALIZATION

Topics in Contemporary Buddhism
GEORGE J. TANABE, JR., EDITOR

*Establishing a Pure Land on Earth: The Foguang Buddhist
Perspective on Modernization and Globalization*
STUART CHANDLER

Buddhist Missionaries in the Era of Globalization
LINDA LEARMAN, EDITOR

TOPICS IN
CONTEMPORARY
BUDDHISM

Buddhist Missionaries in the Era of Globalization

EDITED BY LINDA LEARMAN

University of Hawai'i Press
Honolulu

© 2005 University of Hawai'i Press
All rights reserved
Printed in
10 09 08 07 06 05 6 5 4 3 2 1

**Library of Congress Cataloging-in-
Publication Data**
Buddhist missionaries in the era of globalization /
edited by Linda Learman.
p. cm. — (Topics in contemporary buddhism)
Includes bibliographical references and index.
ISBN 0-8248-2810-0 (hardcover : alk. paper)
1. Globalization—Religious aspects—Buddhism.
2. Buddhism—Missions—History—20th century.
3. Buddhist missionaries. I. Learman, Linda, 1950–
II. Series.
BQ5925.B83 2005
294.3'72—dc22
2004006309

University of Hawai'i Press books are
printed on acid-free paper and meet the
guidelines for permanence and durability
of the Council on Library Resources

Designed by Elsa Carl
Printed by The Maple-Vail Book Manufacturing Group

Contents

Series Editor's Preface

The usual term used to describe the spread of Buddhism is "transmission," which implies the passing down of teachings and practices from masters to disciples in established lineages mindful of preserving past traditions. Buddhism, however, has also been presented to strangers, with successful propagation requiring innovative strategies of interpretation and accommodation. In modern times, the transmitters of Buddhism have been aware of themselves as missionaries not only to their own overseas communities but to foreigners as well. As with commercial and political institutions, Buddhism survives and thrives as a globalized religion in America, Brazil, Hawai'i, China, Nepal, and other localities. It is widely recognized that globalization takes place through localization, but the strategies used by Buddhist missionaries in accomplishing this have not gained widespread recognition through sufficient study.

The present volume goes a long way toward filling this gap in our knowledge. It explores Buddhism as a contemporary religion of immense variation. In these pages, Buddhism appears as Theravada, Mahayana, and new religious movements extending beyond familiar homelands to foreign territory. At the heart of these stories are the missionaries themselves, clerics and laypersons pursuing their mission of propagating Buddhism throughout the world, especially in the West.

George J. Tanabe, Jr.
Series Editor

Acknowledgments

This book is the outcome of the conference The Globalization of Buddhism: Case Studies of Buddhist Missions held in April 2000, at Boston University. I am very grateful to all of the participants, the Anthropology Department of Boston University, and to my advisor, Rob Weller, who first encouraged me to organize a conference on this topic and has given much needed and timely, practical and intellectual support throughout the process. Professor Frank Korom, of the Religious Studies Department at BU, was also very helpful in getting me started; and Peter Gregory, Jill Ker Conway Professor of Buddhist Studies, Smith College, has been an ongoing mentor, for which I am extremely grateful. The Wenner-Gren Foundation, the Institute for the Study of Economic Culture of Boston University, and the Shelley and Donald Rubin Foundation supplied the necessary and much appreciated funding. I am also quite grateful for the cooperation I received from the contributors to the volume; and to Professor George Tanabe, editor of the Topics in Contemporary Buddhism Series; Patricia Crosby, Executive Editor of the University of Hawai'i Press; two anonymous readers; and the managing editor at the press, who all helped turn the manuscript into a well integrated book.

Introduction

Linda Learman

Peter Berger has noted four cultural dimensions of the worldwide communication and economic integration called "globalization": the cultures of international business, of the Western intelligentsia, of American popular tastes and values, and of Evangelical and Pentecostal Protestantism.[1] Although the impact of these cultures may have been the major anthropological narrative of our time, we live in an era in which non-Western traditions, such as Eastern religions, martial arts, and healing practices, have also spread around the world. Globalization has involved multi-directional flows. Given the structures of power over the last century, however, the West has had a predominant role, but not an exclusive one. The Buddhists who are the focus of this book—Theravadins from Sri Lanka; Vajrayana teachers from Tibet; Zen, True Pure Land, Shingon, and Soka Gakkai Buddhists from Japan; and two distinctive Chinese Buddhist organizations from Taiwan—are examples of transnational and cross-cultural movements resulting from and shaped by globalization but also making use of it. In the twentieth century, Buddhist traditions have not only increasingly forged links among themselves in Asia, they have also emerged from Asia, being carried by emigrants, picked up by travelers, and taught by Buddhist missionaries to new peoples of the Western and non-Western world. Moreover, now Western Buddhists are becoming influential propagators of the faith, in the West at least.

Although the papers in this book deal specifically with late-nineteenth- and twentieth-century Buddhist missionaries, Steven Kemper raised the question of whether we should view twentieth-century Buddhist missions as a critical departure from earlier Buddhists' ethos and practice. He referred to Jonathan Walters' dissertation "Rethinking Buddhist Missions," in which Walters rejected the notion that premodern Buddhism was a missionary religion, at least in the Sri Lankan Theravada tradition based on Pali texts.[2] He maintained that the texts customarily used to establish a Buddhist missionary agenda have alternative readings that were totally missed by Buddhologists, who approached their subject with Anglo-American Protestant preconceptions and purposes. "Buddhist mission," he said, "is an Anglo-American construct that has been maintained only by silencing the premodern Buddhists who paradoxically are depicted as agents" (1:5).

While I remained unconvinced by Walter's arguments about premodern Theravada Buddhism, his research into the development of Anglo-American Protestant thinking on the concepts of "mission" and "missionary" is very useful, both for the background it gives for the twentieth-century encounters between Buddhists and Protestants and for the comparative examples it affords. Thus, I shall summarize the varied meanings of "mission" in nineteenth- and twentieth-century Anglo-American discourse, drawing on Walters' and others' work, comparing them to Buddhist examples, and pointing out their impact on the development of Buddhist missions in the twentieth century. Thereafter, I shall describe in broad terms examples of premodern Buddhist "missionary spirit" and move on to a discussion of the cases presented in this book. One of the main contributions of this work is our focus on the active proselytization by Asian Buddhists themselves. The second important contribution is sociological: comparing these cases in light of Buddhist and Western social-science concepts of conversion has allowed us to come up with a typology for missions that not only helps to explain some aspects of our Buddhist data but also should be useful in the study of non-Buddhist "mission" and "missionary" efforts. I am grateful to George Tanabe for precipitating these three types of missions from the data and pointing out their relevance to this study.

ON THE DEFINITION OF MISSIONARY RELIGIONS, MISSIONARIES, AND MISSIONARY METHODS

Walters pointed out that by about the 1840s Buddhism was being called a "missionary religion" in Anglo-American discourse, and the "first systematic attempt to use 'mission' as a comparative category was made by Max Muller . . . in 1873" (99, 105). Of the eight "great world religions," Muller classed Buddhism, Christianity, and Islam as "missionary religions," in contrast to the "non-missionary religions" of Judaism, Brahmanism, and Zoroastrianism (Muller did not include Confucianism or Taoism in either of these typologies; 100, 105).

Walters identified three phases of thinking with regard to "mission" and "missionaries," although with the emergence of each, older models by no means disappeared. In the nineteenth century, the ideal missionary would have four attributes. He would be a scholar, learning the language, customs, and beliefs of others in order to undermine their religion and effect successful conversion; he would be a "civilizer," eradicating customs that were inimical to Christian values, such as cannibalism, suttee, and nakedness, while offering, in addition to the Gospel, literacy, Western medicine, technology, law, and science; he would be an aggressive "saver of souls," working to supplant false religions; and, because of his "missionary spirit," he would be the epitome of Christian life, undertaking hardships, risking martyrdom, and, sometimes, persevering *because* of suffering in order to become close to God (17–22, 27–28, 29 n75, 35–36, 173). This is the model picked up by the Sri Lankan Buddhist Anagarika Dharmapala (1864–1933), founder of the Maha Bodhi Society and one of the most influential missionary figures of twentieth-century Buddhism (see Chaps. 1 and 2); and as will be seen in the essays in this book, whether by convergence or adoption, the roles of scholar, civilizer, and converter to the truth have appeared in most Buddhist missionary agendas, Theravada and Mahayana alike.

The second phase, after World War I, was marked by a reorientation of Anglo-American Protestant thinking. It was characterized by the recognition that mission work needed to be done among the secularized at home. Moreover, missionaries were to place greater emphasis on education, women's issues, and medical, agricultural, and industrial development. This phase was also characterized by more tolerance of other religions, stemming from the idea that all paths lead to the same God and the view that "religion," itself, should be encouraged in order to counteract science, materialism, atheism, and humanism (Walters, 85–90). Influential in Chinese Buddhist circles today (see Chaps. 7 and 8) and an early proponent of studying and learning from Christianity was the Venerable Master Taixu (1890–1947; also spelled Tai Hsü) in Republican China. What he admired, however, was not its central tenets of divine creation and the resurrection, but "its ability to organize and motivate individual adherents in normative modes of belief and practice . . . to engender in diverse adherents a singleness of purpose and unified commitment to mission."[3] Like Dharmapala, Taixu wished to adopt Christian missionary methods to promote domestic religious and social reform and international ecumenical and propagation work.[4]

After World War II, in liberal Anglo-American Protestant circles a third model emerged in which dialog replaced evangelism. For the most liberal, it was accompanied by "universalism," the view that it is possible to find the true essence of religion and that to further the realization of this essence through active engagement with other religious people on an equal footing was good.[5] During this period Buddhist figures have actively engaged in Buddhist–Christian dialog, the Dalai Lama, Thich Nhat Hanh, and Nikkyo Niwano being internationally known examples. Scholars Winston King and David Chappell have observed, however, that unlike their Christian counterparts, most Buddhists have not been very interested in dialog on questions of theology or ultimate reality or in the use of dialog as a means to deepen their own understanding; rather, their motivation for engagement has tended to be to "nurture a sense of global community in a divided world," to promote interreligious cooperation for world peace.[6]

Opting for an "indirect influence of Christianity on non-Christian traditions," as Walters described post–World War II developments, was not acceptable to all Anglo-American Protestant missionaries.[7] A case in point was Pentecostalism. Emerging from the Azusa Street Revival (1906–1909) in the United States and holding that glossolalia and other gifts of the Holy Spirit were signs that the end of the world was close at hand, all early Pentecostal churches felt strongly obligated to undertake evangelical work.

Taking literally the word of the Bible, Pentecostal churches gave (and continue to give) precedence to the "'leading of the [Holy] Spirit' over administrative structures and scientific church growth formulas."[8] In contrast to the paternalistic organizations of more established Protestant denominations—that is, organizations in which church structures, financial backing, and major decision making came from a home church in North America or Europe—beginning in the 1920s Pentecostal mission strategy moved toward the creation of indigenous churches. Pentecostal missionaries became catalysts for locally organized, led, and funded churches. Their principles (articulated by the Presbyterian J. L. Nevius' *The Planting and Development of Missionary Churches* [1886]) were the "three selfs": self-propagation, self-support, and self-government.[9] The earliest missionaries even went into the field without financial backing or pledges, "relying solely on faith and prayer for support."[10]

Given their conviction that "believers can and ought to proclaim their faith wherever they will," nonordained Pentecostals were (and are) encouraged to make converts.[11] Most churches denied women ordination; yet opportunities in actual practice gave them substantial self-confidence, voice, and authority.[12] And throughout most, if not all, of their history, the majority of their missionaries have been married and single women.[13]

Although I have no evidence that they were influenced by Pentecostal examples, two Buddhist movements that share an emphasis on the grassroots, lay-witnessing approach to evangelism not unlike that of the Pentecostals are Soka Gakkai from Japan and the Buddhist Compassion Relief Tzu-Chi Foundation (referred to in Huang's chapter as Ciji, and herein shortened to Compassion Relief Foundation) from Taiwan (see Chaps. 5 and 8). In both movements, women have also been empowered and are one of the driving forces behind these primarily lay organizations (see also LeVine and Rocha on missionary women). Yet there are

notable differences. In contrast to the fragmentation of the Pentecostal movement, both have had strong central leadership, making them a unified force in
their home base and, for the Compassion Relief Foundation at least, tying their
overseas branches closely to it. Moreover, they aim for both world and personal
transformation.

While there is no doubt that most Theravada and Mahayana Buddhist organizations have engaged in what can be seen as "missionary" activity in the twentieth century, a question posed by Walters and picked up in Steven Kemper's essay
(Chap. 1), however, is whether "missions" and "missionaries" can be understood
to be a part of Buddhist institutional history *before* the nineteenth century.

The passage from the Pali canon often used by scholars as emblematic of a
long-standing, *historical* presence of a missionary ideal within the Theravada tradition is the following (I will discuss Mahayana traditions a bit further on):

> Wander about on wanderings [*carikam*], monks. For the good of many folk,
> for the happiness of many folk, out of compassion for the world, for the
> good and the happiness of gods and men, don't two of you go by one [road].
> Preach the Truth, monks, which is lovely at the beginning, lovely in the
> middle, lovely at the end, in the letter and in the spirit. Demonstrate the
> purified holy life which is fully complete. There are beings with little dust
> in their eyes; they are falling away from the Truth because they do not hear
> it. There will be people who understand. . . .[14]

According to Walters, *carikam* means "moving about" or "journey." He translated it as "wanderings," arguing that Rhys-Davids' earlier translation of *carikam*
as "mission" wrongly presupposed a category of "mission." Instead, Walters maintained that ambiguities in the Pali make it possible to read the text in two ways:
one in which the monks are enjoined to wander, with preaching as secondary; and
the other in which monks are sent out specifically to preach. Moreover, despite
the spread of Buddhism through Asia, Walters found that the Pali word for "missionary," *dhammaduta*, is of late-nineteenth-century coinage. There are quite a few
words for "preaching," as, for example, *dhammadana* ("gift of Truth"), *dhammabheri*
("drum of Truth"), *dhammadesana* ("explication of Truth"), *dhammadatha* ("discussion of Truth"), and *dhammadhaja* ("flag of Truth") (204–205, 212). But Walters
wanted to reserve the rubric "missionary" for only those religions for which proselytization is the *defining* and *essential* characteristic (169, 211); a preaching tradition
is not sufficient.

Whether ambiguities allow for both readings or not, I would agree that the

Theravada canon does not take proselytization as its *defining* characteristic. For example, canonical sources suggest that an imperative to spread the Dharma is not intrinsic to arhatship, the difference between a buddha and an arhat being the vow to become liberated so as to liberate others and the subsequent long career as a bodhisattva that finally culminates in buddhahood. Upholding the arhat ideal, the Theravada doctrinally downplays the aspiration for buddhahood, pointing to the Buddha's encouragement of his disciples to make arhatship their goal. In addition, the canons describe Pratyekabuddhas, those who achieve enlightenment without the help of a teacher and do not have disciples.

Thus, while arhats are not defined by a zeal to propagate the dispensation, central concerns have been the example of the Buddha's forty-five years of clearing away the "dust from people's eyes" and his institutionalization of the sangha through the rules for the order, so as to help others realize enlightenment and uphold a means by which the teaching could be maintained and passed on. Walter's argument only holds by using a very restricted definition of "missionary religion"; and it is clear from canonical texts and the sangha's behavior that conversion to a new viewpoint and propagation of the dispensation have been extremely important parts of Theravada Buddhism. At this point, I think that we need to abandon Walter's definition of a "missionary religion" and look at how Buddhists have approached this aspect of their practice.

Erik Zurcher suggested that the above passage does present a missionary ideal, but not one that can be characterized as a "large-scale planned missionary movement"; rather, the spread of Buddhism has depended on "the individual efforts of itinerant monks and preachers."[15] In a similar vein, Walters maintained that the "Protestant" Buddhist missionary movement begun by Dharmapala was a radical break with the premodern Theravada tradition. Perhaps the best evidence that the Theravada sangha was not constituted in the manner of nineteenth-century Protestant missionary organizations was the Protestant missionaries' own assessment that the monks were just too tolerant of other religions and too nonconfrontational.[16]

This does not, however, mean that pre-nineteenth-century Buddhists eschewed all manner of outreach or relied merely on preaching. Mahinda Deegalle, in his article on *bana*, Sinhala vernacular texts used for lecturing that began to emerge in the tenth century and that played an important role in a revival of Buddhism in parts of Sri Lanka from the thirteenth to the fifteenth centuries, showed also that such texts were intended to be read by segments of the population who were generally unable to attend preaching assemblies (that is, by common people in remote areas, sequestered queens, kings and nobles too busy to attend, and senior monks too high in the hierarchy to listen to their juniors).[17] In this we see both public preaching and vernacular texts for private study as methods of outreach, and are reminded that methods of propagation and revitalization have neither been static down the centuries nor, in some cases, so different cross-culturally.

As for twentieth-century missions, however, the experiences of colonial domination and English Protestant evangelizing presented many of the methods, as well as the challenge, to Sri Lankan Buddhists. Their missions' primary supporters were the village intelligentsia and the educated, urban middle class that had emerged over the nineteenth century.[18]

One last point. Walters noted the creation in 1989 in Sri Lanka of the Ministry of Buddhist Religion, a highly organized, state-funded, missionary project.[19] Drawing on an ideal of an Asokan Buddhist state, the ministry focuses on missions at home and abroad, and appears to have a broad base of support. Sinhala Buddhists have, in addition, continued to use much of the nineteenth-century Protestant model, as in

> "letters from the field"; conversion statistics and converts' personal recollections; warnings about the shortages of missionaries in certain parts of Europe and the United States; criticisms of those who slack off at home; missionary biographies; missionary journals; missionary keepsake volumes; scores of missionary societies and institutions for training missionaries; missiology.[20]

In Walters' view, "contemporary Sri Lankan Buddhism is swimming in missionary spirit."[21]

Despite his evaluation of a radical change having taken place in Sri Lankan missionary practice, our two chapters on Sri Lankan missionaries show both substantial borrowings and differences from Protestant models. Kemper emphasizes how missionaries work to make "Buddhism present in the world"; LeVine points out the tension between monks' securing their own salvation, the preservation of the tradition, and working for the secular and spiritual welfare of others.

What of the Great Vehicle (or Mahayana) traditions, in which the liberation of others is said to be an integral part of one's own path? How has the bodhisattva ideal played out historically in terms of a "missionary spirit"?

Studies of the spread of Buddhism to and within China largely uphold Weber's observations on elective affinities, indicating that the religious Taoists were attracted by Buddhist cosmography, ritual, vows, and meditation; the elite intelligentsia, by its sophisticated thought and the model of an aristocratic householder, the Buddhist layman Vimalakirti; political elites, by monks who were adept at rain-making, military and political strategy, miracle working, and Indian medicine; and rural folk, by miracle working, teaching, meditation, Indian medicine, and other good works.[22]

Using archaeological and textual sources, Shufen Liu found that by the early fifth century rural north China was dotted with thousands of Buddhist statuary stelae, which were used as ritual sites, as visualization and teaching aids, and as a means for making merit. In addition to images of buddhas and bodhisattvas, the stelae often showed scenes from popular scriptures, such as the Lotus and the Vima-lakirti Nirdesa Scriptures; from the biography of the Buddha or of his previous births; and pictures of the tortures of hell.[23]

At this time in north China, Buddhist monks led lay associations for public works as well. The then title of itinerant Buddhist monks meant "Master of Chari-table Organizations" (yi shi), and the activities of these associations included build-ing bridges, digging wells, planting trees, feeding the hungry, providing cemeteries, and erecting a stele at the site of each project.[24] Women participated in these asso-ciations, sometimes even organizing them on their own.[25] If monks were enjoined to "remove the dust from people's eyes" through preaching and personal example in the earliest of Buddhist traditions, in fifth-century China they also employed ritual, instruction in visualization, and good works.

Evidence for Mahayana forms of "missionary spirit" can also be found in ca-nonical sources. The strong emphasis in the Lotus Scripture, for example, on read-ing, copying, reciting, practicing, and broadly propagating the scripture (found throughout the scripture); on the development of the moral qualities of forbear-ance and perseverance in the face of physical and verbal abuse when seeking to convert skeptics (in the chapter "The Bodhisattva Never Disparaging"); and on the characterization of the bodhisattva of compassion Avalokiteswara as someone who would appear anywhere in whatever form is necessary in order to save sentient beings (in chapter 25) all strongly suggest purposeful outreach to believers and nonbelievers alike. The first of the four bodhisattva vows—however many beings there may be, I vow to save them all—is another example of such concerns.

The missionary aspect of Mahayana forms of Buddhism has had diverse mani-festations. Dōgen (1200–1254), the founder of Sōtō Zen in Japan, promoted the efficacy of silent meditation, writing of the legendary sixth-century Indian monk Bodhidharma in China that "we still hear the echoes of his nine years facing a wall."[26] In the Tibetan tradition, the great Indian monk Padmasambhava (eighth century) is credited with paving the way for the conversion of Tibet to Buddhism by esoterically subduing and converting the local gods and demons. The Japanese monk Nichiren (1222–1282) courted martyrdom with the belief that in the Dharma-ending age it was one's duty to confront those whose faith was misplaced and convert them to the Lotus Scripture. To suffer hardships in this endeavor alleviated one's past bad karma; to die for the cause was to ensure one's future buddhahood.[27]

As for twentieth-century Brazil, in this volume Cristina Rocha (Chap. 6) notes that Zen missionaries rely on Dōgen's emphasis on silent meditation, while Peter Clarke (Chap. 5) documents substantial reworkings of Nichiren's "missionary spirit" among his heirs in Soka Gakkai.

Stuart Chandler and Julia Huang offer sustained treatments of Taiwan's Master Xingyun and Master Zhengyan, two prominent figures in the reform of Buddhism in Taiwan and in its spread in Chinese communities around the world.[28] Both recognize their indebtedness to Master Taixu, whose thought has had a number of parallels with the Dharmapalan reformation of the Theravada. Indeed, Master Taixu attended a school for Buddhist missionaries that had been set up as a result of Dharmapala's visit to China in 1893.[29] Both these leaders have distanced themselves from "funeral Buddhism," reorienting practice toward this world and to global missions that aim to cross ethnic lines. Rooted in the Mahayana, both share their approach with earlier responses to the Christian challenge.

George Tanabe (Chap. 3) offers a portrait of figures who were instrumental in the development of the True Pure Land Mission to Hawai'i during the early to middle years of the twentieth century, amply demonstrating the deliberate selectivity with which Japanese priests working in an immigrant community approached American civic and Christian traditions.

Gray Tuttle's essay (Chap. 9) offers an exception to this pattern of selective appropriation of Western ways. It gives us a picture of Tibetan Buddhist lamas in China during the early decades of this century and shows how their agenda and methods for spreading the Dharma in the contemporary West are remarkably similar to that earlier model, one that developed along Tibetan Buddhist and Chinese administrative models independently from Western influence, and one that continues to emphasize the supernormal efficacy of ritual.

Therefore, although Buddhist missionaries in the nineteenth and twentieth centuries have certainly been stimulated and influenced by Christianity, they should not be thought of as simplistically imitating or being overwhelmed by Christian ethos and practices. Buddhists already had their own versions of "missionary spirit" and traditions of social responsibility. In addition, and as a number of the chapters in this book note, changes to economic, political, and social conditions during this period—that is, colonialism, nationalism, worldwide economic integration and travel, organizational rationalization, science, technology, and mass communications—have all contributed greatly to the character of twentieth-century Buddhist missionary efforts.

CONVERSION: FOREIGN, DIASPORA, AND DOMESTIC MISSIONS

Kemper noted that most Sri Lankan Theravada missionaries do not seem to spend much time trying to convert others, and Rocha and Clarke found that Zen institutions and Soka Gakkai in Brazil have come to have no denominational barriers, permitting practitioners multiple religious affiliations. Moreover, Chandler and Huang have observed that the vast majority of the new adherents of the Foguang Shan (lit., Buddha's Light Mountain) and the Compassion Relief organizations already think of themselves as Buddhist. Like "missionary," "conversion" and "mission" have more than one meaning.

Building on Jan Nattier's earlier attempt to understand how religions "travel to new places," the essays in this book form the basis for proposing a new typology for the sociology of missionary efforts.[30] Once stated, they seem so obvious as to go without saying; yet once articulated, they help to explain heretofore perplexing data: particularly relevant to the character of missionary efforts and to the role of conversion in the propagation of any religion is whether the target population is a culturally foreign group being introduced to the religion for the first time, a diaspora community drawing on its religious heritage to make its way in a culturally foreign environment, or a domestic audience deemed to be in need of religious revitalization. The essays in this volume deal with all three kinds of missions.

Buddhist scriptures recognize two processes that resonate with Western usages of "conversion," namely, a transformation of character and viewpoint and a change of affiliation. Decisive steps on the path to "enlightenment" (such as the realization of the "four fruits") are the first type of conversion and constitute the goal of practice.[31] They are often accompanied by the second type of conversion, that is, an increasing identification as a Buddhist and an intensification of commitment. They are often marked by taking a particular monk, nun, or layman as one's teacher, undertaking to keep the lay precepts, undergoing ordination, and/or receiving the bodhisattva vows.

Taking the Three Refuges is the Buddhist institutional equivalent of conversion in the sense of a change of affiliation. It is formally marked when a person, in the presence of an ordained member of the sangha, declares their intention to take the Buddha, his teachings, and the sangha as their religious guides, to the exclusion of other paths or faiths. The Pali canon records an instance in which Shakyamuni

Buddha spoke of the first glimpse of nirvana as the time when one becomes a member of the Buddha's lineage (or *gotra*), thus merging the ideas of character transformation and insight with change of affiliation.[32] This has remained a metaphor, however, for the Buddha and sangha have recognized as disciples people who have not yet entered the stream and have understood that people can awaken to the truths of Buddhism without the benefit of the Three Treasures and subsequent institutional affiliation to them (the above-mentioned Pratyekabuddha being a case in point). Moreover, because the Buddha recognized different realms of gods, the sangha also has tended to respect deities and theistic faiths while still maintaining the superiority of Buddhist goals and methods. This respect for spiritual entities may tend to soften the sense of conversion, in the sense of change in affiliation, more than Western observers might expect.

None of the authors in this book deal with conversion in the sense of enlightenment. Indeed, readers may wonder how awakening experiences and the extinction of passions figure into the political agendas, ethnic chauvinism, and generational conflicts that have sometimes characterized the Buddhists described in this book. In his analysis of Dharmapala, however, H. L. Seneviratne noted that meditation was an "ever present undercurrent" in his utopian vision.[33] Dharmapala advocated both "active effort toward liberation" (*paramattha dhamma*) and social service; but he and his successors also believed that social service should take priority, even for the monastic sangha, when the people are poor, unhealthy, uneducated, and "torn by caste division"—hence their two different approaches to mission: an emphasis on economic and social development on the one hand and on meditation and insight on the other.[34] Moreover, other voices in Theravada Buddhism are not well represented in this book. There are, as Kemper points out, Burmese, Thai, and Sri Lankan monks who are dismayed by what they feel is the politicization and worldliness of many Sinhala monks and urge a reform of the "Dharmapalan reformation."[35]

Future research should address how psychological conversion plays a role in the lives of missionaries and the people attracted to Buddhism.[36] For example, Sarah LeVine mentioned that the women in her study were attracted to intensive training by the ideal of enlightenment. After training for some time, they found that what they really wanted was the capacity to help their families and community, and that this could only be accomplished through realizing "no-self" and letting go of greed, hate, and delusive habits of mind. What is more, they experienced their practice to be effective in this regard.[37] In a similar vein, although with no reference to anything that could be regarded as the "four fruits" or *satori*, Huang describes the reorientation of outlook and intensification of commitment of Taiwanese Buddhists in Taiwan and abroad—a domestic and diaspora revival, if you will—by means of bodhisattva service and inspired by the charismatic leadership, example, organizational skill, and political acumen (although the organization is apolitical) of Master Zhengyan, a Buddhist nun.[38]

As for conversion in the sense of change of affiliation, the chapters in this book examine cultural boundaries and how missionaries negotiate them. These are complex processes for which our contributors have enlisted a variety of conceptual and explanatory devices. George Tanabe offers his own particularly well-developed analogy of the "transplantation" and "hybridization" of an immigrant Pure Land temple in Hawai'i. Cristina Rocha employs the "creolization" model from linguisitics, in which elements from Buddhist culture (like "vocabulary") are incorporated into preexisting habits of social interaction and religious cosmology (like "rules of syntax") of Brazilians who take an interest in Buddhism. This process is akin to Richard Payne's use of the term "assimilation." Payne borrows from Piaget the distinction between assimilation and accommodation, in which he uses "assimilation" to mean the incorporation of new cultural elements without making any fundamental changes in worldview or practice, while he adapts Piaget's concept of accommodation to mean the reworking of preexisting beliefs or practices when faced with differences.[39]

Also important to the process of conversion is the means by which cultural contact is made and maintained. Kemper's "ethnoscape" and Payne's "mediascape" draw on Arjun Appadurai's work on the channels for cultural flows.[40] The former refers to people on the move—migrants, tourists, refugees, students, and so on—creating complicated landscapes or networks and pockets of group identity that do not straightforwardly conform to territorial or national boundaries. Missionaries are brokers of the religiocultural boundaries of these ethnoscapes, using a wide variety of "media" to create and broadcast their message.

While no explicit reference has been made to Appadurai's other "scapes" in this work, for example, to "technoscapes," "finanscapes," and "ideoscapes"— that is, the interlocking global technological, financial, and political grids that mark the contemporary world—the essays in this book do point to their impact on Buddhist missions. The Compassion Relief Foundation has chosen highly sophisticated technological media, namely, Western-type medical hospitals, worldwide emergency disaster relief, an international bone-marrow registry, and a television station to spearhead its outreach (Huang). American foreign aid in Nepal has changed the opportunities for local youth so that young men study engineering and economics rather than enter monastic life (LeVine); and there are the political dimensions of Tibetan Buddhist missionary activities (Tuttle).

The interaction between conflicting pressures for cultural survival and efforts at conversion of outsiders is explored in a number of chapters and is particularly important for understanding diaspora missions. At one end of the spectrum are the Japanese-American followers of the True Pure Land School of Buddhism (*Jodo Shinshu Nishi Honpa Honganji*) in Hawai'i. Tanabe argues that, while declining steadily in numbers, they have been remarkably successful in maintaining unchanged their core religious principle of "family, or ancestral, religion," brought from Japan, even as they embraced many formal aspects of Protestant religiosity. He also points to a recurring, though not universal, idea among Japanese Buddhists, namely, that one cannot really understand Buddhism without also being Japanese. This is not the same as asserting a Buddhist identity for a particular ethnic group—for instance, to be Sinhala is to be Buddhist—or the same as a difficult relationship between Buddhists of different cultures who share a temple (see Rocha),[41] for it asserts that authentic Buddhism cannot be truly learned by foreigners. Thus, some Japanese immigrant churches find it hard to embrace foreign devotees (see Tanabe, Payne, and Rocha).

An example of a Japanese immigrant church that emphatically does not share this ethnocentric view is Soka Gakkai in Brazil (see Clarke). In this case the leadership in Japan, President Ikeda, set the course for the organization when he targeted Brazil to be the vanguard for the spiritual transformation of the world. Like the Theravada, Zen, and Tibetan missionaries who sought to spread Buddhism beyond their own ethnic groups, Soka Gakkai in Brazil has been quite successful at attracting nonimmigrant devotees.

Focusing on cultural presuppositions of Americans that have helped to shape conversion patterns, Richard Payne explores the invisibility in the United States of a Japanese Buddhist tantric tradition, Shingon, despite a contemporaneous avid interest among some westerners in Tibetan Buddhist tantra and Zen. As immigrant churches that assimilated Protestant forms, they have not been attractive to westerners who seek something altogether different from their known worlds. His observations may also be relevant to the relative lack of success in reaching beyond their ethnic communities of the two Chinese organizations discussed in this book: both Buddha's Light Mountain and the Compassion Relief Foundation use charitable work and the concomitant pressure for fundraising and proselytizing as their primary means of self-cultivation.[42] Apart from the appeal of Chinese culture to some foreigners (Chandler), these churches' practices are perhaps just too similar to Western day-to-day experience and mainstream American church organizations to be attractive to those who are disaffected with Western religious alternatives.

Class and caste differences need to be reckoned into the analysis of domestic, diaspora, and foreign missions. As Rocha ably points out for Zen Buddhists in Brazil, and LeVine for Newar Buddhists in Nepal, these divides are no less distinct than commonly understood "cultural" ones.[43]

Methods used for reaching beyond ethnic and class barriers for conversions described in this volume include the translation and publication of scriptures, commentaries, and practice manuals into the vernacular (and more and more into English as the internationally accessible language), the preparation of clergy explicitly for missionary work and training them in local languages (again, often English), and the use of the latest technological advances in communications.

Other propagation methods for conversions include building magnificent temples to pique the interest of non-Buddhists (Chandler); establishing personal ties, "links of affinity," which are given important religious significance in Chinese missionary efforts (Chandler and Huang); and the Tibetan use of ritual empowerments, which have been quite successful in attracting devotees in war-torn Republican China and in the modern West (Tuttle). None of these strategies are different from ones used by Buddhists for their own ethnic groups.

The Brazilian missionary to the Sōtō Zen temple in São Paulo described by Rocha, as well as the Theravadin monks described by Kemper, however, have adopted a dual strategy, tailoring their teaching to the respective interests of their diaspora and foreign congregations. As mentioned above, they also both point out that conversion, in the sense of formal affiliation, is not emphasized. While downplaying formal affiliation in some Buddhist missionary circles can have a variety of motivations, it may also draw on Buddhist gradualist models, in which adherents are given only so much teaching as they appear willing to accept, and injunctions against craving, which can be applied just as much to craving converts as it can to sensual desires, intellectual knowledge, or spiritual success.

Similarly, Peter Clarke found in Brazilian Soka Gakkai a "strategy of reflexive syncretism," born of confidence in the power of their own religion, that replaced shakabuku, a strongly exclusive, sectarian approach to conversion. In placing his study in the larger context of plural societies and globalization, he suggests that their further shift toward nonsectarianism—their acceptance of multiple church memberships and the idea that individuals can decide for themselves what is best for them—is a response to a trend in which people seek a religious consciousness beyond any specific religious identity. This latter trend toward "nonsectarian universalism" (my term) contrasts with the "sectarian triumphalism" that has characterized much of the thinking of the True Pure Land Church in Hawai'i described by Tanabe. By "sectarian triumphalism" Tanabe means the belief and practice that only one's own tradition transcends all ethnic and sectarian claims (Tanabe). Earlier in the century, this kind of thinking was used to enlist Buddhist missionaries to further Japanese nationalism and colonialism (Tanabe).

None of the above approaches stands against another trend noted by Chandler, namely, that religious identities are not only reaching across national boundaries, but perhaps in some cases even superseding patriotic sentiment. All of these observations dovetail with Rocha's point that, under the pluralistic conditions of our contemporary world, people are presented with more and more choices, including religious choices, from which they need to construct their own individual identities.[44]

CONCLUSIONS

The chapters in this volume are roughly arranged in the historical order of when a particular Buddhist tradition began to send missions beyond Asia, although many of the essays analyze domestic revivals and diaspora conditions that stimulated an outreach to foreigners in the first place. This ordering is not to ignore the importance of East–East connections, which form an appreciable part of over half of the chapters, some notable examples being the extension of Chinese Mahayana *bhikkhuni* ordination to Theravada nuns, the influence of Sri Lankan Theravada on Buddhism in Nepal and Vietnam, and the financial support offered by Japanese Buddhists to Sri Lanka and elsewhere. All of the essays bring the reader up to the late twentieth century.

What also stands out in the essays is the observation that a globalizing, evangelical Christianity stimulated and/or gave shape to much of what we see as a globalizing Buddhism, including Theravada, Japanese, and Chinese organizations. This should not be taken to mean, however, that Buddhists have not drawn on their own traditions of "missionary spirit" or methods. What is more, the rationalization of organizational life and the sense that the whole world is much more *tangibly* within one's reach, which characterize modernity and of which the Christian missions have been a highly visible example, are probably two of the more lasting recent changes to Buddhist institutions.

Charity, nonreligious education, and other public works are not new to Buddhists; but instead of what has been a more ad hoc and even anonymous approach in some traditions (as Huang points out in Chapter 8),[45] the search for worthy charitable causes and the mobilization for these services on the scale that we see today may be new, especially for Buddhist sects working without the backing of a state. This reflects not only the modern push toward rationalization, but also a shift in thinking to embrace social welfare as an essential component of Buddhist organizational life. The recent salience of social activism also has had Christian and Western stimuli; but given the historical evidence for social service by Buddhists, I suspect that a large measure of this recent thrust comes from the gains in health and human welfare made possible by science and technology, the need for a modern education generated by current economic organization, and favorable political conditions for Buddhist organizations, rather than from the awakening of a new social conscience. In addition, an emphasis on social ethics has not replaced the ultimate, and ultimately legitimating, goal of supramundane insight and compassion, although the latter may become submerged in the exigencies of day-to-day practice or even be lost on some devotees.[46]

Involuntary exile has placed Tibetan missionaries in a very different position from their counterparts in other Buddhist traditions. Without the safety net afforded by immigrant congregations, they have been forced to make a success of the cross-cultural transmission of their teachings quickly. This, together with the esoteric nature of their teachings, may help to explain their success among westerners, in contrast to the ethnic limitations encountered by even such charismatic figures as the Taiwanese Master Zhengyan. What is more, the timing of the exile in relation to the crisis of faith of some American and European youth beginning in the late 1950s and gaining momentum in the 1960s perhaps has been an important factor (see Payne and Tuttle).[47] Last, the separation of politics from mission work is by no means the norm in the Buddhist world (see Kemper, Tanabe, and Chandler), but the theocratic tradition of the Geluk school (and other Tibetan Buddhist schools), which shapes much of the current political agenda of the Dalai Lama, sets it off from the other forms of Buddhism described in this book (see Tuttle).

If understanding the Buddhist impact on cultures outside of its historical milieus in the last 150 years is still in its infancy,[48] the indigenization of Buddhism has been found to be deeply significant and ongoing. Its responses to Christianity and other agents of modernity are examples of this process.[49] Indeed, Peter Gregory has suggested that the changes to Buddhist institutions and doctrines that began during the colonial period are likely to be as significant, in the long run, as the emergence of the Mahayana and the Vajrayana traditions in centuries past.[50] The essays in this book attest to this process of cross-fertilization, yet they show very significant continuities as well.

Last, noting the three kinds of missionary work—namely, domestic revivals, support for diaspora communities, and foreign conversions—helps to explain variable Buddhist attitudes toward conversion and the trajectories of specific missions.

It will also assist in comparisons of Buddhists with other religious people and organizations involved in missionary work.

Notes

I want to thank Peter Gregory, Robert Weller, and Peter Wood for commenting on drafts of the Introduction. Their advice was extremely helpful, though I have not been able to live up to all of it.

1. Peter Berger, "Four Faces of Global Culture," *The National Interest* 49 (Fall 1997): 23–29.

2. Jonathan S. Walters, "Rethinking Buddhist Missions," 2 vols. (Ph.D. diss., University of Chicago, 1992).

3. Don A. Pittman, *Toward a Modern Chinese Buddhism: Taixu's Reforms* (Honolulu: University of Hawai'i Press, 2001), 242–250.

4. Ibid., 105–152.

5. Walters, "Buddhist Missions," 1:92–96, 98.

6. David W. Chappell, "Buddhist Interreligious Dialogue: To Build a Global Community," in *The Sound of Liberating Truth: Buddhist-Christian Dialogues in Honor of Frederick J. Streng,* ed. Sallie King and Paul Ingram (Richmond, Eng.: Curzon, 1999), 4, 22.

7. Walters, "Buddhist Missions," 1:93.

8. Gary B. McGee, "Missiology," in *Dictionary of Pentecostal and Charismatic Movements,* ed. Stanley M. Burgess and Gary B. McGee (Grand Rapids, Mich.: Zondervan, 1988), 609.

9. McGee, "Missions, Overseas (North American)," in ibid., 620.

10. Edward L. Cleary, "Introduction," in *Power, Politics, and Pentecostals in Latin America,* ed. Edward L. Cleary and Hannah W. Stewart-Gambino (Boulder, Colo.: Westview, 1997), 4, 7; and McGee "Missiology," 608.

11. Galilea, as quoted in Edward L. Cleary and Juan Sepulveda, "Chilean Pentecostalism: Coming of Age," in Cleary and Stewart-Gambino, *Power, Politics, and Pentecostals,* 107.

12. Cleary and Sepulveda, "Chilean Pentecostalism," 120n76; and Cecilia Loreto Mariz and Maria das Dores Campos Machado, "Pentecostalism and Women in Brazil," in Cleary and Stewart-Gambino, *Power, Politics, and Pentecostals.*

13. McGee, "Missiology," 613.

14. Walters, "Buddhist Missions," 1:218.

15. Erik Zurcher, *Encyclopedia of Religion,* s.v. "Missions: Buddhist Missions."

16. Walters, "Buddhist Missions," 1:167–169.

17. Mahinda Deegalle, "Buddhist Preaching and Sinhala Religious Rhetoric: Medieval Buddhist Methods to Popularize Theravada," *Numen: International Review for the History of Religions* 44, no. 2 (1997): 189–191.

18. Richard Gombrich and Gananath Obeyesekere, *Buddhism Transformed: Religious Change in Sri Lanka* (Princeton, N.J.: Princeton University Press, 1988), 211–212.

19. Walters, "Buddhist Missions," 2:425–427.

20. Ibid., 425, 428–429.

21. Ibid., 429.

22. Arthur Wright, *Buddhism in Chinese History* (Stanford, Calif.: Stanford University Press, 1959) and "Fo-t'u-teng: A Biography," in *Studies in Chinese Buddhism*, ed. Robert M. Somers (New Haven, Conn.: Yale University Press, 1990), 34–68. Erik Zurcher, *The Buddhist Conquest of China: The Spread and Adaptation of Buddhism in Early Medieval China*, 2 vols. (Leiden: E. J. Brill, 1959), and "A New Look at the Earliest Chinese Buddhist Texts," in *From Benares to Beijing: Essays on Buddhism and Chinese Religion*, ed. Koichi Shinohara and Gregory Schopen (Oakville, Canada: Mosaic Press, 1991). Richard B. Mather, "Vimalakirti and Gentry Buddhism," *History of Religions* 8 (1968): 60–73. Stephen R. Bokenkamp, "Sources of the Ling-Pao Scriptures," in *Tantric and Taoist Studies in Honour of R. A. Stein*, vol. 2, ed. Michel Strickman, *Mélanges Chinois et Bouddhiques* 21 (1983): 434–486. Shufen Liu, "Art, Ritual, and Society: Buddhist Practice in Rural China during the Northern Dynasties," *Asia Major* 8, no. 1: 19–47. Jacques Gernet, *Buddhism in Chinese Society: An Economic History from the Fifth to the Tenth Centuries*, trans. Franciscus Verellen (New York: Columbia University Press, 1995). Max Weber, "The Social Psychology of World Religions," in *From Max Weber: Essays in Sociology*, trans. H. H. Gerth and C. Wright Mills (New York: Oxford University Press, 1958 [1915]), 280–285.

23. Liu, "Art, Ritual, and Society," 32–33.

24. Ibid., 24–26, 28, 31–39; Gernet, *Buddhism in Chinese Society*, 114, 259–277.

25. Liu, "Art, Ritual, and Society," 35.

26. P. T. N. H. Jiyu-Kennett, M.O.B.C., trans.,"Rules for Meditation" ("Fukanzazengi" by Zen Master Dōgen), in *Serene Reflection Meditation* (Mt. Shasta, Calif.: Shasta Abbey, 1989), 1.

27. Jacqueline I. Stone, *Original Enlightenment and the Transformation of Medieval Japanese Buddhism* (Honolulu: University of Hawai'i Press, 1999), 241.

28. See also Chien-yu Julia Huang and Robert P. Weller, "Merit and Mothering: Women and Social Welfare in Taiwanese Buddhism," *Journal of Asian Studies* 57, no. 2 (1998): 379–396. Chien-yu Julia Huang, "Recapturing Charisma: Emotion and Rationalization in a Globalizing Buddhist Movement from Taiwan" (Ph.D. diss., Boston University, 2001). C. Stuart Chandler, "Establishing a Pure Land on Earth: The Foguang Buddhist Perspective on Modernization and Globalization" (Ph.D. diss., Harvard University, 2000).

29. Pittman, *Toward a Modern Chinese Buddhism*, 44–45.

30. Jan Nattier's "Who Is Buddhist? Charting the Landscape in Buddhist America," in *The Faces of Buddhism in America*, ed. Charles S. Prebish and Kenneth K. Tanaka (Berkeley: University of California Press, 1998), 183–195, at 189. Nattier proposed a three-part typology to view the propagation of Buddhism to North America. "Demand-driven" can refer to a Buddhist tradition or organization that is "actively sought out by the recipient"; he or she hears or finds out about it through books or travel and pursues it further on his or her own initiative. This she labeled "Elite Buddhism," as people need the leisure time and the money to pursue their religious interests. Moreover, Elite Buddhists in North America have been strongly drawn to meditation. "Export-driven," or "Evangelical Buddhism," refers to Buddhism that is "sold" or propagated primarily by missionaries. And the third is "Baggage Buddhism," Buddhism that is carried as part and parcel of emigration. This she labeled "Ethnic Buddhism" (Nattier 1998: 189). As with any typology, the conditions on the ground will be much more complicated; and applying them to a broader field than just North America does require some rethinking.

In viewing these essays in light of these typologies, the first thing to be noted is the thoroughly mixed character of the Chinese, Zen, and Theravada organizations described. For example, the Compassion Relief Foundation is both demand-driven and evangelical; some Sōtō Zen missionaries from Japan want to export a different kind of Zen from what their immigrant congregations demand; and "making the Dharma available to the world" — its soft sell, to continue Nattier's metaphor—of the Sinhala Theravada does not stand against its evangelical nature. Her "demand-driven" model probably overemphasizes the efforts of the new converts at the expense of their teachers and their supporters, that is, at the expense of the teachers and congregations who are writing and publishing the materials new converts read and are building and maintaining the centers the new converts visit. Second, labeling the Buddhism brought by immigrants as Ethnic Buddhism downplays the "ethnicity" of the nonimmigrant communities of the host society. We are all "ethnic." The elite vs. ethnic labeling also suggests that immigrants will not be elites in their adopted societies. But this should not be presumed, especially when studying relatively wealthy emigrants (e.g., Taiwanese) to Malaysia and elsewhere. Moreover, these elites are drawn to a charismatic movement rather than to meditation.

31. This is the Theravada teaching of the "Four Fruits" of stream entrant, once-returner, non-returner, and arhat, born of seeing for oneself the law of karma and rebirth and the selfless and impermanent nature of the phenomenal world. These are accompanied by the attenuation and then eradication of the three passions of greed, anger, and delusion. Pure Land scriptures emphasize rebirth into Amitabha's Pure Land, but, strictly speaking, only as a decisive step toward enlightenment and not as the end of practice. *Satori* and *kenshō* in Zen schools refer to a revolution in one's views. Nichiren-inspired Buddhism holds out the promise of realizing buddhahood in an instantaneous change of mind and a future, earthly buddha realm.

32. See Bhadantācaniya Buddhaghosa, *The Path of Purification (Visuddhimagga)*, trans. Bhikkhu Ñāṇamoli, 3d ed. (Kandy, Sri Lanka: Buddhist Publication Society, 1975), s.v. "*gotrabhu*" or "change of lineage."

33. H. L. Seneviratne, *The Work of Kings: The New Buddhism in Sri Lanka* (Chicago: University of Chicago Press, 1999), 102.

34. Ibid., 110–111.

35. See M. Carrithers, *The Forest Monks of Sri Lanka* (Delhi: Oxford University Press, 1983).

36. For a good overview of these kinds of studies, see Julia Day Howell, "ASC Induction Techniques, Spiritual Experiences, and Commitments in New Religious Movements," *Sociology of Religion* 58, no. 2 (1997): 141–164.

37. Private conversation, April 2000.

38. For a very useful analysis of the cultural dimensions of conversion to Christianity in Taiwan, see David K. Jordan, "The Glyphomancy Factor: Observations on Chinese Conversion," in *Conversion to Christianity: Historical and Anthropological Perspectives on a Great Transformation*, ed. Robert Hefner (Berkeley and Los Angeles: University of California Press, 1993).

39. The cross-cultural transfer of Buddhism has been also addressed in other scholarship. See, for example, Zurcher, *The Buddhist Conquest of China*, and "A New Look at the Earliest Chinese Buddhist Texts" (n. 22); Steven M. Tipton, *Getting Saved from the Sixties* (Berkeley and Los Angeles: University of California Press, 1982); Peter N. Gregory, *Tsung-mi and the Sinification of Buddhism* (Princeton, N.J.: Princeton University Press, 1991) and "Describing the Elephant: Buddhism in America," *Religion and American Culture: A Journal of Interpretation* 11, no. 2 (2000): 233–263; Thomas A. Tweed, *The American Encounter with Buddhism: 1844–1912* (Bloomington: Indiana University Press, 1992); Christopher S. Queen, "Introduction" and "Dr. Ambedkar and the Hermeneutics of Buddhist Liberation," in *Engaged Buddhism: Buddhist Liberation Movements in Asia,* ed. Christopher S. Queen and Sallie B. King (Albany: State University of New York Press, 1996), 1–44 and 45–71; Martin Baumann, "Culture Contact and Valuation: Early German Buddhists and the Creation of a 'Buddhism in Protestant Shape,'" *Numen: International Review for the History of Religions* 44, no. 3 (1997): 270–295; Nattier, "Who Is Buddhist?" (n. 30); Sandra Bell, "Being Creative with Tradition: Rooting Theravada Buddhism in Britain," *Journal of Global Buddhism* 1 (2000): 1–23; Matthew T. Kapstein, *The Tibetan Assimilation of Buddhism: Conversion, Contestation, and Memory* (Oxford: Oxford University Press, 2000); and Lionel Obadia, "Tibetan Buddhism in France: A Missionary Religion?" http://jgb.la.psu.edu/2/obadia012. html 2002.

40. Arjun Appadurai, *Modernity at Large: Cultural Dimensions of Globalization* (Minneapolis: University of Minnesota Press, 1996), 27–47 and 48–65.

41. See also Paul Numrich, *Old Wisdom in the New World: Americanization of Two Immigrant Theravada Buddhist Temples* (Knoxville: University of Tennessee Press, 1996).

42. C. Stuart Chandler, "The Dharma of Wealth: The Foguang Perspective on the Role of Capitalistic Enterprise in Buddhist Cultivation," in "Establishing a Pure Land on Earth: The

Foguang Buddhist Perspective on Modernization and Globalization" (Ph.D. diss., Harvard University, 2000).

43. For a sociostructural theory relevant to the study of the lack of interest in immigrant churches by elite and intellectual strata of American society, see Mary Douglas, *Natural Symbols* (London: Barrie and Rockliff, 1970). Max Weber's work on "elective affinities" mentioned above is still extremely useful; see "The Social Psychology of World Religions," 280–285.

44. See also Anthony Giddens, *Modernity and Self-Identity: Self and Society in the Late Modern Age* (Stanford, Calif.: Stanford University Press, 1991).

45. See also Holmes Welch, *The Buddhist Revival in China* (Cambridge, Mass.: Harvard University Press, 1968), especially 76–79, 121–131.

46. For more on "socially engaged Buddhism," see Queen and King, eds., *Engaged Buddhism*.

47. For Zen Buddhism in the United States, see Tipton, *Getting Saved from the Sixties* (n. 39).

48. See, however, Tweed, *The American Encounter with Buddhism* (n. 29), and "Asian Religions in the United States: Reflections on an Emerging Subfield," in *Religious Diversity and American Religious History: Studies in Traditions and Cultures*, ed. Walter H. Conser, Jr., and Sumner B. Twiss (Athens: University of Georgia Press, 1997); Donald S. Lopez, Jr., *Prisoners of Shangri-La: Tibetan Buddhism and the West* (Chicago: University of Chicago Press, 1998); and Richard H. Seager, *Buddhism in America* (New York: Columbia University Press, 1999).

49. Other research includes Gombrich and Obeyesekere, *Buddhism Transformed* (n. 18); Penny Van Esterik, *Taking Refuge: Lao Buddhists in North America* (Tempe: Arizona State University, 1992); Numrich, *Old Wisdom in the New World*; Stephen Prothero, *The White Buddhist: The Asian Odyssey of Henry Steele Olcott* (Bloomington: Indiana University Press, 1996); Alan Sponberg, "TBMSG: A Dhamma Revolution in Contemporary India," in *Engaged Buddhism: Buddhist Liberation Movements in Asia*, ed. Christopher S. Queen and Sallie B. King (Albany: State University of New York Press, 1996), 73–120; Frank Korom, ed., *Constructing Tibetan Culture: Contemporary Perspectives* (St. Hyacinthe, Can.: World Heritage, 1997); Robert Sharf, "The Zen of Japanese Nationalism," *History of Religions* 33, no. 1 (August 1993): 1–43; Seneviratne, *The Work of Kings*; Nancy Smith-Hefner, *Khmer-American: Identity and Moral Education in a Diasporic Community* (Berkeley and Los Angeles: University of California Press, 1999); and Pittman, *Toward a Modern Chinese Buddhism* (n. 3).

50. Gregory, "Describing the Elephant" (n. 39), 250.

1 Dharmapala's *Dharmaduta* and the Buddhist Ethnoscape

Steven Kemper

Buddhism arrived early in Sri Lanka. The dominant tradition dates that arrival to the time Asoka sent out an embassy to Anuradhapura with the doctrine and a sapling of the bo tree under which the Buddha achieved enlightenment at Bodh Gaya. This event and the unbroken descent of Buddhist belief and practice ever after are pivotal facts of Sri Lankan history. The Tripitaka, as well as the commentaries and subcommentaries that explain it, were committed to writing in Sri Lanka, and thus arose another claim to orthodoxy. In time, Sri Lankan Buddhism came to be dominated by one form of belief, Theravada, and Theravada came to be identified with the Sinhala people, the island's dominant ethnic identity.[1] When Burma, Thailand, and Cambodia received Theravada from monks who came from Sri Lanka some 1,500 years after the arrival of Buddhism in Sri Lanka, they referred to it with an eponym—Sinhala Buddhism. Monastic traditions of Sri Lanka became monastic traditions of those countries.[2] These references—authenticity guaranteed by priority, textualization, and continuity, the connection between the religion and an ethnic group, and a sense of authority and missionary responsibility that follows from these other notions—figure in Sinhalas' present-day understanding of their religion and themselves.

An entirely different set of missionary enterprises played a central role in more recent Sri Lankan history. Portuguese rule (early sixteenth century to 1658) brought Jesuits, Dominicans, Augustinians, and Capuchins; the Dutch (1650–1796) drove off Catholic clergy and replaced them with ministers and proponents of the Reformed Church; they were supplanted by British rule (1796–1948) and Methodist and Baptist missionaries. Four hundred years of colonial control along the southwestern littoral made Sri Lanka one of the most thoroughly missionized societies in the world, as each wave of Europeans established schools, converted people, and attended to small communities of the faithful. Well-to-do Sri Lankans became thoroughly exposed to Western religions, learned Western history, played Western games, spoke Western languages, and pursued social practices that derived from alien places. Joined together, two religious traditions—the Buddhist and the Christian—gave direction to the modern practice of Sri Lankan Buddhist missionizing. That practice begins with the initiative of one man, Anagarika Dharmapala (1864–1933).

Dharmapala's youth as the son of a father who made a considerable fortune manufacturing furniture, his early education at the hands of Christian missionaries, his involvement with Henry Steele Olcott, Helena Blavatsky, and the Theosophical Society, as well as the psychological tensions that marked his life—are concerns that are fundamental to his biography but do not need to be repeated here. Commentators have looked to Dharmapala for recuperating Buddhism and Sinhala self-confidence; bringing Buddhist monks, laypeople, ideas and practices into the public arena; rationalizing Buddhism and focusing it on this world.[3] His efforts led to the rise of an activist and secularized Buddhist monkhood and the onset of ethnic chauvinism that now dominates Sri Lankan politics. Dharmapala's foreign involvements are less discussed, but he spent most of the years from 1891 to 1933 living abroad—which is to say, most of his adult life—while traveling five times around the world and periodically returning to Sri Lanka.

Dharmapala's activity outside of Sri Lanka as a *dharmaduta* (messenger of Dhamma) set the course for modern Buddhist missionizing. In so doing, it shaped the lives of monks and laypeople in Sri Lanka and beyond—the dispersal of Sinhalas around the world I will call the Sinhala Buddhist ethnoscape—because his *dharmaduta* work missionized new forms for monks to be monks and laypeople to be laypeople. Appadurai defines an "ethnoscape" in a way that links it to contemporary life, calling it "the landscape of persons who constitute the shifting world in which we live: tourists, immigrants, refugee exiles, guest workers, and other moving groups and individuals constitute an essential feature of the world and appear to affect the politics of (and between) nations to an hitherto unprecedented degree."[4] Although he leaves out missionaries as such, Christian evangelicals, Muslim fundamentalists, and Buddhist monks constitute a globalizing force as important as any other "moving group." Sinhala *bhikkhus* are scattered across the globe, serving Buddhist communities that developed in colonial times in Malaysia and Singapore, and more recently in the United Kingdom, Canada, Australia, and the United States. In sacred sites in India such as Sarnath and Bodh Gaya, Sinhala monks await Sinhala pilgrims and other religious seekers. In places without a Sinhala community—in the Netherlands, for instance, and Brazil—Sinhala monks engage with local Buddhists and non-Buddhists. Together they constitute the Sinhala Buddhist ethnoscape. Extending beyond this Sinhala ethnoscape, and sometimes interspersed with it, lies a broader Buddhist ethnoscape.

Dharmapala's attitudes toward Buddhism are marked by contradictions and hybridity going well beyond the influence of Christianity upon his thinking.[5] He made himself a champion of Sinhala village life, but his attitudes toward villagers were condescending and often contemptuous. His vision of Buddhist social regeneration was motivated by, and framed in terms of, the values of Victorian England. On the one hand, Dharmapala showed the respect for Buddhist relics—remains of the Buddha's body and articles he once used—images, and historical places (of which Bodh Gaya where he had his enlightenment is the most pertinent) one would expect of a Sinhala Buddhist of his time. He writes of growing up in a family where everyone fasted on full-moon days and, on the day of the Buddha's Enlightenment, spent a full twenty-four hours in meditation and study (Guruge, 682). On the other hand, he initiated the process that rationalized Buddhism, creating what Obeyeskere has called Protestant Buddhism, a new way of practicing an old religion marked by a this-worldly asceticism, a code of ethics for laypeople, and an emphasis on doctrine coupled with disdain for the intercession of gods and demons.[6]

Two factors complicate understanding how Dharmapala influenced missionary practice. The first is that he couched his innovations—Christian-influenced, purely Buddhist, and otherwise—in terms of tradition. He spoke of reforming things, returning Sinhalas to piety and orthodox belief and practice, yet our seeing beyond the language of restoration is easy enough.[7] The second complication is harder to sort out, because how Buddhism was propagated before Dharmapala invented modern Buddhist missionizing is problematic. Millennia before colonialism and Christianity entered the Buddhist world, choices confronted the everyday practices of Buddhist monks: were monks to wander about or live "at one place" (ekatra) and "at a fixed residence" (dhruvaśila),[8] were their lives to be solitary or communal, were their days to be lived in villages or forest retreats, and were they to pursue their own salvation or teach the Dhamma for the benefit of others? Over the course of South Asian history, those choices were resolved in ways that generally favored the settled life, communal living situated in village settings where monks shared their learning with other monks and laypeople. But the preeminence of learning is beset by a more subtle distinction. Acting as a repository of Dhamma—committing the teachings to memory and sharing them with others—constitutes the minimal realization of a life of learning; proselytizing non-Buddhists and regarding that function as central to the religious life realizes that role in more outward-looking fashion.

Despite the way in which missionary enterprise figures in modern self-understandings, despite the words of the Buddha that seem to require missionary work— "Go ye now, O bhikkhus, and wander for the gain of the many, for the welfare of the many, out of compassion for the world, for the good, for the gain, and for the welfare of gods and men. Let not two of you go the same way"[9]—and, finally, despite the fact that the religion has obviously been dispersed by some means across Asia, the precolonial history of the Buddhist *sasana* had little to do with missionary work as the notion came to be used after Dharmapala. As Jonathan Walters points out, conversion may not have been integral to early Buddhism or a duty that monks felt compelled to take on.[10] Monks could well have carried the "yoke of learning" (*granthadhura*) without acting on motivations more characteristic of West Asian religious traditions centered on one god, sharp boundaries separating believers and nonbelievers, and an understanding of conversion—as in the case of Christianity—that has it serving as the enactment of one's own faith.

There was little chance that Dharmapala's reinvention of Buddhist missionizing could not have been influenced by Western practices. Consider how the hegemony of Christianity weighed on Dharmapala. His generation found Buddhism pushed out of the public life of the colony, replaced after Anglicanism was disestablished in 1880 by a policy that placed all religions on an equal footing (despite the fact that Christianity remained the religion of those who ruled). Sri Lankans of Dharmapala's class were often Christians, nominal or heartfelt, or Buddhists (and Hindus) who had been educated at Christian schools. They carried Christian names—Dharmapala was born Don David Hevavitarana, three names referencing three ethnic identities—and the English-based education he received put him in closer touch with Western history and culture than with the lives of villagers living only a few miles outside Colombo. Returning Buddhism to its historical place was the first step toward returning Sri Lankans to a way of life, as seen in dress, names, social forms, and values, authentically theirs. But his reimagination of Buddhism was itself influenced by his own life experiences—Victorian propriety, American entrepreneurship, mixed with resentment of Western power and arrogance. And what motivated Dharmapala's missionizing was reactive in a way that efforts to propagate Buddhism in ancient South Asia could not have been, for he was an "antimissionary missionary."[11]

The sixth-century chronicle of the Sri Lankan state, the *Mahavamsa*, begins with an account of the Lord Buddha's three visits to the island, "for Lanka was known to the Conqueror as a place where his doctrine should (thereafter) shine in glory."[12] That chapter concludes with more luminous imagery (1:84): "Thus the Master of boundless wisdom, looking to the salvation of Lanka in time to come . . . visited this fair island three times—he, the compassionate Enlightener of the world—therefore this isle, radiant with the light of truth, came to high honour among faithful believers." That second figure—"radiant with the light of truth"—comes from the Pali *dhammadīpa,* and *dhammadīpa* can be interpreted in two ways—as "radiant with the light of truth" (referring back to Lanka) or as "island of truth." Geiger's translation comes closer to the original, but the second interpretation has the advantage of setting Lanka apart as a special place, the very island of Dhamma. Dharmapala—and the Sinhala nationalists he inspired—favored the latter, and the neologism *dharmaduta* envisioned a role that acted out the responsibility that came with Lanka's being the "island of truth." Even if the term had to be invented, nineteenth-century Sinhala Buddhists must have found the missionary role self-evident. How else to explain the dispersal of Buddhism across Asia? How else to account for the early arrival of the religion in Sri Lanka (and how else to take advantage of the priority of Sinhala Buddhism in the Theravada world)?

Assume that the first "missionary" connection comes by way of the Buddha himself (following the *Mahavamsa*'s account of his flying to Sri Lanka) and the responsibility dates to the life of the founder. Or assume that it derives from Asoka's son and daughter's visit to the island (favoring a realist but still suspect story of one great South Asian king's sending an embassy to another). That connection is virtually as ancient, and better serves Dharmapala's purposes, dismissing an account with mythological exuberance for one that sets a human example for his own missionizing (Guruge, 486). The scholarly consensus focuses on what is implied by archeological and textual evidence, but even those sober facts establish the presence of Buddhism in the island a century before the beginning of the common era. Sri Lankans, in other words, were practicing Buddhism at a time when Britons were an insignificant society living on the margins of the Roman Empire. In that contrast Dharmapala found pathos. Two thousand years earlier Sinhalas were enjoying the glories of great kings, the Dhamma, and a magnificent hydraulic society. At that same point, their colonial masters "painted their bodies and wore skins to ward off the cold" (ibid., 480).[13]

For Walters, the issue is whether Dharmapala's taking on the responsibility of missionizing Buddhism represented a renewal of tradition or an innovation on it. For me, it is enough to emphasize how thoroughly Dharmapala borrowed from Christian practice, innovated, and adapted those ideas to his circumstances. Olcott had shown Sinhalas the virtues of Christian missionary practice. He copied the practice of raising funds at church bazaars. He envisioned Buddhist Sunday schools and urged Buddhists to insist that government make the Buddha's birthday a public holiday on a par with Christmas. Dharmapala learned the arts of propaganda and efficiency from the American, and his newspaper *Sinhala Baudhaya* was nothing if not efficient. It put Dharmapala in a position to propagandize his cause in Sri Lanka even while living as a *dharmaduta* in India. We can attribute these innovations as we like to Olcott's organizational ingenuity, print capitalism, or Christian practice, but what is pertinent here is that Dharmapala invented a missionary Buddhism with modern organizational forms, and this Buddhism is here to stay.

"TO DIE OUT SLOWLY FROM INANITION"

I want to begin with Dharmapala's own vision of Buddhist missionary work—"Buddhism had its missionaries before Christianity was preached. It conquered all of Asia and made the Mongolian mild"—and then consider contemporary efforts to spread the teachings in places as faraway as Brazil and Australia, before returning to a Colombo now linked to Buddhists the world over (Guruge, xvii). Sri Lankan monasteries these days are found in Bodh Gaya and other sacred sites associated with early Buddhism, Indian cities, North America, England, the Netherlands, and Brazil, as well as Malaysia, Singapore, and Indonesia. Dharmapala's outward vision included quite a lot more than conversion. Olcott was the first European to convert to Buddhism, but by my calculation Dharmapala himself converted only a handful of westerners. In this regard I would turn Walters' concerns back on modern *dharmaduta*, because one thing "Buddhist missionizing" did not borrow from Protestantism was its emphasis on conversion proper.[14] The Christian impetus and even the word "*dharmaduta*" make it easy to overlook the simplicity of the project—to make Buddhism present in the world, "bringing knowledge" of the Dhamma.

Dharmapala's efforts, both the missionizing abroad and what could be called either missionizing at home or "internal conversion," were motivated by high colonial pathos.[15] Centuries of foreign rule had put the existence of Sinhalas at risk. "It is, indeed, pathetic," Dharmapala wrote, "to observe that a unique race who had been the custodians of an ancient religious literature for 2200 years, Aryan in origin, should be allowed to die out slowly from inanition. The history of evolution can point to no other race today that has withstood the ravages of time and kept its individuality for so long as the Sinhalese people" (Guruge, 483). The notions that organize this passage—race, Aryan origins, evolution—derive from Dharmapala's education in Christian schools and the popularized science he encountered in journals and newspapers. On his understanding, the source of the problem is also Western: the "ancient race is slowly dying out under the despotic administration of Anglo-Indian bureaucracy."

When Dharmapala ticks off his complaints, it is obvious that he is less upset by despotic administration than by its collateral effects—cultural corruption, dissipation, and lethargy. "Although they are a powerful race today," Dharmapala says of the British, "their hereditary tendencies of primitive barbarism still cling to them. Cruelty, drunkenness, slaughter of innocent animals, wife-beating, roasting the whole ox on feast days, promiscuous dancing of men and women regardless of the laws of decency are vestiges of their primitive customs . . ." (Guruge, 479– 480). The low morality of the British—embodied in the careers of Clive, Hastings, North, Sladen, and Rhodes—has corrupted "unsophisticated Asiatics," and to make matters worse in Sri Lanka, British administrators cut down the highland forests to plant tea, while insinuating opium, ganja, marijuana, whiskey, and arrack into every village (ibid., 482).

The long-term solution is for the British to return to their own island; the short-term solution is for Sinhalas to return to their own religion, now redefined by Dharmapala. By giving up on Buddhism, Sinhalas had given up on being Sinhala. The remedy was activity, recalling the example of Buddhist kings who "spent all their wealth in building temples, public baths, *dagobas* [Sinhala: relic mounds], libraries, monasteries, rest houses, hospitals for man and beast, schools, tanks, seven-storied mansions, water works and beautifying] the city of Anuradhapura" (Guruge, 481). Building a Buddhist temple (Skt. and Pali: *vihāra*) in London, Dharmapala thought, was a way for Sinhalas to return to the tradition of building and to reform themselves in the process. ("Sinhalas do not have the intelligence to give the English anything worldly. The only wealth the Sinhalas can give the English is the noble dharma.")[16] The *vihara* would give them what the Buddha taught, and that knowledge would give them insight: "I am convinced that by the power of the Dhamma they would see the unwisdom of enslaving nations to satisfy their ambitions" (ibid., 740).

What is instructive is that Dharmapala thought that Sinhalas needed to missionize their religion among non-Buddhists for the sake of reforming themselves. He makes his case for his religion's potential for social reformation by quoting Max Muller: "The most important element of Buddhist reform has always been its social and moral code. . . . He whose meditations had been how to deliver the soul of man from misery and the fear of death had delivered the people from a degrading thralldom and from priestly tyranny" (Guruge, 650). The resonance of those words—not merely Dharmapala's engagement with Muller and Western scholarly concerns, but also the transposition by which Buddha's liberating ancient Indians from Brahmin priests becomes the Dhamma's liberating modern Sinhalas from Christian ones—assumes that missionizing is as much involved with reforming society as with setting the individual on the path to salvation. Social reform is not in fact a traditional Buddhist goal; but Dharmapala understands Buddhism as a vehicle for saving the Sinhala people from deracination. Beyond Sri Lanka, Buddhism has more general liberational potential. As a religion of analysis and inquiry into the self, it can liberate a believer in any religion from "priestcraft, materialism, and sheep theology" (ibid., 696).

Olcott reached Sri Lanka in 1880 and immediately took the five precepts in Galle (without regarding his doing so as conversion or even an exclusive commitment to one Asian religion).[17] Once acquainted, Dharmapala and Olcott traveled by oxcart through a part of the island Dharmapala knew no better than Olcott, village Sri Lanka. There Dharmapala encountered a landscape of what he thought of as desolation—the poverty and lethargy of the Sinhala peasantry. In 1890 when Olcott convened a meeting of Buddhists in Madras, Dharmapala joined delegates from Burma, Chittagong, and Japan as the representative of Sinhala Buddhism. Afterward he went north to Bodh Gaya with the Japanese delegate and saw another landscape of desolation, the desecration of the most sacred place in the Buddhist world (Guruge, 649). To this extent, Dharmapala's project was of one piece; he would reclaim the ancient sites, return Sri Lankan villages to the righteousness they had known before colonialism, unite the Buddhist world by way of the Maha Bodhi Society, and missionize Buddhism in non-Buddhist societies as an act of self-reform and world renewal.

Dharmapala's emphasis on clear exposition in preaching the *Dhamma* was applicable to either a local context or a foreign one. To Sinhala audiences, he offered moral instruction and practical advice about handling money, table manners, and personal hygiene.[18] For Western audiences, preaching in a way that resembled a Christian sermon made it an easily recognized social practice. Clarity allowed the brilliance of the Buddha's teaching to be easily communicated, and nothing was lost, he thought, by sloughing off the repetitive and time-consuming quality of the traditional form. Westerners were not likely in any event to be interested in making merit. They could convert by taking the Three Refuges; they could participate if they liked; or they could come and go. The one thing non-Sinhalas were certain to find engaging was meditation. Dharmapala reimagined that practice as something laypeople could pursue; he practiced meditation himself; and he made certain that foreign donors saw him doing so.[19]

The way Dharmapala talks about missionizing cycles ranges between the benign and the ferocious. In 1893 he told the Parliament of Religions that the Chicago meeting recalled Asoka's third-century B.C.E. sending out "gentle teachers, the mild disciples of Buddha," going on to conclude that "the influence of that congress, held twenty one centuries ago, is today a living power, for you everywhere see mildness in Asia" (Guruge, 655). In order to make the "Mongolian mild," however, Buddhism had to "conquer" Asia (xvii). Although the British have brought Sri Lanka "opium, ganja, whisky, and other alcoholic poisons as well as every kind of abominable vice . . . to undermine the vitality of our people . . . [w]e, on our part, should with a loving heart, give the Britishers the ennobling and purifying faith of our Tathagato" (ibid., 764). He described his own mission in even milder terms: "I have come to the West . . . not to convert Westerners to Buddhism, but to bring some knowledge of a religion that . . . has quickened the peoples of Asia to higher achievements" (ibid., 681). The distinction between conversion and "bringing knowledge" is worth reiterating. By not imposing Protestant ideas about conversion, Dharmapala gave the West a Buddhism more agreeable to seekers abandoning religious traditions that insist on religious identity as an exclusive commitment.[20]

Obeyesekere makes a great deal of the contrast between Dharmapala's invocation of mildness and his "oedipal rage."[21] Although Dharmapala frequently spoke of compassion (Pali: *maitreya*), he did not visit much of it on westernized Sri Lankans, including his own family. He turned against his father ("the wild elephant with a walking stick," Guruge, 242) and his brother ("an elephant doctor," ibid., 243), despite the fact that it was their money which supported his early missionary efforts. Joining forces with the two outstanding monks of his day, he preferred the company of Mohottivatte Gunananda, (1823–1890), the fiery orator, over Hikkaduve Sumangala (1827–1911), the scholarly administrator (ibid., 232). In speaking of the Japanese victory over the Russians in 1905, Dharmapala described the defeat in terms that are at once religious and bloodthirsty: "A day of triumph for Buddhism. The Christian god lies prostrate before Buddha. His head is crushed, he lies expiring."[22] Although he drew a distinction between Christian missionaries and Buddhist ones—Christians are high-living, corrupt, meat-eaters; Buddhists are peaceful, righteous, and vegetarian—he also took pleasure in discovering that Buddhists had set fire to a Catholic church in Anuradhapura.[23]

These contradictions can be read in several ways—poetic excess, the evolution of a human being who is both charismatic and fallible, or the ugly face Dharmapala showed minorities in Sri Lanka (as opposed to his inclusive feelings toward Buddhists and non-Buddhists beyond it). Dharmapala brought great intensity to the project of reform, and he was incapable of recognizing the virtue in Sri Lanka's being a multiethnic society. The balance of power had swung, Dharmapala thought, to the Sri Lankan minorities—he reviled Tamils, Muslims, and even immigrants from Kerala (too few in number to count as a minority community)—and Buddhist "mildness" too closely resembled the inanition he wanted to put right. He had this same ambivalence toward the monkhood. "In all Buddhist countries," he argued, "the Bhikshus monks with a few exceptions, have failed to influence the people" (Guruge, 328). More Buddhist mildness will not right the balance; "de-voted enthusiasts" need to be "zealous" in spreading the religion (ibid., 328). The emphasis on activism has important consequences for the Buddhism Dharmapala envisioned: "Greater than the bliss of sweet Nirvana is the life of moral activity" (737).

As Dharmapala understood things, the inanition of his coreligionists could scarcely be traced to the Buddha's own life:

> The Blessed One worked daily for 22 hours, from His 35th year to His 80th Year. . . . The ancient Rishis counted time in years, but our Lord counted time by hours. An hour under the Dispensation of the Buddha is equal to a year and the Gospel of Activity was what He preached day after day for 16,200 days, and each day He was engaged in doing good to the world of gods and men twenty-two hours. During the forty-five years His blessed life was spent for 256400 [sic] hours in working for the welfare of the world. (Guruge, 737)

While Dharmapala calibrates the Buddha's life on a hyperbolic scale, he interprets that life in an even more exotic manner, melding the "this-worldly asceticism" that Obeyesekere associates with Protestant Buddhism with a Taylorist fixation on small units of time—not unimaginably long Hindu intervals—for productive work.[24]

There are inconsistencies here that go beyond the activity Buddhism requires and the peace it offers. Dharmapala redefined the nature of a Buddhist sermon (Pali: *bana*), sloughing off the incantatory parts and reducing the night-long act of merit making to something resembling a Christian sermon (*dhammadeśana*). And while he insisted on the rationalistic character of the religion, he also propagated meditation as an important part of Buddhist religiosity. In describing both the coming of the Sinhala prince Vijaya to Sri Lanka and the subsequent founding of Buddhism in the island, he read the mythological details out of the stories (Guruge, 479 and 485). He excluded popular religion, astrology, and necromancy from the practice of enlightened Buddhism in Burma and Sri Lanka (ibid., 637–638), arguing that Buddhism was "pure science" with no room for theology or the worship of the Hindu gods (*devas*) who formed an integral part of Sinhala Buddhism from Dharmapala's time to the present (ibid., 658). But he also told a British audience that, although the Buddhist doctrine is called atheistic, "Buddhism teaches that we are surrounded by gods or devas. Buddha taught there are many gods. One god can illuminate ten thousand world systems. Such mighty gods exist. Divine beings exist from eternity to eternity. The Buddha was no atheist. He was a super-divine-devatideva [the god of gods]" (ibid., 669).[25]

I mention these complications to foreground the role the Maha Bodhi Society played in the evolution of the Buddhist ethnoscape, for it developed in similarly convoluted ways. Dharmapala founded the society to restore the sacred site of Bodh Gaya, a place that preserved material evidence of the Enlightenment and a living connection to the Buddha. For Olcott, by contrast, relic veneration was superstition—he thought that the Tooth Relic in Kandy was an animal bone—and Dharmapala's interest in relics played a role in the two men's estrangement.[26] But the irony is surely this. However unlikely venerating the physical remains of a man who taught the doctrine of no-soul (and however inconsistent with the rationalistic Buddhism Dharmapala generally favored), the veneration of relics and the practice of pilgrimage that it inspired had surprising results. They created a nexus for a Buddhist ethnoscape that transcends the Sinhala influences on its twentieth-century reconstruction. Relics have a prelapsarian centrality for all varieties of Buddhism that enables the Maha Bodhi Society to be nonethnic, nonsectarian, and inclusive of women.[27] In that regard, relics come to play a progressive role in the universalist Buddhism Dharmapala created abroad.

THE MAHA BODHI SOCIETY

Dharmapala first learned of the wretched condition to which Bodh Gaya had been reduced indirectly by reading Edwin Arnold's account in a London newspaper. "Vandalism," Arnold wrote, "has made havoc of the graceful life-like statues of the Glorious Tathagata; and it is certainly painful . . . to wander round the precincts of the holy tree and see scores and hundreds of broken sculptures lying . . . on brick heaps scattered; some delicately carved with incidents of the Buddha legend, and some bearing clear and precious inscriptions . . ." (Guruge, 589). That vandalism derives from the Buddhists' losing control of the place; toward the end of the sixteenth century the Bodh Gaya temple fell into Hindu control. By Dharmapala's time a lineage of Shaivite priests held sway over the temple, conducting their own rituals. Dharmapala was not the first outsider to find Hindus presiding over the site. In attempting to restore the Buddhist character of Bodh Gaya, Dharmapala followed in the wake of a Burmese king who had started to restore the place in 1833.[28] That effort came to naught, but was succeeded in the 1870s by the Burmese king Mindon's attempt to carry on the work, and a final Burmese initiative under Thibaw, who sent Burmese monks to reside in a rest house he built.[29] Burmese patronage was superseded by a government of Bengal project with a different conception of restoration work (itself guided by a small stone model found among the ruins).

Dharmapala arrived in Bodh Gaya in January of 1891. By May he had started a branch of the Maha Bodhi Society, "the first Buddhist organization in the history of modern Buddhism to begin a propaganda for the dissemination of the Dhamma in non-Buddhist lands" (ibid., 732), and by July he brought four Sinhala monks of the Ramanna *Nikaya* (monastic community) to reside in the Burmese rest house.[30] The ethnic markers were at cross-purposes with Dharmapala's intention to establish Bodh Gaya as a shrine and pilgrimage site for all Buddhists.[31] But a religious difference immediately outstripped ethnic and sectarian divisions, and Dharmapala threw himself into removing the Shaivites from the temple. Although he established branches of the Maha Bodhi Society elsewhere and trained monks for *dharmaduta*, it is unclear how wholeheartedly Dharmapala "brought knowledge" of the Dhamma to Indians. In print his feelings were clearer. There he melded personal salvation with social reformation by asserting that "the people of India were happy in the Buddhist period. Our Lord Buddha opened the gates of Immortality to all without distinction of Caste, Colour, and Sex."[32]

Dharmapala did not linger in Bodh Gaya, moving the Maha Bodhi Society to Calcutta and founding the *Maha Bodhi Journal* in 1892. The journal led to his being invited in 1893 to attend the Parliament of Religions in Chicago. Before he went, he visited Arakan (where Buddhists raised funds to rent a house in Calcutta), Rangoon, Sri Lanka, and England. In Chicago, he gave the Three Refuges to a New York businessman, Charles Strauss, an act that might be considered the first conversion in America.[33] He convinced Paul Carus to establish a branch of the Maha Bodhi Society in Chicago.[34] On his way back to Sri Lanka he visited Hawai'i (meeting a wealthy American woman who became his chief lay supporter), Japan, China, Thailand, and Malaysia (Guruge, xxxvi–xxxvii). In Colombo he raised funds for the purchase of Maha Bodhi Village, and in 1894 arranged the first organized pilgrimage of Sinhala Buddhists to Bodh Gaya. As Dharmapala's efforts to restore the site to Buddhist control got under way, relations with Bodh Gaya's Shaivite priest became more contentious, culminating in the priest and his helpers removing (and throwing into a nearby pond) the Buddha image Dharmapala had brought from Japan. Dharmapala sued, and he was able to regain control of the Burmese rest house and install the Buddha image there (where it remained until 1910 when a judge ordered it transferred to Calcutta).

In his own life Dharmapala pursued the zealous activity he advocated for the reformation of Buddhism and Buddhists. In a letter to a British official in Sri Lanka, he insisted: "I have to be active and activity means agitation according to constitutional means" (Guruge, 753). He traveled the world, making a second trip to the United States in 1896, another trip to Japan (his third) in 1902, followed by a third to the United States in 1902, a fourth in 1913, and a fifth in 1925, besides periodically returning to Sri Lanka. The organizational skills he saw in Olcott he applied to the Buddhist cause, establishing branches of the Maha Bodhi Society in Madras and Kushinagar in 1900, purchasing land at Sarnath in 1901, and founding industrial schools (which he had first seen in the United States and Europe) in Sarnath in 1904 and Sri Lanka in 1906. That same year he also established a Sinhala Buddhist newspaper in Colombo and the Maha Bodhi Press. In 1920 he completed construction of a Buddhist *vihara* in Calcutta. In 1926 he established the headquarters of the British Buddhist mission in London and in 1930 built a *vihara* at Sarnath.

THE INSTITUTIONAL LIFE OF DHARMADUTA

Dharmapala established a school in Colombo to begin the training of missionary monks, sending them on to India for higher education. But the school never amounted to much, and after his lifetime no one institution developed for propagating Sinhala Buddhism.[35] As is generally the case with Dharmapala's innovations, his influence was wide but diffuse. In Colombo that influence ran, first, through two colleges of monastic learning, Vidyodaya and Vidyalankara, which had been established in the late nineteenth century, and later, through a monastery, Vajirarama, which began with a modernist and foreign-facing orientation. For all of Bodh Gaya's importance as a focus of Buddhist feeling, these institutions have played a much greater role in the propagation of Buddhism abroad. They have been sending institutions; Bodh Gaya has been a receiving institution. The World Fellowship of Buddhists is another vehicle for mission work, led by monks and laypeople. Although its membership is truly worldwide, it was founded in Colombo, and Sinhala Buddhists have always played a dominant role in the organization.

In its Sri Lankan context, the Maha Bodhi Society began on the grounds of Vidyodaya.[36] Monks educated there—Kalukondayave Pannasekhera (1895–1977), Hinatiyana Dhammaloka (1900–1981), and Hendiyagala Silaratana (1913–1982) are leading examples—absorbed Dharmapala's concern for the desolation of Sinhala villages and attempted to invigorate them by programs fixed on village development and the eradication of crime, temperance, vegetarianism, and proper female behavior.[37] They were missionaries to their own people. Dhammaloka used to wait at the Kompanna Veedya train station as Colombo office workers were heading home from work. There he would preach in a public arena (one that has a Christian precedent but no Buddhist one), and preach so quickly that he could deliver his message in the brief time during which trains paused to pick up passengers (putting into practice Dharmapala's emphasis on the Buddha's Taylorism).[38] In Heenatiyana, a village notorious for cattle theft and gambling, he established a conciliation board, voluntary labor campaigns, and meditation classes, as well as a school where he trained monks for *dharmaduta*.[39]

Vidyalankara monks, by contrast, applied the nationalist and political aspects of Dharmapala's program to everyday life. Although the distinction between the "Marxist-dominated and anti-imperialist Vidyalankara and the conservative Vidyodaya" sometimes grows blurry, Seneviratne castigates the Vidyalankara monks in particular for pursuing a Marxism that evolved into a Buddhist socialism and then into a Sinhala chauvinism.[40] Vidyalankara monks such as Walpola Rahula and Yakkaduwe Pragnarama carried Dharmapala's ideas forward even more aggressively than the Vidyodaya monks, insisting that a monk's obligations lay in this world, guiding laypeople, speaking out on political issues, and defending the nation. Rahula wore a beret in Paris, while Pragnarama kept a beard, slept during the day, and carried on his affairs at night. In pushing the limits of decorum, such figures redefined the rôle of a monk. That was their point· Rahula once supported a young monk who had received a law degree and wanted to practice law.[41]

The connections among these institutions are multiple and cross-cutting. Palane Vajiragnana (1878-1955) was one of the monks Dharmapala considered a "hero-giant," suitable for use as an example to cast shame on the Colombo elite. He was educated at Vidyodaya by Hikkaduve Sumangala, who also served as the president of the Maha Bodhi Society. Vajiragnana developed Vajirarama into a temple with a self-consciously modern and active relationship with the outside world, and in the 1920s he delivered the first Buddhist sermon broadcast on radio. His sermons applied the Dhamma to everyday problems. His students went further afield. Although he spent the great majority of his life in Sri Lanka, Madihe Pannasiha (1913-) established the first Sri Lankan *vihara* in North America. Palane Vajiragnana's other students became relentless *dharmadutas*. His senior student Narada (1898-1993) established a tradition of travel that mimicked Dharmapala's high energy, traveling to Vietnam thirty-five times.[42]

When Dharmapala finished the Mulagandakuti Vihara in Sarnath, he invited Narada to participate in the opening celebration. Although he was relatively young, Narada possessed the skill *dharmaduta* monks need most—a world language—and conducted the ceremony in English on behalf of a senior monk who lacked it.[43] In the 1950s Narada spent some years at the London Buddhist Vihara, which Dharmapala had established in 1926, using it as a base for forays into nearby places in continental Europe. There he began a practice of writing short pamphlets—"Buddhism in a Nutshell" suggests their function—that introduced Buddhism to both westerners and Sri Lankans. Eventually Vajirarama became the base for his work, although he continued to make regular *dharmaduta* journeys abroad.

Narada brought saplings from the bo tree at Anuradhapura to places he visited and as early as 1935 planted one at Borobudur while on a lecture tour of Java, following suit in Dar-es-Salaam, Singapore, Malaysia, India, and Nepal.[44] But the focus of his travels was Vietnam, where he distributed saplings from Saigon to Hanoi.[45] He followed the Dharmapalite practice of visiting the poor and needy, and in the 1970s visited military hospitals to bring comfort to patients, as well as organizing the recitation of protective verses at the Jetavana Vihara, the headquarters of the Theravada monkhood in Vietnam.[46] The biographer of his brother monk Piyadassi says that Narada cleared the way for Piyadassi's later work by weaning Vietnamese away from Cao-Dai: "Through his influence people gave up the ritualistic type of Buddhism and instead followed the intellectual and philosophical aspects of the Theravada teaching."[47] In Southeast Asia, the thrust of *dharmaduta* work paralleled efforts in Sri Lanka to move people from one kind of Buddhist practice to another. But rather than simply following Dharmapala's insistence that ritual is bad and real Theravada is not ritualistic, Narada and Piyadassi retained the chanting ritual—Piyadassi's biography notwithstanding—and the Xa Loi temple in Saigon where Narada resided draws Buddhists because it has what other Vietnamese temples lack, a Buddha relic.

The cover of Abeyesekera's biography depicts Piyadassi in a lonely setting, barefoot, with his begging bowl swung over his shoulder. His description of Piyadassi as a "wandering monk" evokes an image of missionary Buddhism that resonates with the life of the early monkhood. But Piyadassi (like Narada and other *dharmaduta* monks today) had a fixed residence, and the photographs at the end of Abeyesekera's text better suggest the contexts where Sinhala monks pursue *dharmaduta* these days: feeding kangaroos in Australia, administering the eight precepts to a Swiss lawyer in a forest hermitage in Kandy, addressing the World Fellowship of Buddhists in Bangkok, speaking to students at the University of Stockholm, establishing a ritual space in the Netherlands, and trekking up Monte Bianco in Italy (165–190). By the early 1990s Piyadassi had traveled around the world thirteen times.[48]

Sometimes contacts between Sri Lankan Buddhists and other parts of the Theravada world developed from the opposite direction. As LeVine (Chap. 2) shows, a Theravada tradition was reawakened in Nepal early in the twentieth century by a monk named Pragnananda, who led a long monastic life of sixty-four years. During this time, he was expelled from Nepal and tried to reestablish pilgrimage to Lumbini.[49] His student Amritananda was given lower ordination in 1936 (by the same Burmese monk who had ordained Pragnananda), and Amritananda was sent to Colombo for further studies. He received his higher ordination from Palane Vajirarama and returned to Nepal in 1942. He and his teacher were banished from Nepal in short order, and he went back to Sri Lanka. In 1946 Amritananda returned with Narada. They gained an audience with the Nepalese king, and *bhikkhus* were allowed to stay, restoring Theravada. Amritananda, by then a member of the global Theravada establishment, was back in Colombo in 1950 for the inaugural conference of the World Fellowship of Buddhists, and he hosted the group's fourth and fifteenth conferences in Nepal.[50]

When Sri Lankan monks go on *dharmaduta* missions these days, they typically tie together a number of stops that take them entirely around the world. Piyadassi's world mission of 1991 entailed a representative variety of activities. In the Netherlands he served as chief guest at the opening of a new monastery and officiated at a robe-offering ceremony at a temple in The Hague.[51] From there he flew to Rome, where he gave a talk on "The Central Concept of Buddhism" to the United Nations Food and Agriculture Organization, before visiting the first Theravada *vihara* in Italy at Seeze. He flew on to France, giving a similar talk at the UNESCO headquarters, then visited his longtime lay supporters at the Vietnamese center and led a program of meditation and discussion sessions. In Switzerland he taught meditation. After a stop in Sweden, a month-long program of activities followed in England, as he moved among the London Buddhist Vihara, the Thames Meditation Center in Sussex, the Saddhatissa International Center in Surrey, and the Buddhist Cultural Institute in London. Crossing the Atlantic, he spent the first half of 1992 in Los Angeles, venturing out to New York, Washington, D.C., Montreal, Toronto, Calgary, Edmonton, Vancouver, and San Francisco. In Japan he visited with the chief monk of the Kōdō Kyōdan Sect and lent his support to the World Tathagata movement in Korea. On his way home, he made stops in Indonesia, Malaysia, and Singapore.

THE SINHALA BUDDHIST ETHNOSCAPE

Whatever other effects nineteenth-century missionary discourse exerted on how Sri Lankans—monks, laypeople, historians of religion, and other academics—have conceptualized *dharmaduta*, Piyadassi's travels suggest that he does not spend a lot of time trying to convert non-Buddhists. He pastors to a flock that has spread itself around the globe. He leads meditation sessions. He talks about Dhamma to interested non-Buddhists. The skills required to do so entail considerably more than textual knowledge. On Piyadassi's interpretation of *dharmaduta*, a monk needs to have knowledge of several languages; he urges young monks to acquire more than a knowledge of Sinhala, Tamil, Pali, and Sanskrit. "Most of the Sanskrit and Pali works, their commentaries, and interpretations are found in English," he writes. "English, therefore, is a must for every bhikkhu."[52] This is even more important for a monk intending to work overseas: without it, "one becomes a dumb animal in foreign soil." The virtues of a world language duly noted, the argument that knowing English is a monk's access to Buddhist doctrine should give the Pali Text Society cause for reflection on hybridity and unintended effects.

In the West, the *dharmaduta* monk needs an additional skill. He must acquire comparative knowledge:

> In the West in particular, the bhikkhu would cut a sorry figure without the knowledge of other isms. The Western mind is an inquiring mind. They are fed up with their traditional religious beliefs, with the catastrophic wars and threat of impending nuclear disasters. The Westerner's great and immediate need is a new way of life. That is the task the Buddhist monk has to fulfil in the modern day world.[53]

On the Sri Lankan front, Piyadassi urges reform, in this case reforming the reformation, namely the political activism and secularization associated with the Vidyalankara monks. As young monks became increasingly involved in political movements in the late 1980s, he made comments that were framed abstractly but referenced Sinhala society's anxiety about monks' involvement in nationalist organizations. He tied his vision to the need for a monk to be a "practical" person, which he defines as a person who "practices" meditation.[54] A monk cannot describe the benefits of meditation without having studied both *vipassana* (Pali: mindfulness) and *satipathana* (Pali: insight) meditation. Disaster occurs when a monk commits himself entirely to the life of this world—social service, hospital welfare work, teaching in schools. Piyadassi's energetic pursuit of *dharmaduta* work owes to Dharmapala, even as he opposes the "this-worldly" orientation that Dharmapala introduced to the monkhood.

Sinhala monks nowadays regard *dharmaduta* as an ancient and fundamental part of the monastic life. A small number of Sinhala monks reside permanently overseas as *dharmaduta* monks, and a larger number periodically go out on *dharmaduta* trips. Their activities border on the entrepreneurial. When they establish

Buddhism in exotic places, they benefit themselves. Seneviratne pulls no punches about foreign travel.[55] It provides upward mobility for monks and redounds to their economic advantage. I once saw Mapalagama Vipulasara—a monk easy to recognize because of his goatee—in the Bangkok airport when he was returning from a conference. As he made his way to the departure gate, he had so many electrical appliances in his two baggage carts that he had to ask another traveler to push one for him. Members of the Sri Lanka monkhood have a neologism for foreign travel. They call it *videsagatavima* ("enforeignization") and recognize what spending time abroad does for a monk's career. It achieves the same result that foreign residence does for a Sri Lankan in business, civil service, or academic life: it confers status. That monks know how many trips to Vietnam they have made or how many times they have flown around the world suggests the same conclusion.

Before his death Vipulasara served as general secretary of the Maha Bodhi Society, and to that extent he carried on the *dharmaduta* role in an organizational setting that began with Dharmapala and Olcott. But his other offices indicate just how far the proliferation of voluntary organizations has come in modern Buddhism. Besides serving on the Kalyani Samagi Dharma Maha Sangha Sabha (the board that manages his monastic community), he was involved with the World Bhikkhu Congress, the Sri Lanka Korea Cultural Association, the Sri Lanka Supreme Sangha Council (organizer/secretary), the Jathika Kala Peramuna (founder), the Sri Lanka Buddhist Congress (president), the Japan–Sri Lanka Center in Japan, the Asian Buddhist Peace Council (vice president), the Lanka Kala Sangamaya (patron), the Board of Management of the Buddhist and Pali University, and the All Religious Leaders' Council. Japan loomed large in Vipulasara's travel overseas, and in 1975 he established the Japan Sri Lanka Friendship Society.[56] In the years that followed Sri Lankan relics were sent to Japan, Sinhala dance troupes appeared there, and one of the monk's students was ordained as a Sōtō Zen monk, taking his training in that tradition at the Eihei Temple in Chubu.[57] In such lives the Sinhala Buddhist ethnoscape meets the Buddhist ethnoscape headlong.

When Sinhala monks travel overseas, their destination is likely to be one of two types of monasteries.[58] The first is the universalistic monastery that Dharmapala envisioned. He wanted the London Buddhist Vihara to spread the teachings to the British, not serve Sinhalas living in England. When he established the London *vihara* in 1926, it became the first Theravada Buddhist temple located beyond the continent of Asia.[59] Circumstances forced the *vihara* to close at the time of the Second World War, and it has moved several times from one residence to another. Its functions have also changed over time because it now serves Sinhalas living in London and beyond. But the most changed circumstance is external to the temple.

It is now one of fifty-one Buddhist temples, foundations, and centers in London.[60] In this context, it makes sense to qualify the expression "universalistic" by saying that, while each of these groups is likely to welcome outsiders, all but two have a doctrinal tradition. Dharmapala's Buddhism for non-Buddhists was Theravada (of the Sinhala variety); nowadays some of these centers are as eclectic as the one that practices both Theravada and Mahayana, and some are innovative (the Heart of London Sangha, Community of Interbeing, describes itself as "Vietnamese Zen" and "engaged Buddhist").

Universalistic Theravada temples have grown up in other Western contexts. Most were established by westerners who arranged for a Sri Lankan monk to live at the temple, give Dhamma talks, and teach meditation. The Buddhayana temple in the Netherlands has been universalistic in a doctrinal way. The Dutchman who started the temple took the name Anagarika, linking himself to Dharmapala, and Piyadassi has been a regular visitor.[61] But Anagarika Dhammawirantha also maintains connections to Tibetan and Mahayana monks, who give talks and teach meditation at the Buddhayana center, the name suggesting an attempt to transcend sectarianism. And the center has acquired another universalizing element by default. Although its focus falls on Dutch people interested in Buddhism, Sri Lankans living in Europe also take part in the temple's activities.

The other form Sri Lankan temples assume overseas is the ethnic temple, serving Sinhala expatriates. The distinction between the two types is seldom impermeable, temples focused on westerners often including local Sinhalas, and Sinhala temples abroad reaching out to local people. Postwar Malaysia provides a case in point. Worried about the influence of Christian schools and the prospect of their children converting, Sinhala Buddhists in Kuala Lumpur wrote the principal of Vidyalankara, asking him to send them a monk to reside at the Brickfields Vihara. Kirinde Dhammananda arrived in 1952 and set about refurbishing the temple, preaching in Sinhala, counseling people, and establishing a Sunday school.[62] In 1963 he organized the Buddhist Missionary Society, which publishes pamphlets and books, usually in English, but also translated into Chinese and Indonesian. He usually preaches in English (as do his students), traveling around Malaysia and Singapore in a way that makes Dhamma available not only to Sinhalas, but also to other English-speaking Southeast Asians and Europeans.

Dhammananda has ties to Mahayana monks in Malaysia, an openness he traces to the Buddha's knowing nothing of sectarian distinctions.[63] The main Sinhala temple in Singapore, Lankaramaya, provides a more extreme example of the ethnic temple, demonstrating that ethnic distinctions mean quite a lot to Sinhalas. The membership of Lankaramaya is almost entirely Sinhala, and even though the *vihara*'s charter makes no reference to ethnicity, its activities exclude the participation of people who do not speak Sinhala. Dhamma discourse is done in the Sinhala style (the very form that Dharmapala rejected); the giving of alms to monks and the chanting of *pirit* are emphasized, as is the veneration of a Buddha image and relics brought from Sri Lanka. These religious activities are supplemented by cultural ones, including the teaching of Sinhala for children and the celebration of the Sinhala New Year. Where the universalistic temple brings something new to non-Buddhists, the ethnic temple allows Buddhists to hold on to their traditions in a new and often threatening setting.

Sometimes monks prove to be more willing to adapt their lives to an exotic setting than their supporters would like; sometimes they are less eager to adapt than their lay supporters; sometimes the temple ordains non-Asians as monks and welcomes converts and religious seekers; sometimes it remains an ethnic enclave. A Sinhala temple was established in Sydney in 1990, appropriating the name Lankaramaya as a sign of both its intentions and inspirations. The exclusivity of the Sydney temple made one Australian Buddhist of Sinhala origins upset enough to set up a web page to air his views. His objections to the Lankaramaya model derived from his conception of Buddhism as a missionary religion:

> While there are now a large number of Sri Lankan monks in Western countries they are not engaged in dhamma-duta work, but in catering for the Sri Lankan communities abroad. In effect they are denying the universalistic character of Buddhism [and] returning it to the particularistic mould of ethnic religion in contravention of the clear injunctions of the Buddha.[64]

From Gunasekara's point of view, spreading Buddhism does not require knowledge of Pali, sitting on the floor, or Asian attire. All that is needed to restore Buddhism's universalistic nature is avoiding the *bana*-style preaching of the Lankaramaya kind in favor of the Dhamma discussion that Dharmapala advocated.[65]

THE BUDDHIST ETHNOSCAPE

There is a network of Sinhala monks spread around the world bringing Dhamma to westerners (from London and Los Angeles to Rio), "theravadizing" local systems of belief and practice among non-Theravada Buddhists (in Singapore, Malaysia, Vietnam, and Nepal), catering to the everyday needs of Sinhalas in foreign contexts, maintaining sacred sites in India (Bodh Gaya, Sarnath, Sanchi, Savatti,

Amaravati), and serving pilgrims of all kinds.[66] This network depends on laypeople who serve as supporters (*dāyakas*) for those monks, and it would not exist without them. In most contexts *dāyakas* are local Buddhists, but in India the situation is less clear. Are those supporters local Buddhists or Sinhalas now on pilgrimage? Are they local non-Buddhists or foreign Buddhists? These questions address two issues: just how successful was Dharmapala in "bringing knowledge" of Dhamma to India and at what point does the Sinhala Buddhist ethnoscape yield to the Buddhist ethnoscape.

Dharmapala is missing from Trevor Ling's treatment of the revival of Buddhism in India, which does not say much about the Maha Bodhi Society either. Instead he emphasizes that modern Buddhism has attracted two types of Indian adherents, which he typifies by drawing a distinction between Nehru and Ambedkar.[67] As secular intellectuals both were drawn to Buddhism because of their disenchantment with caste society and its inequities, a connection Dharmapala first struck. However impressed he may have been by Buddhism as a teaching, Nehru never became a Buddhist, and Indians like him have gravitated instead toward groups such as the Maha Bodhi Society. Although they became Buddhists, Ambedkar's Dalit followers, by contrast, have not looked to the society or to non-Indian monks who live in India for leadership. Either Dharmapala regarded India as important for its sacred sites and relics (and converting Indians was incidental) or his missionizing—in India as in the West—did not have a great investment in conversion as such. As it has turned out, the Maha Bodhi Society has had greater relevance to Buddhists living outside of India than to local people.[68]

New Indian Buddhists have no obvious connection to the Maha Bodhi Society. Ambedkar did not learn of Buddhism by way of either Dharmapala or the society. As a student, Ambedkar was given a Marathi-language biography of the Buddha, and that account sparked his lifelong interest.[69] Nor did the society play much of a role in his conversion some forty years later. After he announced in 1935 that he would not die a Hindu, the Maha Bodhi Society invited him to become a Buddhist, just as he received proposals from followers of other Indian religions— Islam, Sikhism, and Christianity—urging his conversion.[70] Initially he planned the event (as well as the mass conversions that would follow) for Mumbai, but he was persuaded to move the ceremony to Nagpur because of his reform campaigns there and the presence of substantial numbers of Dalits in that part of eastern Maharashtra.[71] Neither place qualifies as a Buddhist sacred site. In other words, the social reform that the mass conversion of Dalits to Buddhism represents follows neither from the reestablishing of the Buddhist sites of north India nor from Dharmapala's insistence that Buddhism offers India a chance at its own reformation.

The Maha Bodhi Society's example led to the proliferation of transnational Buddhist voluntary organizations such as the World Fellowship of Buddhists (WFB). It was more directly an outgrowth of the Ceylon Buddhist Congress and carried on both organizations' interest in fostering Buddhism by extending it in transnational directions. The WFB held its first conference in Colombo in 1950 and its second in 1952 in Japan, drawing Buddhists of various ethnic origins and sectarian identities. Although conferences have taken up education, social action, and doctrinal issues, spreading the teachings has been in the forefront.[72] Those early meetings led to the reinvigoration of Theravada in Nepal and the founding of several Theravada monasteries in Vietnam.[73] Narada's thirty-five visits put contact between Sinhala Buddhism and some 150,000 Vietnamese followers of Theravada on a regular basis.[74] In this context, *dharmaduta* has produced the internal conversion of Theravada Buddhists to practices Dharmapala endorsed, such as relic veneration.

Japanese delegates attended those first meetings of the WFB, and in meeting with other Buddhists, some became interested in organizational unification and others were impressed by Theravada's claim to being the original form of Buddhism.[75] As a result, Japanese laypeople have become involved in Sinhala Buddhism in a variety of ways: offering to protect the Tooth Relic with bullet-proof glass, organizing peace marches to respond to the ethnic conflict, establishing free nurseries and schools, and supporting village temples. Tracing out the upturn of Japanese charity and presence in Sri Lanka during the late 1980s and early 1990s, Seneviratne points to a local backlash against the considerable money and power that has flowed into the hands of Sinhala monks from Japanese supporters.[76] The most notorious controversy was the allegation that Pelpola Vipassi (who enjoyed the support of one of the world's richest men, Ryoichi Sasakawa) intended to establish Mahayana Buddhism in Sri Lanka. However baseless the allegation, the furor it created indicates the limits of the Buddhist ethnoscape.

But there are counterindications. The presence of voluntary organizations and the practice of regular visits have meant the cross-fertilization of, and challenge to, various forms of Buddhism. Having studied in Japan, a Sinhala monk returned to the island and constructed a Japanese-influenced temple outside of Colombo where nowadays *dāyakas* purchase space to commemorate their parents by installing their ashes in small shrines. Another Sinhala monk renovated Sanchi Vihara in India, splitting his time between Sanchi and his temple in Colombo. Japanese lay supporters brought one of that monk's students to reside in Japan, where in time he was appointed the chief Theravada (*sanghanāyaka*) of Japan.[77] It hardly seems likely that Japanese Buddhists will gravitate toward Theravada or

Sinhalas adopt Mahayana, but Buddhist influences nowadays move in both directions.

If the Buddhist ethnoscape has a center of gravity, it is the sacred sites of north India, because their historical importance, prelapsarian quality, and material potency draw together Buddhists of all kinds. Colombo organizes a specifically Sinhala Buddhist ethnoscape, its centrality deriving not from relics but from those self-understandings with which I began—the island's crucial role in the historical unfolding of what became "Buddhism" and a gathering sense that Buddhism is a missionary religion with responsibilities to all kinds of people. In many overseas settings, circumstances are making Sinhala Buddhism less Sri Lankan; in places such as Vietnam, Sinhala Buddhist missionaries are making local Buddhism more Theravada (in its specifically Sinhala form). Besides the interaction of particularisms that attach to ethnic identities—Sinhala and Japanese are the pertinent ones—the Buddhist ethnoscape is structured by a second dialectic between doctrinal forms such as Theravada and a generic Buddhism that is developing in Western venues. Amid their individual projects Buddhist missionaries negotiate their way through these force fields. And as for inanition, Dharmapala's indictment cannot be raised against today's monks. In the national election of December 2001, a Buddhist monk was elected to a seat in the Sri Lankan parliament.

Notes

1. I have used the expression "identity" rather than "community," not wanting to reinscribe here the mythology of an unchanging Sinhala ethnic group that begins with Vijaya and continues to the present. The best critique of that notion is R. A. L. H. Gunawardana, "The People of the Lion: The Sinhala Identity and Ideology in History and Historiography," in *Sri Lanka: History and the Roots of Conflict*, ed. Jonathan Spencer (London: Routledge, 1990), 45–86.

2. Walpola Rahula, "A Challenge for the Maha Sangha," *Daily News*, January 2, 1988.

3. See Gananath Obeyesekere and Richard Gombrich, *Buddhism Transformed: Religious Change in Sri Lanka* (Princeton, N.J.: Princeton University Press, 1988), 202–240.

4. Arjun Appadurai develops the "ethnoscape" notion in two articles: "Disjuncture and Difference in the Global Cultural Economy," and "Global Ethnoscapes: Notes and Queries for a Transnational Anthropology," in Appadurai, *Modernity at Large; Cultural Dimensions of Globalization* (Minneapolis: University of Minnesota Press, 1996), 27–47 and 48–65 at 33. Dharmapala himself thought he lived in a radically shrinking world—"aeroplanes have brought England within ten days distance from Ceylon"—but his evaluation takes shape against a backdrop of travel by ocean liner; Ananda Guruge, ed., *Return to Righteousness: A*

Collection of Speeches, Essays, and Letters of Anagarika Dharmapala (Colombo: Government Press, 1965), 672.

5. Leading sources include Gananath Obeyesekere, "Personal Identity and Cultural Crisis: The Case of Anagarika Dharmapala of Sri Lanka," in *The Biographical Process: Studies in the History and Psychology of Religion*, ed. Frank E. Reynolds and Donald Capps (The Hague: Mouton, 1976), 221–252; and H. L. Seneviratne, *The Work of Kings: The New Buddhism in Sri Lanka* (Chicago: University of Chicago Press, 1999).

6. Gananath Obeyesekere, "Religious Symbolism and Political Change in Ceylon," in *Two Wheels of Dhamma*, ed. Bardwell Smith (Chambersburg, Pa.: A. A. R. Monograph No. 3, 1972), 58–78.

7. Sometimes he does so himself. In speaking of Christian reformation, he reveals a more constructionist attitude to tradition: "Christians ought to reform Christianity by eliminating the Old Testament and all those passages in the New Testament that show Jesus to have been quick-tempered and intolerant" (695).

8. Sukumar Dutt, *Buddhist Monks and Monasteries in India* (London: George Allen and Unwin, 1962), 54.

9. T. W. Rhys Davids and Hermann Oldenberg, *Vinaya Texts* (New York: Charles Scribner's Sons, 1899), *Mahavagga* I.11, 112.

10. Jonathan S. Walters, "Rethinking Buddhist Missions" (Ph.D. diss., University of Chicago, 1992). Walters makes his case for a nonmissiological reading of the "Buddha's Great Commission" by arguing that the string of datives ("for the sake of . . .") modify not the primary command, "wander," but the secondary command, "Let not two of you go the same way," and by concluding that the Pali is ambiguous (219n. 37). That ambiguity allows the missiological reading but does not warrant assuming that early Buddhists heard the "Commission" in the same way.

11. Dharmapala learned that role from Olcott, himself an "antimissionary missionary." See Obeyesekere and Gombrich, *Buddhism Transformed*, 204.

12. Wilhelm Geiger, trans., *Mahavamsa* (Colombo: Ceylon Government Press, 1960), 1, 20.

13. These images of early Britons are the product of a classical education. A nineteenth-century student reading Julius Caesar (*The Conquest of Gaul*, book 5, part 2) and Tacitus would have encountered accounts of "barbarians" wearing skins and painting their bodies blue or tattooing themselves, although those images were applied to the Picts or Caledonians; Charles Thomas, *Celtic Britain* (London: Thames and Hudson, 1986), 169. By the first century B.C.E., Britons were wearing clothes made of flax, not animal skins.

14. As sympathetic as I am to Walters' intentions, his definition of missionizing is so specifically Western that Buddhist monks of any historical period would virtually have to be Christians to qualify as what he calls "missionaries."

15. See Clifford Geertz, "'Internal Conversion' in Contemporary Bali," in *Malayan and Indo-*

nesian Studies Presented to Sir Richard Winstedt, ed. J. Bastin and R. Roolvink (Oxford: Oxford University Press, 1964), 282–302.

16. Ananda Guruge, ed., *Dharmapala Lipi* (Sinhala) (Colombo: Government Press, 1991), 286, quoted by Seneviratne, *The Work of Kings*, 37.

17. See Stephen Prothero, *The White Buddhist: The Asian Odyssey of Henry Steel Olcott* (Bloomington: Indiana University Press, 1996).

18. Seneviratne, *The Work of Kings*, 47.

19. Naranvila Dhammaratana, *Hadipannala Pannaloka* [Sinhala] (Sandalankava, Sri Lanka: Sandalanka Co-operative Society, 1954), 120–121, cited by Seneviratne, 212n. 32.

20. Mellor argues that what often makes Buddhism attractive to English people is its emphasis on self, which in the European tradition derives from the Reformation and the Enlightenment. According to this logic the English are drawn to a religion that offers a way to analyze the self by a predisposition to believe that knowledge about the self is the individual's principal obligation in life and the key to spiritual growth. Mellor does not say as much, but in a sense there is no need for English people to convert to Buddhism—they are already engaged in a project that is Buddhist in spirit. Philip A. Mellor, "Protestant Buddhism? The Cultural Translation of Buddhism in England," *Religion* (1991): 21, 73–92.

21. Obeyesekere, "Personal Identity and Cultural Crisis," 240–243.

22. Quoted in Michael Roberts, "For Humanity. For the Sinhalese. Dharmapala as Crusading Bosat," *Journal of Asian Studies* 56, no. 4 (November 1997): 1006–1032 at 1023.

23. Ibid., 1026.

24. Obeyesekere and Gombrich, *Buddhism Transformed*, 231.

25. Obeyesekere says that Dharmapala "emphasized the doctrinal aspects of Buddhism and scorned the intercessionary powers of *devas* (gods) and demons" in "Personal Identity and Cultural Crisis," 249. Making a distinction between the "original pure form" and "the mystical aspects superadded," Dharmapala characterized Buddhism as a great religion satisfying various kinds of spiritual needs (Guruge, *Return to Righteousness*, 670). *Deva* worship has lived on in Sri Lanka, and some cults have grown enormously, especially Skanda or Murugan, but Sinhala Buddhism, once installed in non-Buddhist contexts, has emphasized meditation and doctrine.

26. Obeyesekere, "Personal Identity and Cultural Crisis," 239. Dharmapala says he broke off his friendship with Olcott after he discovered that a copy of the Tooth Relic that had been given as a gift to Olcott had been placed under a shelf; Guruge, *Return to Righteousness*, xxxix. For his part, Olcott also opposed Dharmapala's zeal to confront the Hindu priest of Bodh Gaya. See K. D. G. Wimalaratna, "The Buddhist Revival and the Maha Bodhi Society," *Daily News*, June 1, 1991. A holy place used by two religious communities must have had its appeal to the ecumenical Olcott, whatever his views about venerating relics.

27. On February 15, 1998, an ordination ceremony for 140 women was held at Bodh Gaya,

reestablishing the order of nuns in Sri Lanka, Thailand, Tibet, and India where no women have been ordained for some eight centuries. The ceremony was organized by Master Xing-yun, the founder of Foguang Shan in Taiwan (see Chandler, Chap. 7 in this volume), but included the participation of Kirinde Dhammananda, P. Somalankara, and Mapalagama Vipulasara (the president of the Maha Bodhi Society of India), as well as Thich Nhat Hanh, the Dalai Lama, and the Supreme Patriarch of the Cambodian monkhood. The monkhood in Sri Lanka continues to oppose attempts to restore female ordination. "World Buddhists Affirm Equality of Women in Unprecedented Ordination Ceremony," January 30, 1998, http://www.prweb.com/releases/1998/prweb3407.htm.

28. Aryadasa Ranasinghe, "How Anagarika Dharmapala Saw Buddhagaya Viharaya in 1891," *Daily News*, April 27, 1999.

29. D. C. Ahir, *Buddhism in Modern India* (Delhi: Sri Satguru Publications, 1991), 108.

30. I suspect that Dharmapala's choosing Ramanna monks was strategic. Especially during the early years of this ordination tradition, whose establishment dates to 1864, the Ramanna monks were known for their piety, energy, and learning. See Kitsiri Malalgoda, *Buddhism in Sinhalese Society, 1750–1900* (Berkeley and Los Angeles: University of California Press, 1976).

31. Prothero, *The White Buddhist*, 158–159. He said he wanted Bodh Gaya to function for Buddhists as the holy sepulchre, Zion, and Mecca did for Christians, Jews, and Muslims

32. "Why India Should Become Buddhist?" *Maha Bodhi Journal* 32 (October 1924). At the very end of his life Dharmapala wrote another article also envisioning the conversion of Indians to Buddhism, "Return of Buddhism to India," *Maha Bodhi Journal* 40 (October 1932).

33. See Rick Fields, "Divided Dharma: White Buddhists, Ethnic Buddhists, and Racism," in *The Faces of Buddhism in America*, ed. Charles S. Prebish and Kenneth K. Tanaka (Berkeley and Los Angeles: University of California Press, 1998), 196.

34. Martin J. Verhoeven, "Americanizing the Buddha: Paul Carus and the Transformation of Asian Thought," in Prebish and Tanaka, eds., *Faces of Buddhism*, 218.

35. According to Gombrich and Obeyeskere, the Maha Bodhi Society controls and sponsors all Sinhala Buddhist temples outside of Sri Lanka, *Buddhism Transformed*, 206. The Sri Lankan *vihara* in Washington, D.C., however, was set up by the Sasana Sevaka Society, the Sri Lankan government, and American Buddhists; "Piyadassi Nayaka Thera on Global Dhamma Dhuta Mission to Show Peaceful Path to Progress," *Daily News*, November 22, 1991. The Lankarama Temple in Singapore is administered by the Singapore Sinhala Buddhist Association. "Call to Lankans to Fund Buddhist Temple in Singapore," *Daily News*, July 5, 1988.

36. K. D. G. Wimalaratne, "The Buddhist Revival and the Maha Bodhi Society."

37. Seneviratne, *The Work of Kings*, 65–129.

38. "Monk of Simplicity and Learning," *The Sunday Times*, December 11, 1994.

39. K. Samarakone, "A True Disciple of Buddha," *Daily News*, August 9, 1989.

40. Seneviratne, *The Work of Kings*, 131.

41. "Ven. Rahula Backs Bhikkhu Lawyer-Aspirant," *Daily News*, January 28, 1978. Rahula argued that "no Buddhist precept prohibited Ven. Sumana's taking his oath as an attorney. Those who opposed this move were ignorant of both the dhamma and the vinaya. . . . Society needed 20 to 30 bhikkhus . . . who were conversant with the law."

42. "Narada Maha Thera's Fifth Death Anniversary Falls Today," *Daily News*, October 2, 1987.

43. Nemsiri Mutukumara, "The Venerable Narada Maha Thera" (Colombo: Government Printing Department, 1983), 6. This is a pamphlet published for the cremation ceremony of Ven. Narada.

44. Yoneo Ishii, "Modern Buddhism in Indonesia," in *Buddhist Studies in Honour of Hammalava Saddhatissa*, ed. Gatare Dhammapala, Richard Gombrich, and K. R. Norman (Nugegoda: University of Sri Jayewardenepura, 1984), 111.

45. "Narada Maha Thera's Fifth Death Anniversary Falls Today," *Daily News*, October 2, 1987.

46. "Ven. Narada Maha Thera in Vietnam," *World Buddhism* 22, no. 9 (April 1974): 351. The Jetavana (Vietnamese: Ky Vien) Temple in Saigon was built in 1952. Vo Van Tuong, *Nhyng Ngoi Chua Noi Tieng Viet Nam* (The sacred pagodas of Viet Nam) (Hanoi: Nha Xuat Ban Van Hoa-Thong Tin, 1994), 588–589.

47. Kirthi Abeyesekere, *Piyadassi, the Wandering Monk: His Life and Times* (Colombo: Karunaratne and Sons, 1995), 75. To call it a heterodox form of Buddhism is to shortchange the wildly eclectic character of Cao-Dai belief and practice.

48. Nemsiri Mutukumara, "Piyadassi Nayaka Thera on Global Dhamma Dhuta Mission to Show Peaceful Path to Progress," *Daily News*, November 22, 1991.

49. "Pioneers of Nepali Buddhism Honoured Today," *Daily News*, June 12, 1993.

50. "Ven. Piyadassi Leaves on 'Dhammaduta' Mission," *Daily News*, October 1, 1987. These same intergenerational, transnational connections characterized Piyadassi's seventh visit to Indonesia. The sapling that Narada had planted at Borobudur did not survive the renovation of the place, but the connections he first established in the 1930s continue to the present. At the invitation of Indonesian Buddhists, Piyadassi returned in 1987 to celebrate Vesak at Borobudur.

51. "Piyadassi Nayaka Thera on Global Dhamma Dhuta Mission," *Daily News*, November 22, 1991.

52. Nemsiri Mutukumara, "Mental and Physical Discipline for Bhikkhu Education," *Daily News*, August 17, 1987.

53. Ibid.

54. Ibid.

55. Seneviratne, *The Work of Kings*, 341.

56. His images now reside in temples in New York, Washington, D.C., Berlin, Paris, Singapore, Hong Kong, Kuala Lumpur, Sydney, and Toronto. K. Rupasinghe, "Ven. Mapalagama Vipulasara Thera," *Daily News*, March 15, 1990.

57. "Sinhala Mahayana Bhikkhu at Eiheiji Temple," *Daily News*, March 15, 1989.

58. The distinction between Asian immigrants and American converts has been true of most varieties of Buddhism in America. In Theravada temples, the parallel congregation phenomenon occurs "under a single temple roof and at the direction of a shared monastic leadership." Paul David Numrich, *Old Wisdom in the New World: Americanization in Two Immigrant Theravada Buddhist Temples* (Knoxville: University of Tennessee Press, 1996), 63.

59. Ernst Benz, "Buddhism in the Western World," in *Buddhism in the Modern World*, ed. Heinrich Dumoulin (New York: Macmillan Publishing, 1976), 312. A Buddhist Society, led by Christmas Humphries, had begun to meet as early as 1907. It borrowed from various traditions, although initial interest fell on Theravada and its emphasis on renunciation of the world.

60. See http://www.buddhanet.ent/euro_dir.

61. "Buddhism Gaining a Foothold in Holland," *Daily News*, September 3, 1987. Unlike Dharmapala, who took full ordination in the last stage of his life, the Dutchman started his adult life as a monk but found it difficult to manage a monastic existence in Holland.

62. "Malaysian Buddhist Leader to Be Honoured," *Daily News*, December 6, 1991.

63. Malaysian Buddhists maintain a webpage, listing both Chinese monks and Dhammananda as leading figures and praising Dhammananda for his preaching to all Malaysians; http://www.founder.net.my/~ybam/english/ebuddhism/chief.htm.

64. V. A. Gunasekara, "Ethnic Buddhism and Other Obstacles to the Dhamma in the West," *BuddhaZine*, The Buddhist Society of Queensland, Australia, http://buddhanet.net/bsq14.htm, 5.

65. In the late 1980s the Lankaramaya incumbent insisted that the temple was reaching out to serve the religious needs of "Chinese, Indians, Sinhala, Tamil, Europeans and other Asian communities in Singapore." "Call to Lankans to Fund Buddhist Temple in Singapore," *Daily News*, July 5, 1988.

66. Numrich provides an appendix listing Theravada temples in the United States. There are eight Sinhala temples (as against 11 Burmese, 34 Lao, 34 Kampuchean, and 55 Thai temples), *Old Wisdom*, 149–153.

67. Trevor O. Ling, *Buddhist Revival in India: Aspects of the Sociology of Buddhism* (New York: St. Martin's Press, 1980), 59.

68. Ambedkar Buddhists have not been very interested in ordination themselves, settling for trained laypeople who function as social workers, ritual specialists, or missionaries. On some accounts, Ambedkar Buddhists have found non-Indian *bhikkhus* in India "aloof" and "indifferent." Ibid., 110.

69. M. S. Gore, *The Social Context of an Ideology: Ambedkar's Political and Social Thought* (New Delhi: Sage Publications, 1993), 217.

70. Ibid., 144.

71. Vasant Moon, *Growing up Untouchable in India* (London: Rowman and Littlefield, 2001), 149.

72. Joseph M. Kitagawa and Frank Reynolds, "Theravada Buddhism in the Twentieth Century," in Dumoulin, ed., *Buddhism in the Modern World*, 59.

73. Heinz Bechert and Vu Duy-Tu, "Buddhism in Vietnam," in Dumoulin, ed., *Buddhism in the Modern World*, 190.

74. My colleague Trian Nguyen says that 150,000 undercounts the number of Theravada Buddhists in Vietnam by a factor of three or four. These communities, located in the southern part of the country, especially along the Cambodian border, are long-standing and not Narada's converts.

75. Heinrich Dumoulin, "Buddhism in Modern Japan," in Dumoulin, ed., *Buddhism in the Modern World*, 237.

76. Seneviratne, *The Work of Kings*, 214–220.

77. "Ven. Pannatissa Worked to Propagate Buddhism," *Daily News*, October 24, 1991. Also see Seneviratne, *The Work of Kings*, 213–215. As in the case of Banagala Upatissa's appointment as *sanghanayake* of Japan, the proliferation of grandiloquent titles for offices of no responsibility is a by-product of both the *dharmaduta* ethic and monkly self-promotion.

2 The Theravada Domestic Mission in Twentieth-Century Nepal

Sarah LeVine

Almost eighty years ago, a Buddhist revival was launched in the Newar community of the Kathmandu Valley, Nepal. Although it had a dual focus, Tibetan and Theravada, the Theravadins have had a greater impact. Factors involved in the Theravadins' success include, first, the social conditions that made Newar Buddhists more receptive to the "modernist" message of the Maha Bodhi Society than to Mahayana philosophy and practice; second, the strategies selected by the Theravadins to put their movement on a firm footing; and third, the support received from Buddhists and Buddhist institutions elsewhere in Asia. Following a discussion of some enduring weaknesses of the monks' order, my focus will be on the growth and development of the nuns' order and its impressive contributions to the Buddhist community. For the first five decades of the order's existence in Nepal, female recruits took the Ten Precepts as "ordained lay women." But after being encouraged to do so by the Dalai Lama in his address to the first International Conference of Buddhist Women in Bodh Gaya in 1987, Nepali nuns started taking full ordination *(bhikshuni upasampada)* according to Chinese rites. As of 2003, more than one-third of Nepali nuns, defying their monk preceptors, have taken full ordination abroad.[1]

BACKGROUND TO A MISSION

Since the beginning of recorded history Hinduism and Buddhism have coexisted in the Kathmandu Valley (the "Nepal" of premodern times), and although Nepalese kings seem almost always to have been Shaivite Hindus, at the same time they were the principal patrons of many Buddhist institutions and major ritual events.[2] The last kings of the Newars, a Tibeto-Burman people who until recently were the numerically and culturally dominant ethnic group of the Valley, were defeated in 1768–1769 by the Nepali-speaking Gorkha king Prithivi Narayan Shah.[3] More than a century later, the British Resident Surgeon Daniel Wright estimated that Vajrayana Buddhism—whose clerics were married priests, the descendents of monastics who had abandoned celibacy for householder life—was practiced by two-thirds of the Newar population.[4]

But strong as the Buddhist community may have appeared to Wright, in reality it was under great pressure. Thirty years earlier, in 1846, following a bloody coup that he appears to have engineered himself, a courtier and military commander named Jang Bahadur Kunwar had placed the Gorkha king Rajendra under virtual house arrest. Having changed his family name to Rana and upgraded his caste from warrior to princely status, Jang Bahadur took the titles of "Maharaja" and hereditary "Prime Minister," and thenceforth ruled the Gorkha Empire—which was only officially renamed "Nepal" in 1930—as his private fiefdom.[5]

In 1854, following a trip to Europe where he was impressed by the French focus on codification, Jang Bahadur promulgated the Nepalese Legal Code (Muluki Ain). This imposed both a standardized legal code throughout the kingdom and a "national caste hierarchy"[6] that incorporated myriad castes and ethnic categories and, through the application of a religious paradigm, legitimized inequality.[7] Jang Bahadur's objective in melding an extremely diverse population into a unified Hindu state was to centralize authority—nominally in the hands of the king but actually in his own—and to emphasize Nepal's "unique" religious identity, whose prestige, he hoped, would protect his country's independence from the British, who had assumed control of most of the Indian subcontinent. As Burghart pointed out: "Rana identity became double talk. . . . It declared its modernizing intentions to the agents of modernity and its traditionalizing intentions to the agents of tradition. . . . Gorkha's religious identity served to resist imperialism, but as a mode of resistance, religion became a counter for tradition."[8]

Jang Bahadur was succeeded by brothers, nephews, and great-nephews. Over a period of 105 years (1846–1951), while four kings were restricted to their palaces, ten Rana maharajas and prime ministers maintained autocratic rule and brahmanical orthodoxy in Nepal. Buddhist institutions, stripped of royal patronage, declined, and Newars were politically and economically motivated to identify themselves as Hindus, at least for official purposes. By the end of the Rana era, few Newars other than those who could not deny their religious affiliation because of caste ascriptions, still publicly acknowledged their Buddhism. It was among these high-caste Newar holdouts that the movement to modernize Newar Buddhism found its first recruits.

In the 1920s and early 1930s a few young Newar men and women who regarded their traditional laicized form of Vajrayana Buddhism as baroquely ritualistic and doctrinally obfuscated and their priests as elitist and scripturally ignorant, began to search for a "purer" model.[9] Some looked north to Tibet. The Kathmandu

Valley, which stands on an ancient trade route between the Gangetic Plain and the Trans-Himalayan region, was a conduit for the transmission of Buddhism from India to Tibet between the seventh and the thirteenth centuries. Thereafter Tibetans came to regard the Valley as a "province" of the Tibetan hinterland and visited the great Kathmandu Valley stupas of Namobuddha, Svayambhu, and Bauddha on pilgrimage to the north Indian sacred sites. Although in the early years of this century the small group of Tibetan monks who resided in the Valley were primarily concerned with caring for the stupas and ministering to pilgrims,[10] from time to time celebrated lamas would arrive from Lhasa and elsewhere, and the teachings they offered would attract Newar Buddhists, many of them traders with close ties to the Tibetan plateau, as well as Tibetans.

In 1924, a Nyngmapa monk Kangtse Lama caused a sensation in Kathmandu. He had prostrated his way all the way from Kiyrong in Tibet, an ordeal that had taken him more than three years. As the guest of Dharma Man Tuladhar, a Uray merchant with extensive business in Tibet, the lama gave teachings in Kimdo Baha, a Vajrayana Buddhist monastery near the Svayambhu stupa, where each day he attracted more and more people, most of them Newars. After teaching the preliminary practices of Tibetan Buddhism (Kunzang lama'l sheling ngon-dro) to a cumulative total of several thousand people, Kangste Lama returned to Tibet in the spring of 1925, leaving his devotees bereft.[11] But they soon turned to another Tibetan Buddhist teacher, a native of Kashmir named Tsering Norbu, who, with government permission, established himself in a hut on Nagarjuna Hill overlooking Svayambhu. Although he did not know Kangtse Lama personally, he accepted the lama's disciples and undertook to give them further instruction in Tibetan Buddhism. Some of his devotees were Tibetan and some Newars, including a handful whom he ordained as novices. After two years he was expelled, having repeatedly come into conflict with the government because he sent his red-robed disciples into the city to collect alms—a practice the Ranas harshly condemned, given the strict rules of commensality laid down by the Nepal Legal Code. Accompanied by five Newar novices, Tsering Norbu went first to India and thence made his way back to Tibet.[12]

In 1927 it might have appeared that the Newars, having an elective affinity for the Tibetan tradition, had found an alternative Buddhist model that suited them well. But although Kangtse Lama and Tsering Norbu had sown the seeds of revivalism, it was Theravada missionaries arriving in the Valley just a few years later who reaped what the Tibetans had sown. Tibetan pilgrim teachers continued to visit the Valley, and some had considerable impact; again, from time to time Newars would take vows as Nyngmapa and Karma Kagyupa monks. But after the great interest that Kangtse Lama and Tsering Norbu aroused in the 1920s, their successors never again achieved such wide appeal.

While some Newar Buddhist "seekers" looked—and traveled—to Tibet, others looked and traveled to India, where they encountered Maha Bodhi missionary monks at Buddhist sacred sites. Convinced that the Theravadins' "modernist" interpretation of Buddhist teaching was what they had been seeking,[13] they took novice ordination (*pabbajjaa*) and went on to Burma and Sri Lanka, where they studied in monastic institutions and took higher ordination (*upasampadaa*).[14]

These young Nepalese Theravadins were reformers not revolutionaries; far from rejecting the religion of their ancestors, their goal was to purify it, namely, to rid it of magical practices, ritual sacrifice, and caste distinctions absorbed in medieval times from Hinduism, and to rebuild the community by reintroducing monasticism and educating the laity, the great majority of whom had no understanding of such fundamentals of Buddhist doctrine as the Four Noble Truths. Other than for the small priestly and merchant elite who were eligible to take esoteric initiations, Nepal Buddhism was a social and apotropaic rather than a soteriological religion. While emphasizing generosity to neighbors and kin and giving donations (*daana*) to the monastery and its community (sangha), it provided life-cycle and protective rituals and a community focus.

When the reformers returned to Nepal after ordination they found harsh opposition from the Rana regime, which regarded new ideas, whether political, religious, or literary, as a threat to the status quo.[15] They harassed, imprisoned, and even exiled the Theravadins through 1951 when, after their ousting and the restoration of monarchial power, the missionaries were finally free to put their reforms into effect.[16] In the years following the "coming of democracy" (*pvajatantra*), the Theravadins launched a wide-ranging program of teaching, monastery construction, scriptural translation, and vernacular publication that soon won them a strong lay backing.[17]

THE ROOTS OF THERAVADA SUCCESS 1923–1951

The Ranas went to great lengths to protect Nepal from contamination, both by democratic and egalitarian ideas, which were circulating in India, and by Christianity, whose missionaries had been active in Bengal since the late 1700s. Furthermore, for decades their efforts were largely effective: the malaria-infested border region blocked movement into and out of the country; only a handful of westerners were permitted to enter Nepal; and Nepalis from the Kathmandu Valley who wished to travel to India could do so only in the dry season with government permission.

But the Ranas' determination to seal off the country and prevent the infiltration of pernicious foreign influences was defeated, first by the mercenary soldiers, known as Gurkhas, who, under the terms of the Sagauli Treaty (1816) with the British, were recruited in ever greater numbers into the Indian army.[18] They were followed to their posts in India and in Buddhist Burma, which became a British colony in 1885, by Newar Buddhist goldsmiths belonging to the priestly Shakya caste. Though a few settled permanently in Burma, most traveled back and forth, carrying with them a familiarity with Burmese Buddhism.

A second factor allowing the infiltration of Buddhist modernist ideas was the Ranas' craving for foreign goods. Despite their refusal to permit all but a handful of westerners into the country, they, their captive kings, and their courtiers developed an insatiable appetite for Western luxuries, the supplying of which required the development of trading networks in India. The majority of these traders were Newar merchants from the Kathmandu Valley, many of whom also had business in Tibet.[19] When, after the Younghusband expedition of 1904, the India–Tibetan trade was rerouted from Patna–Kathmandu–Shigatse–Lhasa to Calcutta–Kalimpong–Gyantse–Lhasa, some traders settled in Calcutta, where they encountered and were impressed by Maha Bodhi Society missionaries who, led by their Sri Lankan founder Dharmapala Anagarika (see Kemper, this volume), had had their headquarters in that city since 1892.[20]

Nepalese students were a third conduit for "pernicious" ideas. In the early years of the twentieth century, the Ranas finally acknowledged their need for Western-educated bureaucrats. Since Jang Bahadur's time, the Ranas had had a palace school in which Indian, and sometimes British, teachers were employed to instruct their sons and the sons of their counselors and courtiers;[21] but until 1918 when Tri Chandra College was established, no Western-style institution of higher learning existed in Kathmandu. Thus the government was obliged to send some young men, including some Newars, to India, where they were exposed not only to the incendiary ideas of the Free India movement but—at least from a Newar Buddhist perspective—to the equally radical ideas of the Maha Bodhi Society.

The first Newar to embrace Buddhist modernism was a young Shakya from Patan named Jagat Man Vaidya, whose father was a court physician. In 1923 Jagat Man arrived at Calcutta University on a government scholarship to study commerce, a subject that Tri Chandra College did not offer. After meeting Dharmapala Anagarika, an experience so compelling that he likened it to meeting Shakyamuni

Buddha himself,[22] he changed his name to Dharmadittya Dharmacarya, donned a yellow robe, and dedicated himself to the revival of Newar Buddhism. His strategies in this regard included publishing a journal in Hindi, Nepali, and Newari, and learning Pali, which equipped him to translate and publish anthologies of excerpts from canonical texts in Newari and Nepali. In addition, he founded a Buddhist laymen's organization in Kathmandu during his summer vacation and, in 1928, organized an all-India Buddhist conference in Calcutta whose focus was the status of Buddhism in Nepal. Most important, although he himself was never ordained as a monk, he pushed for the reestablishment of a monastic order. As a result of these activities he neglected his university studies, failed his exams, lost his scholarship, and had to return to Nepal. He spent the rest of his working life in the employ of Bajra Ratna Kansakar, a wealthy Uray merchant who, having himself been a devotee of Dharmapala in Calcutta, became a generous financial backer of the Theravada mission in Kathmandu.

Why did the Maha Bodhi Society's modernist message have a greater impact on Newar Buddhists than that of the Tibetan lamas? First, the Tibetan language presented a major problem. Although many Newars who had spent time in Tibet spoke Tibetan, not only are written and colloquial Tibetan very different, but the language of the Dharma is virtually unintelligible to the untutored layman. It was very important that the Maha Bodhi Society had published Pali texts in Hindi, which virtually all literate Nepalese could read, and also that Dharmadittya Dharmacarya, the erstwhile commerce student, had translated lengthy canonical passages into Newari.

Second, Tibetan Buddhism is tightly organized, with a clearly defined hierarchy that only gradually permits non-Tibetans a position of some standing. Although from time to time Newars had taken ordination, there is no record of any having risen in the hierarchy. Rather, they remained as devotees of *rimpoches* and lower-level lamas. The closed Tibetan system could hardly have appealed to most Newar Buddhists, whether to prospective monks or to the Newar laity, who were used to having full control of their temples.

The radical simplicity of Theravada Buddhism also held great appeal for the Newars. To focus on the figure of the monk and on the strict worship of the Buddha alone struck the reformers as a much more effective way of changing Newar Buddhism than to adopt esoteric Tibetan practices that would only have compounded the mysteries of their traditional Buddhism.[23]

Last but not least, the reformers were drawn to Theravada Buddhism because it came not from the north but from the south, the source, for Nepalese people, of all things modern and progressive. Although Payne notes in this volume that Tibetan Buddhism, as transmitted to the West in the post-1959 diaspora, has had a markedly reformist character, in the 1930s, the Tibetan Buddhism with which Newar Buddhists were familiar both in Kathmandu and Tibet itself was still deeply conservative.

The first cohort of Nepalese monks and nuns were largely drawn from two upper castes, Shakyas and Urays, who, given their involvement in international trade, may have been more familiar with the outside world—and more receptive to new ideas—than were members of other Newar Buddhist castes. Moreover, in the 1920s the Uray trading community became alienated from traditional Buddhism by a bitter dispute with their Vajracharya household priests. It was resolved only by a court decision in the 1950s, by which time many Uray families had given up calling on their priests to officiate at ritual occasions and were turning instead to Theravada monks.[24] The other group—aside from Vajracharya household priests—at the apex of the Newar Buddhist caste system are Shakya temple priests who, through the 1950s, still called themselves "Shakyabhikshu." As Shakyas are not household priests (purohit) and do not have patrons (jajmaan), their priestly status does not provide them with a livelihood. Traditionally their work has been goldsmithing and image making. Shakyas then, like Urays, had little to lose by shifting their religious affiliation and financial support from traditional to reformist religious institutions.

The Theravada sangha could not have survived the years of Rana persecution without the moral and practical support of the Maha Bodhi Society. The entire first generation received first ordination from its missionaries, in particular from Chandramani Mahasthavira, a Burmese monk who, with Dharmapala's support, had established, in 1902, a monastery at Kushinagar, the town close to the Nepalese border where the Buddha died (attained final release, parinibbaana).[25] Chandramani and other monks in Sarnath, Bodh Gaya, and Calcutta welcomed the Nepalis, gave them novice ordination, and organized their passages to Burma and Sri Lanka, where they received higher ordination and religious training (see Kemper, Chap. 1 this volume). On return, most passed through Kushinagar, where Chandramani taught them Maha Bodhi mission strategies in large part borrowed from Protestant missionaries in Sri Lanka and Bengal.

By the 1940s, serious opposition to the Rana regime had mobilized, provoking a major crackdown not only on political "subversives," but on the Theravadins too.[26] In 1944, the police stopped a monk from giving the Ten Precepts to a female recruit and immediately thereafter ordered monastics living in Kathmandu and

Patan to desist from teaching, performing rituals, or ordaining novices. When they refused to comply, they were exiled to India where they joined other Nepalese emigrés at Sarnath. There they founded the Dharmodaya Sabha, the Buddhist Society of Nepal, with the Burmese monk Chandramani as president, a position he held until his death at age ninety-six in 1972.[27] Only after the intervention in 1946 of the prominent Sinhalese monk Narada Mahasthavira did the government permit the Theravadins to return to Kathmandu. Even so, for the remaining four years of the Rana regime, their activities were closely monitored.[28]

TRAILBLAZERS

Central to the survival of the movement were a handful of charismatic individuals who combined imagination, energy, and determination with an unusual ability to communicate. One of the most interesting was a monk named Mahapragya.[29] Prem Bahadur Shrestha and a Hindu by birth, after participating enthusiastically in both Hindu and Buddhist devotional activities as a youth in Kathmandu, he left his wife and family to wander from temple to temple and teacher to teacher in north India in search of a more profound spiritual truth than he believed Nepal could provide. In 1924 he was back in Kathmandu, where he heard Kangtse Lama's discourses on Tibetan Buddhist practice. When the lama left for Tibet, Mahapragya followed and received ordination as a Nyngmapa monk across the border in Kiyrong. He subsequently returned to the Valley, where he spent two years as a disciple of the Kashmiri lama, Tsering Norbu. When his teacher was expelled to India by the Ranas—in part this was because, by accepting Mahapragya (who had been born a Hindu) as his disciple Tsering Norbu had broken the law against conversion—Mahapragya and four Newar novice companions elected to go on pilgrimage with him to Bodh Gaya. There, according to his autobiography, teacher as well as disciples were so impressed by the Burmese missionary monks they encountered that they took novice ordination according to Theravada rites. From Bodh Gaya the group proceeded to Calcutta where they met Dharmadittya Dharmacarya. Although Mahapragya, in particular, was much stirred by what he had heard and read in Bodh Gaya and Calcutta, he still considered himself Tsering Norbu's disciple, and, when his teacher invited to him to Tibet, he accepted.

In 1927, making yet another turnabout, Mahapragya was ordained as a Geluk monk in Lhasa and, because his teachings on the Lam Rim Path were thought to be so effective, received authorization to ordain novices himself. But instead of remaining in Lhasa and pursuing further studies, he wandered about central Tibet, living on alms. As a result of the altitude, the harsh climate, and a steady diet of *tsampa*, he became very sick and, returning to Lhasa, was treated by a Uray doctor (*vaidya*) named Kul Man Singh Tuladhar, who restored him to health.

Having convinced his doctor to renounce lay life, abandon his wife and child, and take ordination with the new name Karmasila, Mahapragya set off with him to Shigatse. After almost a year meditating in a cave, the two men left for India, dissatisfied with the "fruits" of their retreat. Mahapragya had been mulling over what he had learned about Theravada Buddhism in India and now was eager to learn more. Arriving in Kushinagar, he and his companion committed themselves to Chandramani's tutelage and soon received novice ordination—Mahapragya for the second time. When, in 1930, Mahapragya and Pragyananda—as Kul Man Singh/Karmasila had become at Theravada ordination—returned to Kathmandu in their ochre robes and began to preach in public places, where they attracted not only enthusiastic devotees but enduring government hostility.

In 1946 Mahapragya disrobed and married a widow in Kalimpong. While earning his living as a photographer, he continued to teach Theravada Buddhism in the large Newar community of Kalimpong. He also published a book in Newari entitled *The Sensible Buddhist Life*, which over the years reached a wide readership. Eventually he once again renounced householder life, returned to Kathmandu, and settled in a small house that his devotees built for him near the city center. Since he had broken the celibacy vow and hence was "one who had fallen" (*paaraajika*), he was definitely barred from ordaining as a monk a second time. Thus he called himself "Buddhist sage" (*bauddha rishi*), rather than monk (*bhikkhu*), and wore a long beard and maroon Tibetan dress. A dynamic preacher and teacher, he continued to attract a large following until his death in 1978.

Women, too, were among the Buddhist revival's earliest recruits. In the 1920s, a few Uray wives and widows studied Buddhist books with a widow named Laxminani Tuladhar. Hearing of their activities, Prime Minister Chandra Shamsher Rana summoned them to his palace and told them their behavior *ill befitted* females. According to Hindu tradition, religious texts were for male eyes only. He ordered them to return to their houses and take care of their families![30]

Laxminani, the leader of the group, had lost her husband and children within a short period and turned for solace to the Tibetan monks—first Kangtse Lama and later Tsering Norbu. One of the very few literate Newar women of her generation, she read whatever Buddhist books in Newari, Nepali, and Hindi she could lay her hands on and taught her illiterate friends what she learned.[31] In the early 1930s, she converted to Theravada Buddhism. In the aftermath of the great earthquake of 1934, having enraged her in-laws by distributing the contents of their shop to starving townspeople, she and five of her followers traveled to Arakan in Burma.

There they took the Precepts and received Dharma names. Since the Theravada *bhikkhuni* ordination lineage had died out a millennium earlier,[32] they were given the appellation *anaagaarikaa,* meaning "female homeless one," by their preceptor.

Although as "ordained lay women" they were excluded from the Nepalese monastic order, on their return to Kathmandu, having nowhere else to go, they settled in Kimdo Baha, the same monastery in which Kangtse Lama had electrified large audiences with his teachings years before. Their housemates at Kimdo were an eclectic group of monastics—a handful of Tibetans, a half-dozen Theravada monks, a Vajrayana tantric with his two shakti consorts, and three Newar nuns who had preceded them into "homelessness" in 1931.[33]

Despite having to contend with government persecution and the determination of the *bhantes* (monks) to keep the *gurumaas* (mother-teachers, as nuns were called locally) subordinated, Dharmacari (Laxminani's ordination name) held her own. Eventually, tired of harassment by their male companions and lay gossip—rumor had it that Dharmacari had given birth to a baby fathered by a monk—the nuns moved to separate quarters that Dharmacari built with personal funds and donations from her devotees. The nunnery soon became a center of learning for Buddhist women from the Kathmandu Valley and beyond, a role it played until Dharmacari died at age eighty—within months of Mahapragya—in 1978.

STRATEGIES FOR SUCCESS 1951–1980

Shortly before the ousting of the Ranas and the "restoration" of the monarchy in 1951, the Theravadins listed their objectives in the journal of the Buddhist Society of Nepal, which was being published in Kalimpong, India, due to government censorship. Their objectives, many adopted from the Maha Bodhi Society's program, were:

1. To open Buddhist schools all over Nepal;
2. To build a *vihara,* as the Theravada monasteries are called, in every town or village with a substantial Newar Buddhist population, and to have one or two monks in residence to provide religious instruction and free medical services;
3. To publish canonical texts and other books in Nepali and Newari;
4. To educate Nepalis to propagate Buddhism;
5. To publish two journals, one in Nepali and one in English;
6. To persuade Nepalese officials to preserve ancient Buddhist monuments at Lumbini and Kapilavastu;

7. To encourage Buddhists of other countries to visit Nepal and offer facilities to Buddhist scholars;
8. To guard against members of other faiths making converts within the Buddhist community.[34]

As soon as they were permitted to work openly, the Theravadins set about making their blueprint a reality. But they faced many obstacles, not the least being their small number—in 1950 there were only about twenty monks and novices, and thirty nuns—and lack of government backing. In Thailand and Burma, Buddhism is the state religion; until its disestablishment by the British in the nineteenth century, Buddhism was the state religion of Sri Lanka too, and although it languished during the colonial period, in the early decades of the twentieth century Buddhism, in its modernist form, received the endorsement of the nationalist movement. Moreover, the constitution that Sri Lanka adopted after independence in 1947 afforded Buddhism special state protection. Initially the Nepali Theravadins found King Tribuvan well-disposed toward Theravada Buddhism, as it was a welcome alternative to the brahmanical orthodoxy of the Ranas, his erstwhile juilors. In 1955, however, with King Tribhuvan's death and the succession to the throne of his son King Mahendra, state backing for the Theravada movement, brief as it had been, soon disappeared.

What alternative sources of support were available? On the one hand, there was a small group of progressive Newar Buddhist merchants who were disaffected with traditional Buddhism; and on the other, there were the foreign networks that the Theravadins had begun to develop during their years of training and exile abroad.

A Nepalese law forbade religious conversion.[35] Thus the Theravadins were only permitted to approach people who were already Buddhist by birth. Although they might, with impunity, have sought converts among Tamangs and other submontane ethnic groups who followed the Tibetan tradition, their efforts in the early years were primarily focused on their own Newar community. They soon realized that Newar Buddhists needed to be wooed with what was familiar as well as with what was new. In a word, to be acceptable, Buddhist "modernism" would have to be domesticated,[36] or, to borrow the concept that Tanabe uses with regard to Japanese Buddhism in Hawai'i (see Chap. 3), "cross-pollination" would have to take place.

The monks chose carefully where to incorporate local practice and where to take a stand against it.[37] Male members of the lay community, which at this point was still largely drawn from the upper castes, were accustomed to being centrally involved in the running of the ancient monastic institutions (*bahaaas*) to which, by virtue of patrilineal descent, they belonged. Similarly, they expected to be centrally involved in the new *viharas*—for which they were now providing land, construction and maintenance costs. Thus the monks needed to allow the laity a much more prominent role in the administration of their *viharas* than was the case elsewhere in the Theravada world.

Second, although Buddhism itself rejects caste within the sangha, caste in some form is a reality in a number of Buddhist societies, including that of the Newars.[38] At least since the fourteenth century, if not long before, it has been a highly stratified society. Furthermore, even if the Newar caste system had once been quite flexible, in 1854 Jang Bahadur Rana's legal code had established an immutable six-level hierarchy with rules of commensality that all Newars—Hindu and Buddhist alike—were required to obey.[39] Thus a majority of laypeople and most monks also were opposed to monks'—all of whom, at this juncture, were from upper castes—accepting boiled rice (*kacca bhat*), their staple food, as alms from people belonging to a caste lower than their own.[40] This meant that, since middle-caste farmers composed the majority in most Newar communities, the alms round produced very little food, and sometimes none at all.[41] Thus, although the monks' alms round was a prominent feature in some of the Buddhist countries where the Nepali monks had received their training, back home they were soon obliged to abandon it. They asked instead that devotees donate uncooked food and cash directly to the monastery, and they promoted other ways by which merit could be earned, such as sponsoring rituals, providing robes (*civara*), financing the publication of Buddhist books, and going on pilgrimages.[42]

The monks initiated vigorous campaigns against certain practices that they identified as Hindu—principally, blood sacrifice to family deities. But others, such as the performance of death rituals (*shraddha*) for the ancestors, they endorsed. In addition they endorsed certain Vajrayana practices. These included putting on plays based on Buddhist stories and making the month of Gunla (August-September), traditionally a time of intense devotional activity, a period of daily preaching in the monastery itself and in public spaces. They also encouraged the singing of devotional songs at public events. Whereas traditional Newar Buddhist groups had sung hymns (*strota*) on festival days in front of the main shrine of a temple, the Theravadins composed their own songs, which they had lay members of the community sing both in the new *viharas* and in alcoves in the old monasteries. Stimulated by regularly scheduled competitions, these *gyanmala* (garland of wisdom) groups, as they were called, proliferated and soon became a prominent feature of Theravada community life.

Resolved to simplify or even eliminate rituals they deemed anachronistic or overly elaborate, the monks began to assume certain functions of Vajracarya household priests, such as the administration of life-cycle rites, including an alternative to a ritual for preadolescent Newar boys of nonpriestly castes (*kaytaa puuja*). The nuns followed suit with a Theravada alternative to the girls' puberty rite (*barha tayegu*). Children who participated in these alternative rites spent a week or ten days in a monastery or nunnery dressed as novice monks (*saamaneras*) and probationary nuns (*rishini*); they took eight or ten precepts, memorized texts to chant during Buddha Puja (the principal Theravada devotional ritual) and studied core doctrines of Buddhism. These temporary ordination rites became popular both with parents, who could thereby avoid the expense of providing a feast for several hundred kinfolk and friends, as the traditional rites required, and with children, who enjoyed living and playing with age mates away from home.[43] Just as Soka Gakkai's success in Brazil in recent decades has resulted in part from incorporating practices from other religions, notably Roman Catholicism (see Clarke, Chap. 5), so too has the incorporation of numerous Hindu and Vajrayana practices helped Theravada Buddhism to broaden its appeal. Newars have embraced this "cross-pollinated" message because it seems to point the way to a wider world without requiring that one stray too far from the familiar: to the intensely community focused religion of the ancient monastery has been added the textually focused religion of the *vihara* in which, with like-minded people, the devotee may work out his or her own salvation with diligence. Although help in this regard is available from monks and nuns, in sharp contrast with traditional Newar Buddhist practice no priestly intercessor is necessary.

But while the Theravada lay community expanded rapidly in the years following the ousting of the Ranas, recruits to the monks' order remained few and far between. The monastic tradition in Newar Buddhism had died out many centuries ago, and the fact that it was taking more than one generation to become firmly reestablished should hardly come as a surprise. First, the celibacy rule was exceedingly difficult to keep, and monks too often lapsed. Second, before the 1970s, given that few Nepali children, other than elite males, had any formal schooling, secular education was considered unnecessary for a monk. So novices spent most of their time doing domestic work: they cleaned the rooms, cooked the food, washed the clothes, and massaged the backs and limbs of their teachers. Meanwhile the religious instruction they received was limited. They learned to chant in Pali with little understanding of what they were chanting; they read vernacular translations of *Jataka* stories and verses from the *Dhammapada*; and sometimes they learned to practice meditation techniques, notably *anapana*, which focused on watching the breath, and *kesaloma,* which involved contemplation of bodily decay as a means of understanding impermanence *(anicca).* All the novices were being equipped to do was to perform daily devotional rituals, receive donations, and serve as fields of merit, a career that few boys or their parents found attractive.

Given that rigorous religious training could only be had abroad, Bhikkhu Amritananda, the secretary of the Dharmodaya Sabha (the Buddhist Society of Nepal), was assiduous in his efforts to develop networks that might provide it. At the Fourth World Fellowship of Buddhists Conference, held in Kathmandu in October 1956, six months after the celebration of the 2,500th anniversary of the birth of the Buddha, the Buddhist world made much both of the central role of Nepal as the birthplace of the Buddha and of the nascent Nepalese Theravada community's need for foreign support.[44] Amritananda, who had been trained in Vajirarama Monastery in Colombo in the 1930s and 1940s, began to travel abroad to Theravada countries and also to Communist China, Mongolia, and North Vietnam in order to strengthen ties and make new ones with people and institutions that might provide training for Nepalese novices. While Amritananda's trips to communist countries did not bear fruit, Nepalese novices began to receive invitations and sponsorship from Buddhist institutions in Burma, Sri Lanka, and, later, in Thailand and Taiwan as well. Attempts to secure the help of foreign missionaries was less successful, however. Some came to visit but very few stayed on.

MISSION ACCOMPLISHED: WHAT LIES AHEAD?

Without doubt, the charismatic Theravadin pioneers accomplished a great deal. Indeed, by the end of the twentieth century every goal set by the Dharmodaya Sabha in 1950 had been met. By selectively incorporating features of traditional Newar Buddhism into their modernist framework, the Theravadins had offered their devotees freedom to pursue personal goals within familiar sociocentric structures. They had put in place a multifaceted program to serve a burgeoning community, whose members had found in the Theravada movement a way of defining themselves as progressive without being obliged to turn their backs on traditional ritual or renounce core beliefs.[45] By 2000, in addition to being close to completing the translation into Newari of the entire Pali canon, they had published more than five hundred vernacular books on Buddhist topics, which they encouraged— even hounded—their devotees to read.

But their achievements do not obscure serious structural flaws. Among these are the continued lack of support from the government. According to the constitution adopted after the 1990 revolution, Nepal is defined as a "multi-ethnic, multilingual, democratic, independent, indivisable, sovereign, Constitutional Monarchical Kingdom"; nevertheless, it remains *Hindu*.[46]

Again, the first charismatic generation, all of whose members are either dead or very old, has not been replaced. Today the sangha lacks leadership strong enough to bring consensus on issues of policy and practice. Networking by Bhikkhu Amritananda and others provided religious training for recruits to the order, but this has come at a price. For the most part, novices go abroad in adolescence and stay abroad for many years in countries where not only is Buddhism the state religion, with all the prestige that implies, but that are far more developed and affluent than their own. To the seventeen-year-old Nepalese novice newly arrived from a village in the Kathmandu Valley, the sumptuous wats of Bangkok look more like palaces than monasteries, and the resident monks, with their plethora of possessions, including laptop computers, boom boxes and TVs, more like sons of privilege than ascetics. Meanwhile, outside the monastery walls life in the streets—through which novices pass daily on the alms round—beckons seductively. The meditation centers of Rangoon and Sagain, where young Nepali monks and nuns are also trained,[47] may be somewhat more austere, but even so, they too are lavishly supported and equipped by the Burmese laity, which, according to some estimates, give one-quarter of their annual income in *daana*. Many Nepali novices never make it back to Nepal. With their near-native fluency in the language and their degrees from Buddhist universities, whether as monks or, after disrobing, as laymen, they make a life for themselves in Sri Lanka, Thailand, and elsewhere.

When those who resist the lures of Colombo and Bangkok do return home, not only do they feel like strangers in their impoverished native land, but they find, instead of a cohesive community whose leaders are in agreement on goals, a collection of individuals trained in different countries, wedded to different traditions, each with his own priorities and constituency. In the post-mission era, the frontier mentality of each man (monk) for himself has failed to shift to one of collaboration. In the absence of energetic and appealing leaders offering them challenging roles, the exigencies and tedium of monastic discipline are more than most can tolerate for long. Ashok, a monk newly returned from training in Vajirarama, in a suburb of Colombo, which gave social work and *buddha dharma* equal emphasis, reported that several abbots had invited him to live in their monasteries but he had refused.[48] "I could see the monks in those places weren't doing anything—just performing (protective) rituals, receiving donations, and eating in the houses of devotees. . . . All most of them do is give laypeople the chance to earn merit. But I was trained to do work among the poor and that's what I intend to do, not sit in the vihara!"[49]

Offered a room in the corner of a dilapidated Newar monastery, Ashok accepted it. He lived by himself, did his own housekeeping, and, with little support from the community, which had never had a Theravada monk living in their midst before, began putting a program of his own design in place. His living conditions were not easy: his roof leaked; he sometimes went without a main midday meal; his nights were frequently disturbed by local people coming to the courtyard to feast and get drunk. But at least, as he said, he was doing what he had been trained to do.

Unfortunately, only a few monks of Ashok's generation have the determination to pursue their own goals. Most, lacking Ashok's purposefulness, become discouraged. Keshab, who returned after ten years in Thailand to live in the same monastery as his teacher, failed to find the guidance he needed to make his way in the steadily secularizing culture of Kathmandu. "My guru kept me in the monastery. . . . So there I was, day after day. He didn't let me use my training. He had no plans of his own for me, and he rejected mine." After three years of increasing boredom and irritation Keshab, potential leadership material, returned to Thailand, where he disrobed.[50]

For a while it looked as if *vipassana* (insight) meditation, introduced to Nepal in the early 1980s by the celebrated Burmese "teacher-monk" Mahasi Sayadaw and the Indian lay meditation master S. N. Goenka, would provide a new focus for the sangha. Prior to this time most monks who studied abroad learned meditation practices that they would teach to other monks and to a select group of especially devout laypeople; but for the most part the laity regarded meditation as esoteric and not for them. Today, by contrast, in addition to two large meditation centers in Kathmandu and a third at Lumbini, most *viharas* offer daily meditation sessions.

But despite the great interest generated by *vipassana* in the lay community, long-standing problems still threaten the sangha with stagnation. Not least of these is the failure to retain recruits. The sangha emerged from long years of persecution under the Ranas numbering only 20 monks; thirty years later, there were 60 monks and 72 novices, many of whom were in training abroad and, as it emerged, disrobed on completion of their studies.[51] In 2001 there were reported to be 161 Nepali monks and novices.[52] But although boys and young men continue to join the order, the problem of "seepage" is far from solved: those 161 include dozens who, though still "on the books," went abroad for training and whose whereabouts are no longer known. In sum, it is thought that, without informing their teachers back home, they simply disrobed.

Ex-monks cite various reasons for their decision to disrobe, lack of "job satisfaction" being the one they discuss most freely. However, sexual frustration appears to be the main reason, although they are more likely to say that their families pressured them to marry than to admit that they left the order because celibacy had become intolerable. Elsewhere in the Theravada world temporary ordination is a prominent feature of religious life: Thai and Burmese males are required to ordain for at least a short period prior to marriage, and although these days many ignore the rule, a majority continues to conform. Should a monk disrobe even after a period of several years, few will find fault with him. But Thailand and Burma are Buddhist countries in which there is no shortage of monks who ordain for life. Nepal, on the other hand, is the world's only official Hindu kingdom. The Theravada Buddhist lay community consists of only a few thousand committed members for whom each monk represents a significant investment of time, money, and hope. Such a small community cannot afford for its monks to disrobe and, despite the frequency of this occurrence, is dismayed when they do. One abbot, who had sent fifteen novices to Thailand, none of whom had returned, lived in a great echoing monastery with three other monks, one of whom was an octogenarian while the other two appeared to be mentally ill. Of his revolving-door efforts at recruitment, he remarked resignedly, "Perhaps Newar men aren't really suited to be monks...."[53]

THE GENDER GAP

Today it is the nuns' order, not the monks', that provides the Theravada community's most vigorous leadership. While, in a rapidly secularizing society that is ever more closely tied into the once remote wider world by the internet and cable TV, a monastic career holds little appeal for the brightest and best young Newar men, young Newar women, some of whom are from well-to-do families and already hold university degrees, continue to renounce lay life. Already by the 1970s, Vajracharya, Shakya, and Uray families, well placed to receive the first fruits of the "foreign aid economy," were sending their sons to newly established secondary schools; if afterward they sent them abroad it was to universities in Britain, China, and the United States to study engineering and economics rather than *buddha dharma* in monastic institutions in South and Southeast Asia. Whereas in the first mission generation, monastic recruits had come exclusively from the upper castes, by the 1980s middle- and occupational-caste boys, some from deeply impoverished families, had replaced them. Ordination offered them the education that their parents could not provide.

But although recruitment of monks from privileged backgrounds has now almost entirely ceased, young women from Buddhist families are quite likely to see the monastic life as a prestigious career choice. In their view, far from being intolerably restrictive, celibacy offers a precious freedom, a liberation from an arranged marriage and the "tyranny" of the joint family—still the domestic arrangement of choice for the majority of Newars—and an opportunity to focus on meditation practice, perform meaningful work in the community, and travel abroad. Were there space to accommodate them—nunneries are generally less spacious and less well-equipped than monasteries—the nuns' order would have many more recruits than it does. Furthermore, unlike the monks, once having "shaved their heads," few nuns return to lay life.[54]

Almost from the outset in the 1930s and 1940s, nuns outnumbered monks. But in the first missionary cohort virtually all of them—including their leader, Dharmacari—were widows and rejected wives at the margins of Newar society. Although at that time neither monks nor nuns had been to school, all the monks had somehow acquired literacy skills before joining the order, whereas this was true of few nuns.

After ordination, most male novices had the chance to study abroad, where they learned Pali and Sanskrit, Burmese or Sinhala, and some, English or Japanese. They were absorbed into a tradition with its own particular worldview and, on returning to their homeland, attempted to live according to its values. Some were impressively productive: they translated scriptures and wrote commentaries and textbooks; they set up health clinics and established primary schools in the capital; they preached the Dharma in remote villages and on the radio, and later, on TV.

Meanwhile, in their monasteries these monks reproduced their gurus' tastes and esthetics, down to the smallest detail. The chair on which a monk sat, the small round table at which he ate, the cushion on which he meditated, as well as the books he read, might replicate exactly what he had seen in his Burmese teacher's rooms. This identification with the guru was rarely reinforced by face-to-face contact, however. Decades might go by before a student had the opportunity to visit his teacher, if he ever did. In the meantime, reluctant to share his intimate concerns with colleagues trained under different teachers in different countries, he kept them to himself. A missionary, albeit a missionary working in his own society, could feel extremely isolated.

In contrast, few in the first generation of nuns were equipped to do much more than chant and perform Buddha Puja, for which they received alms. If ever they traveled outside the country, they went as pilgrims, not as students. In 1944/45 the monks who were living in Kathmandu were expelled to India, where they energetically developed networks among Maha Bodhi missionaries at Sarnath, Bodh Gaya, and Calcutta that in time would provide sources of funding and opportunities for study abroad. Meanwhile, the nuns, led by Dharmacari, took themselves off to Trisuli, a market town with a large Newar population less than one day's journey from the capital. Unlike the monks' exile, theirs hardly gave them the chance to make influential contacts.

But in the 1960s a handful of young nuns who had had the opportunity—rare for female recruits—to study in Burma, returned to Nepal. The leader of the group was Dhammawati, a Shakya woman then aged twenty-eight, who had just attained the Dharmacarya, the highest level of Buddhist studies, in Kemarama nunnery in Moulmein.[55] Invited to remain in Burma where she had already developed a reputation as an able scholar and teacher, she made the decision to return to her country to teach the Dharma in her own community. She recalled many years later that coming back to Nepal was like going to hell from heaven. Whereas in Burma women were almost the equals of men—and nuns almost the equals of monks—in Nepal "they were down, down, down."[56] Within a short time she found herself in conflict with the senior monks, who barred her, as a ten-precept laywoman, from preaching in their *viharas*, even though as a Dharmacarya holder—a distinction no Nepalese monk at that date had achieved—technically she was better qualified than anyone else in the community to do so. But she bit her tongue and decided that the best strategy would be to construct a life for herself and her companions that would allow them as great a degree of independence as possible from the monks. Instead of joining Dharmacari and the other formerly married nuns in Kimdol Vihara, she and her "virgin" companions decided to live separately.

With donations from relatives and friends, Dhammawati built a nunnery in the center of Kathmandu, which she named Dharmakirti Vihara. Over the next decade she and her colleagues created their own program of teaching, publishing, and social service, while ignoring as far as possible the senior monks' attempts to restrict their activities. Dharmakirti Vihara soon took over from Kimdol Vihara as a meeting place and focus of religious activity for Theravada laywomen.[57]

Although the nuns were earning the respect and esteem of the community, their model of how to proceed was still based on what had become familiar to them in the nunnery where they had all been trained in Burma. In their view, only religious education was necessary for a nun; secular education was peripheral to their interests and a distraction. When young recruits to the nuns' order asked permission to continue with their studies, their elders strongly discouraged them. One nun remembers that, although after a long battle she was permitted to enroll in the university, her abbess, Dhammawati, required her to do so as an "external student." As a nun, it would be inappropriate for her to attend lectures with members of the opposite sex!

Not until the late 1980s did Dhammawati change her views in this regard. Invited to the first International Conference on Buddhist Women at Bodh Gaya in 1987, she was exposed to the views of nuns and laywomen from many countries, many of whom were struggling to attain equality and respect in societies as male-dominated as her own. She had never much valued secular education until the conference where, because she knew no English, the language in which the proceedings were conducted, she was dependent on a male interpreter, a devotee from the Dharmakirti community who had accompanied her to India.

Dhammawati herself had had no formal secular schooling; she had learned to read at home from the tutor her father had engaged to teach her brothers. Until now, her educational model had been Burmese, which focused on mastering Sanskrit and Pali and committing the Tripitaka to memory. Bodh Gaya opened up a new world to her. She started to imagine how different things could be in her community and soon resolved, despite the financial burden this would involve, to provide the young nuns in her charge with as much secular education as their talents merited.[58] Whereas once she had actively discouraged them from studying, now, having understood that gender equality would never be conceded by the monks but would have to be *claimed* by nuns who were as well-prepared as they, she *insisted* that they study. Most important, although it was too late for *her* to learn English or Chinese, now was *their* chance. In Bodh Gaya she had come to realize that the cutting edge of Buddhism was not in conservative Burma or Thailand as she had long believed, but in Taiwan and Sri Lanka. For Nepalese nuns, participation in modern international Buddhist discourse required their knowing modern, international languages as well as Sanskrit and Pali.

As of 2003 virtually all Nepalese nuns under the age of thirty are enrolled in educational programs. The younger ones study in government schools and the older ones in colleges. At least two dozen are studying abroad, many in institutions to which Dhammawati's contacts, carefully cultivated since Bodh Gaya and at subsequent international meetings, have given them access. Although the majority are studying in nunneries, Nepalese nuns are also enrolled in Buddhist colleges and universities in Burma, Thailand, Sri Lanka, and Taiwan. Whether, as a result of exposure to the lures of economic development in these countries, these young nuns eventually will disrobe like the novice monks remains to be seen.

A second equally important outcome of the 1987 Sakyadhita conference has been the nuns' success in their pursuit of full ordination. At Bodh Gaya, Dhammawati heard the Dalai Lama himself encourage nuns, in whose tradition female ordination had either never been established (Tibet) or, as in the case of Theravada, had died out, to take higher ordination from Chinese or Taiwanese Mahayana monks and nuns whose ordination lineages had survived.[59] Almost to a man, Theravada monks maintained—and today still maintain—that Theravada nuns' ordination, having vanished, could never be revived. Furthermore, in their view the Chinese ordination rite is inauthentic so far as Theravada nuns are concerned, even though it is believed to have been brought to China in 433 C.E. by Sri Lankan nuns.[60] Indeed, until she heard the address of His Holiness and the protracted discussions of the issue during conference sessions, this had been Dhammawati's own view. Knowing that the senior Nepali monks would never give their consent, in December 1988 Dhammawati and two other nuns traveled secretly to the United States to take full ordination according to Chinese rites at the Taiwanese Foguang Shan Buddhist Order's California branch Hsi Lai Monastery in Los Angeles. By 2003, despite the entrenched opposition of their monk preceptors, of the roughly one hundred members of the nuns' order who are old enough to ordain (twenty years), forty-two had traveled to China (Guangdong, December 1997; Shanghai, May 2002), Taiwan (Foguang Shan Monastery, on several occasions), and India (Bodh Gaya, 1998) to take full ordination.[61] The *Bhikkhuni Vibanga* (Deportment rules) require that ten fully ordained nuns as well as ten fully ordained monks, all of whom have themselves been ordained for at least twelve years, be in attendance at a nun's full ordination rite. In 2010 the waiting period will have expired, and for the first time in history full ordination for nuns will be available in Nepal.[62] Although to date the senior nuns admit that finding ten monks who are willing to participate in the ritual might still be difficult, they are optimistic. They believe that everything, even the most recalcitrant opposition, is impermanent.

CONCLUSION

With very few exceptions, the senior members of the Nepali monks' order who, as novices and young missionary monks, once represented the dedicated, scholarly, and energetic best of Buddhist modernism have become, in old age, arch-conservatives. Their response to the massive socioeconomic changes that are sweeping Nepal, as well as everywhere else in the region, is to dig in their heels and refuse to adjust to a changed reality. "It is only because of the Vinaya that Buddhism has survived for 2,500 years. If we relax the rules now, we are lost," one abbot intoned to me. Laypeople still respect the monks; they have not forgotten their good work, but they are deserting their monasteries—elaborate structures built with Thai and Malaysian funds—and are flocking to the more easily approachable *gurumaas* whose nunneries, built with local contributions, are generally more modest. For today, with the exception of a very few young monks, it is the *gurumaas* whose Dharma talks people want to hear. Approaching seventy, Dhammawati is still a workaholic, and several of her disciples are cut from the same cloth. Whereas once it was the monks who preached the Dharma in Newar villages, now it is the nuns in their spotless pink and orange dresses who travel by bus, truck, bicycle, and on foot beyond the limits of the Newar world to Tibetan Buddhist settlements in the Himalayas and to Muslim villages in the Terai. It is they, rather than the monks, who are the Theravada missionaries of the new millennium.

Notes

1. This paper is based on fieldwork carried out in Nepal in 1997–1998; June–July 1999; January–February 2000, March 2001, and April 2002.

2. T. Riccardi, "Buddhism in Ancient and Early Medieval Nepal," in *Studies in the History of Buddhism*, ed. A. K. Narain (New Delhi: B. R. Publishing, 1980).

3. See L. F. Stiller, *Rise of the House of Gorkha* (Delhi: Manjushri Publishing House, 1973).

4. See D. Wright, *A History of Nepal* (New Delhi: AES Reprints, 1990 [1877]).

5. For a history of Rana rule, see A. Sever, *Nepal under the Ranas* (Delhi: Oxford University Press, 1993).

6. See A. Hofer, *The Caste Hierarchy and the State of Nepal: A Study of the Muluki Ain of 1854* (Innsbruck: Universitätsverlag Wagner, 1979).

7. J. Pfaff-Czarnecka, "Vestiges and Vision of Cultural Change in the Process of Nation-building in Nepal," in *Nationalism and Ethnicity in a Hindu Kingdom: The Politics of Contemporary Nepal*, ed. D. Gellner, J. Pfaff-Czarnecka, and J. Whelpton (Amsterdam: Harwood Academic Publishers, 1997), 425.

8. J. Burghart, *The Conditions of Listening: Essays on Religion, History and Politics in South Asia*, ed. C. Fuller and J. Spencer (Delhi: Oxford University Press, 1996), 273.

9. For an account of the introduction of Theravada Buddhism to Nepal, see R. Kloppenborg, "Theravada Buddhism in Nepal," *Kailash* 5 (1977): 301–321.

10. For Kathmandu stupa renovations, see N. Gutschow, *The Nepalese Caitya* (Stuttgart: Edition Axel Menges, 1997). For relations between Tibet and Nepal in the premodern era, see T. Lewis, "Newars and Tibetans in the Kathmandu Valley: Ethnic Boundaries and Religious History," *Journal of Asian and African Studies* 38 (1989): 31–57.

11. Kangtse Lama's teachings were first translated into colloquial Newari and then rephrased in more religious language by a *pandit* (religious scholar).

12. For a detailed account of the reception of Kangtse Lama and Tsering Norbu in the Kath-

mandu Valley, see S. LeVine and D. Gellner, *Rebuilding Buddhism: Theravada Revivalism in Nepal* (forthcoming).

13. The concept of Buddhist modernism was first formulated by H. Bechert, who described the movement's intellectual and organizational origins in *Buddhismus Staat und Gesellschaft in den Landern des Theravada Buddhismus*, vol. 1 (Wiesbaden: Alfred Metzer, 1966).

14. Bhikkhu Amritananda Thera, *A Short History of Theravada Buddhism in Modern Nepal* (Kathmandu: Anandakuti Vihara Trust, 1986).

15. P. Onta, "Creating a Brave New Nepali Nation in British India: The Rhetoric of Jati Improvement, Rediscovery of Banubhakta and the Writing of Bir History," *Studies in Nepali History and Society* 1, no. 1 (1996): 37–76.

16. Bikkhu Amritananda Thera, *Short History of Theravada Buddhism in Modern Nepal*, n. 14.

17. See Kloppenborg, "Theravada Buddhism in Nepal," n. 9; and H. Bechert and J. U. Hartmann, "Observations on the Reform of Buddhism in Nepal," *Journal of the Nepal Research Center* 8 (1988): 1–28.

18. See B. Falwell, *The Gurkhas* (London: Allen Lane, 1984); M. Des Chene, "Relics of Empire: A Cultural History of the Gurkhas 1815–1987" (Ph.D. diss., Stanford University, 1991); Sever, *Nepal under the Ranas* (n. 5), 197, 277.

19. See T. T. Lewis, "Buddhist Merchants in Kathmandu: The Asan Twah Market and Uray Social Organisation," in *Contested Hierarchies: A Collaborative Ethnography of Caste in the Kathmandu Valley, Nepal*, ed. D. Gellner and D. Quigley (Oxford: Clarendon, 1995), 38–79; K. Lall, *The Newar Merchants in Lhasa* (Kathmandu: Ratna Pustak Bhandar, 2001).

20. For Dharmapala Anagarika's activities in India, see Maha Sthavira Sangharakshita, *Flame in Darkness: The Life and Sayings of Anagarika Dharmapala* (Pune, India: Triratna Grantha Mala, 1980); Sinha Ratnatunga, *They Turned the Tide: The 100 Year History of the Maha Bodhi Society of Sri Lanka* (Colombo: Government of Sri Lanka Printing House, 1991).

21. The Ranas' school, later known as Durbar High School, was established in 1853 in Thapothali Palace. It was moved outside to a building north of Rani Pokari by Ranoddip Singh Rana, and again to a building west of Rani Pokari by Sir S. J. B. Rana, who in 1894 permitted commoners to attend. See Sever, *Nepal under the Ranas* (n. 5), 224.

22. Dharmapala himself is said to have seen Jagat Man as a messenger sent from heaven to propagate Theravada Buddhism in Nepal, the land of the Buddha's birth. See V. P. Lacoul, *The Place of Dharmacarya in Returning "Sthaviravad" to Nepal and Reviving Nepal Basha* (Kathmandu: Malati Lacoul, 1985).

23. LeVine and Gellner, *Rebuilding Buddhism*, (n.12), (forthcoming).

24. See C. Rosser, "Social Mobility in the Newar Caste System," in *Caste and Kinship in Nepal, India and Ceylon*, ed. C. von Fürer-Haimendorf (Bombay: Asia Publishing House, 1966), 68–139.

25. Sthavira Sangharakshita, *The Rainbow Road: From Tooting Broadway to Kalimpong, Memoirs of an English Buddhist* (Birmingham: Windhorse, 1997), 396–400.

26. For an account of these years, see J. Fisher, *Living Martyr Individuals and Revolution in Nepal* (New Delhi: Oxford University Press, 1997); W. Hoftun, W. Raeper, and J. Whelpton, *People, Politics and Ideology: Democracy and Social Change in Nepal* (Kathmandu: Mandala Book Point, 2000).

27. Chandramani visited Kathmandu and Terai towns, which had sizable Newar Buddhist populations fairly frequently, but he never lived in Nepal.

28. Bikkhu Amritananda Thera, *Short History of Theravada Buddhism in Modern Nepal*, n. 14.

29. The details of Mahapragya's life are taken from Darasa Nevami, ed., *Autobiography of the Late Buddhist Yogi Mahapragya* (in three parts; Kathmandu: Rishi Ashram, 1983, 1989, and 1995), and from interviews with his disciples.

30. Details of Dharmacari's life are taken from M. B. Shakya, "Bhikkhuni Dharmacari: A Short Biography," unpublished MS (n.d.), and interviews with her disciples.

31. The books Laximani read included Pandit Nisthananda's 1914 Newari translation of *Lalitavistara* and Dharmaditya Dharmacharya's translations of canonical Pali texts.

32. *Bhikkhuni* ordination had died out in India by the tenth century and in Sri Lanka by the eleventh. Although *bhikkhu* ordination also died out in Sri Lanka at various points during the second millennium, each time it was revived by monks from Burma and Thailand to whom the Theravada ordination lineage had been transmitted. By contrast, since the *bhikkhuni* ordination lineage had never been established in either country, retransmission to Sri Lanka was an impossibility. P. Skilling, "A Note on the History of the Bhikkhunisanga (II); the Order of Nuns after the Parinirvana," *WFB Review* 30, no. 4, and 31, no. 1 (1993/94).

33. S. M. Tuladhar, "Kindo Baha: A Center for the Resurgence of Buddhism in the Kathmandu Valley," *Lost Horizon* 3 (1996): 7–12; Kloppenborg, "Theravada Buddhism in Nepal," n. 9.

34. Kloppenborg, "Theravada Buddhism in Nepal," n. 9.

35. Under the most recent constitution (1990) it is still illegal to proselytize and in particular to offer inducements to convert; however, violations are no longer prosecuted.

36. In his study of narratives and rituals of Newar Buddhism, T. Lewis uses the term "religious domestication" for the process whereby certain features of the north Indian Mahayana textual tradition were selected for adoption in the Kathmandu Valley while others were ignored. See T. Lewis, *Popular Buddhist Texts from Nepal* (Albany: State University of New York Press, 2000), xxx. The term might usefully be applied to the reverse process, whereby the Theravadins selected certain features of Newar Buddhism in order to make their message locally acceptable.

37. Bechert and Hartmann, "The Reform of Buddhism in Nepal," n. 17.

38. See D. Gellner, "Buddhism, Women and Caste: The Case of the Newars of the Kathmandu Valley," in *Buddhist Women and Social Justice*, ed. Karma Lekshe Tsomo (Albany: State University of New York Press, in press).

39. See Gellner, "Introduction," in Gellner and Quigley, *Contested Hierarchies*, n. 19.

40. On certain ritual occasions, male members of Newar priestly castes receive alms from the middle and lower castes; however, on these occasions the rice donated is either uncooked or cooked in milk, which is believed to be much less susceptible to pollution than rice boiled in water. See D. Gellner, *Monk, Householder and Tantric Priest* (Cambridge: Cambridge University Press, 1992), 180–181.

41. See R. B. Vandya, *Sanghanayaka Ven. Pragyananda Mahastabir (A Concise Biography)* (Kathmandu: n.p., 1986).

42. Ibid.

43. L. Kunreuther, "Newar Traditions in a Changing Culture: An Analysis of Two Prepubescent Rituals for Girls," in *Anthropology of Nepal: Peoples, Problems and Processes*, ed. M. Allen (Kathmandu: Mandala Book Point, 1994), 339–347.

44. Kloppenborg, "Theravada Buddhism in Nepal," n. 9.

45. T. T. Lewin, "The Tuladhars of Kathmandu: A Study of Buddhist Tradition in a Newar Merchant Community" (Ph.D. diss., Columbia University, 1984).

46. See Constitution of the Kingdom of Nepal 2047 (1990; Kathmandu: Law Books Management Board, 1992).

47. The author interviewed Nepali monks and nuns studying in Bangkok in July 1998 and March 2001, and Nepali nuns studying in Burma in April 1998.

48. Training at Vijirarama was much influenced by the Sarvodaya Shramadana movement. Founded in 1958 by Dr. A. T. Ariyaratne, who was influenced by the teachings of Mahatma Gandhi and Anagarika Dharmapala, the movement reinterpreted the Dharma to focus on social action and selfless service for humanity as the highest form of religious practice. Although originally a lay movement, Sarvodaya has had a major impact on monastic training. "*Sarvodaya*" refers to the movement's objective: the establishment of a new, nonviolent socioeconomic order in which human potential for spiritual achievement is to be realized. See G. D. Bond, "A. T. Ariyaratne and the Sarvodaya Shramadana Movement in Sri Lanka," in *Engaged Buddhism: Buddhist Liberation Movements in Asia* (Albany: State University of New York Press, 1995), 121–146.

49. Ashok (pseudonym) was interviewed in Kathmandu in January 1997.

50. Keshab (pseudonym) was interviewed in Bangkok in July 1998.

51. R. C. Tewari, "Sociocultural Aspects of Theravada Buddhism in Nepal," *Journal of the International Association of Buddhist Studies* 6, no. 2 (1983): 67–93.

52. Bhikkhu Kondanya, *Charumati Voice* (Kathmandu, 2001).

53. Interviewed by the author in May 1998.

54. S. LeVine, "At the Cutting Edge: Theravada Nuns in the Kathmandu Valley," in *Innovative Buddhist Women: Swimming against the Stream*, ed. Karma Lekshe Tsomo (Richmond, Surrey: Curzon 2000), 13–29.

55. M. K. Shakya, *Snehi Chori (Beloved Daughter): A Biography of Anagarika Dhammawati*, translated from the original Burmese by the Reverend Ra We Thon in 1963 (Kathmandu: n.p., 1967).

56. Details of Dhammawati's life after her return from Burma are taken from the author's interviews with her in 1997.

57. S. LeVine, "Financing a Mission: Support for the Theravada Nuns' Order of Nepal," *Journal of the International Association of Buddhist Studies* 24, no. 2 (2001): 217–240.

58. By the 1980s, nunneries were beginning to accept recruits as young as ten years old. Some had discovered a vocation after spending time as *rishini* (probationary nuns) in the nunnery; a few were orphans who had been brought to the nunnery by relatives. See S. LeVine, "Dharma Education for Women in the Theravada Buddhist Community of Nepal," in Tsomo, *Buddhist Women and Social Justice*, n. 38.

59. See Karma Lekshe Tsomo, ed., *Sakyadhita: Daughters of the Buddha* (New York: Snow Lion, 1988).

60. See K. A. Tsai, "The Chinese Buddhist Monastic Order for Women: The First Two Centuries," *Historical Reflections/Reflections Historiques* 8, no. 3 (1981): 1–20.

61. For Chinese and Taiwanese Buddhist involvement in the reintroduction of female ordination into Theravada Buddhism, see Y. Li, "Ordination, Legitimacy, and Sisterhood: The International Full Ordination Ceremony in Bodh Gaya," in Tsomo, *Innovative Buddhist Women*, 168–200n54.

62. Although five records and a few inscriptions written in Sanskrit, including one from the sixth century C.E., indicated that there were nuns in the Kathmandu Valley in ancient times, there is no evidence of the existence of a *bhikkhuni* ordination lineage, whether Theravada Mahasanghika or Mulasarvastivada. The likelihood is that the nuns mentioned in these inscriptions had been ordained in India, or else, even though they are referred to as "*bhikshuni*," they were not fully ordained nuns. See P. Skilling, "A Note on the History of the Bhikkhuni-sanga," n. 32.

3 Grafting Identity: The Hawaiian Branches of the Bodhi Tree

George J. Tanabe, Jr.

Japanese Buddhism in Hawai'i for the last thirty years has been suffering a slow but certain death. Temple memberships continue to drop, rural temples often do not have permanent ministers, and, most ominous, young people are noticeably disinterested. Temple leaders and ministers constantly worry about the bleeding, unable to stop the flow. In the early 1960s there were about fifty thousand Buddhists in Hawai'i, of whom about half belonged to the Honpa Honganji sect. Today there are approximately twenty thousand Buddhists, of whom eight thousand are Honpa members.[1] The numbers decline year by year, quietly because there is no overt pressure forcing the exodus, voluntarily because people freely choose not to belong.

The most widely recognized cause of this demise is Americanization of Japanese Americans. Like other immigrant groups, Japanese Americans have been following a straight-line model of acculturation by which each succeeding generation becomes more American, less Japanese. Language is the most obvious indicator: the first generation (*issei*) spoke only Japanese, the second generation (*nisei*) was mostly bilingual, and the third generation on (*sansei, yonsei*, etc.) speak only English. Traditional customs have followed the same linear decline. Of the many agents of Americanization the Buddhist temples themselves played an extremely important role in promoting the making of good civic and cultural citizens of America. Temple members worked hard to ensure that their children would be more successful Americans than they, and their resultant success is a matter of record and intense pride. They untied the ties of Japanese cultural and religious attachment and let go of their youth, and many of those who left the temples did not return. Victims of their own desired success, the temples unwittingly slit their own wrists, committing slow suicide.

Although local Buddhist temples borrowed Christian-style pulpits, pews, organs, Sunday schools (now called Dharma schools), and hymnals, these adaptations have not gone far enough to satisfy those who find the temples too Japanese for their American tastes. The perceived pattern of temple assimilation, however, is still understood along the lines charted for the acculturation of the people: a straight line of increasing Americanization. The difference between the two is one of degree, and both lines charted on a graph would be parallel, the one for temple assimilation being below that for the people. The gap between the two is the reason for the departure of the young people. Revival, if there is to be one, must take the form of increased Americanization on the part of the temples in order to close the gap, to make the two lines coincide, to replace, in effect, the ethnic Japanese elements with American ones.

Employing ideas of assimilation, acculturation, adaptation, and syncretism, this linear model of social process can be traced back to sociologists active at the University of Hawai'i in the twenties and thirties. In 1920 Romanzo Adams was appointed the first professor of sociology and economics at the university and continued to be the guiding inspiration for a generation of faculty and students carrying out research in Hawai'i. His view of cultural assimilation was the classic melting-pot model, which posited an ever-increasing blending of cultures that made up a thick brew he called Americanism.

While most Japanese Americans in Hawai'i have embraced the melting-pot ideal instead of an ideology of multicultural diversity that locates identity in a single (ironically, nondiverse) culture, the Buddhist temples have locked themselves into a religious culture that is westernized on the surface but remains unassimilated at its core. This has not been due to a deliberate social ideology, but to a conservatism rooted in the very heart of Japanese Buddhist missions that did not seek to convert foreigners but to maintain the home culture and religion. This nondiversified religious core keeps Buddhism essentially Japanese, and is thus a showcase for multicultural diversity in modern Hawai'i.

The problem with Adams' melting-pot model is not that it is wrong—it accurately describes the assimilative process Japanese Americans have chosen—but that it does not explain how or why Buddhist temples remain outside the pot, refusing to be melted at their core. It does not explain the historical development of local Buddhism, which embarked in the early twentieth century on a conscious campaign to assimilate itself into the American melting pot, but then followed a bumpy road of *decreasing* Americanization, at least in doctrinal and ritual terms. The call for a nonethnic or transethnic universal Buddhism, which a model of linear assimilation would expect in later rather than earlier stages, was made in the early twentieth century, peaked around the thirties, and now remains a mostly forgotten vestige in the postwar period, even though calls for an internationalized or globalized Buddhism are periodically heard.[2] In important ways, there has been an increase in a Japanization representing a reversal of the assimilation process.

By their nature, models of assimilation are interested in adaptive change and ignore inherited elements that refuse to change. What we need, therefore, is a more complex model that can account for the nonassimilation of the discrete ingredients of the tossed salad as well as the assimilation of the melting pot. Instead of using lines in a geometry of change, I propose an organic model drawn from horticulture. The use of plants as cultural metaphors is not *new*, and we commonly speak of seeds of change, branches of institutions, roots of identity, the flowering of culture, and so forth. This diction, in fact, was used often by the early Buddhist leaders in Hawai'i. Horticulture is particularly suggestive of human affairs because it deals with the invasive methods of manipulating growth through transplanting, cross-pollinating, pruning, and grafting. Cultural processes can be fruitfully subjected to horticultural analysis, and after defining these manipulative techniques, I will argue that the transplanted rootstock of Japanese Buddhism established itself firmly in Hawai'i's soil and continues to exist unmodified as a family or ancestral (and therefore mostly ethnic) religion. I shall also argue that a variety of branches were grafted to the transplanted tree with different degrees of success, and that cross-pollination, also known as hybridization, seldom, if ever, took place. Put in terms of the melting pot, which can be correlated with hybridization, or in chemical terms with "alchemic absorption,"[3] my argument is that assimilation did not take place in the temples where it counted the most, at the core. The value of this arboreal model is that it allows us to see divergent genetic identities of different and even foreign branches growing on a rootstock that nourished the branches without changing its own ancestral identity.

HORTICULTURAL MANIPULATIONS

TRANSPLANTING

Transplanting is the removal of a plant in enough of its entirety to replant in another location. The plant remains the very same organism moved from one place to another. While different environmental factors can modify its growth patterns, they do not change the basic genetic identity of the plant.

PROPAGATION BY CUTTING

A new plant can be started by taking a cutting from a parent stock, rooting it, and planting it apart from its parent. It is a form of cloning through an asexual process that produces identical stock. As with transplanting, the new plant is genetically identical to its parent.

CROSS-POLLINATION

Cross-pollination, cross-breeding, or hybridization occurs when the pollen from the flowers of two different plants are mixed to produce seeds resulting in plants that combine the characteristics of the parents and therefore are not identical to either parent. If cross-pollination, which can take place between plants of the same species, occurs between two species, then a third species bearing the combined characteristics of its parents is produced. A cross between a red rose and a white one will produce a pink blossom. Unlike the results of transplanting or propagation by cutting, the new plant is genetically different in slight but very significant ways from its parents.

MUTATION

A spontaneous shift in the genetic identity of a plant can take place within itself (that is, without cross-pollination) through responses to the environment. Most mutations are deleterious and, being the result of natural internal changes, are not the results of horticultural manipulations.

GRAFTING

A scion, which consists of a branch or bud from one plant, can be grafted to a host plant and continue to grow symbiotically but without changing its genetic identity. Within the same genus, grafting can take place between different species without any changes occurring to either species. A lemon branch, for instance, can be grafted to a lime tree and will produce lemons that are genetically identical to the parent lemon. It is a form of propagation by cutting, except that the branch does not produce its own root system and lives off the root and stock of its host instead.

PRUNING

The trimming of branches changes the physical shape of the plant and encourages new growth but does not alter its genetic identity.

The most important of these terms for my analysis are cross-pollination and grafting. When two cultural or religious species meet to produce something *new*, then that social process can be likened to cross-pollination. As a hybrid, the new creation must be significantly if not essentially different from either of its parents. Bred from a horse and a donkey, a mule is not just a novelty but is something new. When terms such as "syncretism" or "assimilation" are used to describe the adoption of a Shinto *kami* into a Buddhist temple (or vice versa), hybridization is not involved, as the *kami* can still be recognized genetically as a non-Buddhist deity even though it may be treated as a buddha or bodhisattva. As Ian Reader and I have pointed out, the association of the Shinto *kami* and Buddhist deities in Japan is but a gathering of gods that retain their unique identities, and since new deities are not produced, hybridization is absent. Buddhist-Shinto syncretism is a tossed salad, not a melting pot.[4]

In horticultural terms, Buddhist-Shinto syncretism of the deities is a graft in which scions retain their unique identities apart from the host stock. Just as a lemon growing on a lime tree is a novelty but not a new fruit, so a Shinto *kami* can flourish at a Buddhist temple and still remain genetically a *kami*. Grafting was the dominant technique used by Buddhists in Hawai'i because it allowed the rootstock to remain unchanged. The genetic identity of that rootstock, however, was not the same as that for the bodhi tree in India or China because cross-pollination in addition to grafting took place in Japan to produce a hybrid Buddhism unique to Japan. Upon transplantation to Hawai'i, hybrid Japanese Buddhism became the rootstock onto which grafts were made, but cross-pollination seldom if ever took place. There is as yet no hybrid Hawaiian Buddhism, for the rootstock remains locked in the double helix of Japanese Buddhism and Japanese ethnicity. The case of the Honpa Honganji shows that its particular combination of religion and ethnicity has resisted hybridization and remains a purebred religion of family ancestry instead of the community at large.[5] Like Japanese ethnicity itself, Buddhism is transmitted primarily within non-hybrid bloodlines. Once the integrity of the ethnic lineage is disrupted through intermarriage (that is, cross-breeding), it becomes difficult for the mongrel line to nurture purebred Buddhism. Most attempts at cross-pollinating Buddhism itself failed quietly, but the first person to try it in Hawai'i was publicly humiliated.

THE DANGERS OF CROSS-BREEDING

Cross-breeding Buddhism with Christianity in Hawai'i put an end to the clerical career of Kagahi Sōryū (d. 1917), the founder of Jōdo Shinshū (Nishi) Honpa Honganji in the islands. As a young priest in Kyushu, Kagahi had heard many stories of hardship from friends and neighbors receiving letters from those who had gone to Hawai'i as contract laborers on the sugar plantations. Determined to help, Kagahi went to the Honganji headquarters in Kyoto in January 1889 and requested that priests be sent to Hawai'i. With a budget already strained by overseas missions in China, Korea, and Taiwan, the sectarian officials could offer only their sympathetic support for Kagahi's idea but no funds. Undeterred, Kagahi secured private funding and set sail for Hawai'i. Arriving in Honolulu Harbor on March 2, he called on Consul-General Ando Tarō, who advised him, "when in Rome do as the Romans do," advocating that Japanese living in a Christian country should therefore become Christians. That same evening, Kagahi, paying no heed to Ando's advice, conducted the first Shinshū ceremony in his room at the Kojima Hotel, striking a tiny gong that rang out a sound never heard before in Honolulu.

By the time he returned to Japan in October 1889, Kagahi had visited the islands of Hawai'i, Maui, and Kauai; secured enough donations to purchase a lot in Honolulu; and built a temple in Hilo. As many of the Japanese laborers had come from areas in Japan where Shinshū was well established, Kagahi found many willing supporters. Kimura Saiji was one of the most enthusiastic, especially because he had consciously reaffirmed his faith in Amida after being tempted to convert to Christianity while he had been a student in France. A labor supervisor in the Bureau of Immigration, Kimura was well known among the Japanese. Much of Kagahi's success was due to Kimura's efforts but so too, inadvertently, was his downfall.

In one of their many discussions, Kimura told Kagahi that he believed Amida to be identical to the Christian God. Kagahi seems not to have responded in any particular way to this statement, and besides, except for Consul-General Ando's advice, there was little need to worry about Christianity since he would be working among people who were already Buddhists by custom, if not belief. Buddhist missionary work (kaikyō) did not call for converting Christians or even defending the faith. Rapidly increasing in numbers, the Japanese in Hawai'i would comprise 40 percent of the population by 1920, by which time Hawai'i was called the "Japanese village in the Pacific." As Stuart Chandler and C. Julia Huang point out in their essays included in this volume (Chaps. 7, 8), the modern Foguang Shan and Ciji movements outside of Taiwan minister primarily to overseas Chinese. Although the word "mission" can be used to describe these efforts, there is a fundamental difference between diaspora missions serving those who are already Buddhists and foreign missions designed to convert non-Buddhists. Buddhism in Hawai'i was diasporic, and ministering there was not very different from temple work in Kyushu.

Arriving back in Japan in October 1889, Kagahi gave an enthusiastic report of his successes and the prospects for vigorous mission work among Japanese Buddhists in Hawai'i. This time the headquarters responded with positive support. The Overseas Mission Association issued a call for *kaikyōshi,* "priests who open up the teachings" in new places. The term is usually translated as "missionary," and though it can include the work of converting foreigners, in the context of Kagahi's mission it was understood that converting and serving non-Japanese were not involved. The call was met with eager responses, and everything went well for Kagahi—until he made the mistake of saying that Amida should be identified with God as an expedient means *(hōben)* of propagating Buddhism in a Christian society. Kagahi's stand would have made sense if his objective had been to convert Christians, but that was not the case. He may have thought that there was a legal requirement for all religions in Hawai'i to recognize the existence of God.[6] Unfortunately for him, however, he published his opinion in a widely read journal and caused a huge controversy. His supporters turned against him; even his teacher, who was also his father-in-law, censured him. Kagahi was stunned. He left the priesthood and sought refuge in his family temple in Oita, where he wrote his memoirs, *Hawai'i kikō* (Hawai'i journal). He died in 1917, unrecognized for his pioneering efforts.[7]

As Japanese Buddhism has a long history of using expedient means to justify all kinds of unlikely alliances, Kagahi's downfall is a bit surprising. It would seem that his proposal for relating Amida to God was not so different from the Buddhist-Shinto syncretism that was so prevalent in Japan. While Jōdo Shinshū orthodoxy rejected linkages with the *kami,* it also taught, as Rennyo did, respect for them. Kagahi's proposal, however, went far beyond the pattern of grafting *kami* to Buddhist deities. The theory of *honji suijaku* (original ground, manifest traces), which was developed to justify Buddhist-Shinto associations, did not assert an equal identity between the gods, but an unequal relationship in which both sides retained their essential identities, the Buddhist deities being in the superior *(honji)* position. Kagahi's proposal, in contrast, was to *equate* Amida with God in a melting pot that threatened the loss of Amida's (and God's) identity. A grafting of distinct and unequal parts would be acceptable, but an amalgam of identical and equal parts was anathema. It smacked of something new, of hybridization.

TRANSPLANTING THE TREE

Between 1889 and 1897, individual priests followed Kagahi's pattern of going to Hawai'i with the blessing but not the financial support of the headquarters. In 1897 the headquarters sent Miyamoto Ejun to survey conditions. Miyamoto returned with petitions for more ministers, and the headquarters finally sent its first official *kaikyōshi* in October 1897 with the understanding that the laborers in Hawai'i would provide all of the financial support. The *kaikyōshi* were referred to as missionaries, but their mission was to serve native Japanese, not to convert others. In January 1898, Satomi Hōji was sent as the first *kantoku*, or bishop, as he was called in Hawai'i. In June he returned to Japan for health reasons and to recruit more priests. When he went back to Hawai'i in early 1899, he took with him Imamura Emyō (also Yemyō), a graduate of Keio University trained to speak English and imbued with the ideals of reformers like Fukuzawa Yūkichi and Kiyozawa Manshi. It was a time of rapid expansion, and the growing number of priests established temples wherever Japanese laborers had settled in the growing number of plantation communities.

The temples provided many social functions, but the basic religious service they offered consisted of funeral and memorial services. Working conditions on the plantations were harsh—even Imamura, who was not given to emotional extremes, thought that workers were treated like "slaves and horses"[8]—and it was not uncommon for them to die of illness or accidents at a young age. Okano Jusuke reported that, in the early days before the arrival of the Buddhist ministers, the dead were buried in crude boxes without benefit of religious rites; when it was discovered that a certain Teraoka Tosuke was a lay Buddhist trained to recite the *Amida Sutra* and the *Shōshinge*, he was called upon to perform funerals. Okano estimated that Teraoka conducted no less than four hundred funerals.[9]

Because the early laborers were primarily single men, it cannot be said that the first forms of Buddhism were centered in the family. Imamura's initial assignment was at plantation camps in rural Oahu, and his primary task was to reach hard-drinking, whoring, bad-tempered men who were not interested in sermons on Amida's compassion. Often ridiculed and rejected, Imamura felt himself to be a failure, but he persevered in the face of this seeming futility because he was convinced that Buddhism could improve the lives of the Japanese men in a way that Christianity could not. Japanese Christian missionaries had been active in the plantation camps before the Buddhist priests arrived, and, unlike their Buddhist counterparts, they enjoyed the financial support of their home churches. Imamura was convinced, however, that the Christian ministers were taking the wrong approach by preaching temperance and abstinence to men whose primary solace came from alcohol and sex. The Christians failed to treat them "as Japanese" and expected them to conform to Western norms of puritanical behavior. Rejected for his own straitlaced manner, Imamura was not puritanical and did not condemn alcohol and sex.[10]

The way to deal with the "bad-tempered" men was to create a surrogate family for them. Rather than condemning their behavior, the "primary mission of the Honganji in Hawai'i is to provide comfort by being loving fathers and mothers to these orphans" (Imamura 1918, 27). This was not yet the family Buddhism centered on the ancestors, but it was clearly familial in a way the Christianity preached by the moralists was not. It also treated the men as Japanese, and Imamura was confident that Buddhism would prevail over Christianity. But Christianity was not the only unsuitable religion for the rough kind of people who were in Hawai'i. With sectarian specificity, Imamura argued that Tendai and Shingon were too aristocratic, that Jōdo and Zen were for samurai. Only Shinshū was appropriate for the common laborer. "We do not despise eating meat, do not forbid having wives, and pay no attention to whether one is rich or poor, high or low class, educated or uneducated, foolish or wise. Ours is a teaching of equality. Wealthy people value it, and laborers love it. Foreigners respect it, and believers embrace it" (ibid., 26). While Imamura was not concerned about converting non-Japanese, he was keenly aware that he needed to win the respect of the Christian community and to defend his sect against the claims of other Japanese Buddhist organizations. Mission work was more than ministering to his own kind in an overseas setting; it involved active persuasion to show the general community that Shinshū could hold its own, and even do better than Christian and other Buddhist claims.

The combination of universal egalitarianism with sectarian triumphalism is a recurrent theme in Imamura's writings, one that was also being developed by other Buddhist leaders in Japan at the time. Imamura made this egalitarian ideal the centerpiece of a new Buddhism that purported to transcend ethnic and sectarian boundaries, but like so many claims about universalism it was made on his Shinshū terms—only his sect could transcend all sects. Arguing that his universal Buddhism was appropriate for all, Imamura was keenly aware that such a new formulation would be needed in any approach to non-Buddhists but it was not really necessary for his own mission, for the Japanese were already Buddhists. After twenty years of successful mission work, Imamura knew that the real reason why the Shinshū movement had succeeded is that most of the laborers came from Hiroshima, Yamaguchi, Kumamoto, and Fukuoka, places where Shinshū was well established, not because of his message of egalitarianism.

> Such rapid progress of our mission work is mainly due to the fact that our countrymen here—most of them—came over to Hawai'i from that part of the country where our faith held its firm ground during many hundred years. [The] seed was already sown, and we have had only to foster it.[11]
>
> For twenty years until this day we have succeeded in our mission because the seeds that had already been planted in the old country bore fruit.

In this sense we must understand that the success of Shinshū in Hawai'i is not an accident. When a ditch is constructed, the water flows; and when the pods open, the beans fall out.[12]

Imamura's horticultural imagery of seeds and fruit is not specifically that of transplanting, but the idea is still the same: the laborers from Japan were already Shinshū seeds transported to Hawai'i to sprout and bear their predictable fruit. The ministers did not have to convert them. Ōtani Kōmyō (1885–1961), a high-ranking Shinshū priest, also put it in the horticultural terms of transplantating: "The trunk of the tree has been created, and from it will grow branches, leaves, flowers and fruit. There is great promise for Buddhism in Hawai'i."[13]

Shinshū was thus transplanted to Hawai'i not just by the ministers but by the people themselves. The environment was different, but the core religious need was for funeral services for men who were single but still sons and brothers. Precisely because they were single, Imamura aimed at creating a family for them by being their loving father. In a short time, with the arrival of picture brides and other women, real families needed the traditional religion of funerals, memorial services, and ancestor veneration. Ancestors and family exist in bloodlines, and the rites of memorialization were inseparable from ethnicity, at least for as long as family lineage remained Japanese.

Rooted in the family, the transplanted bodhi tree also had the budding branches of an egalitarian Shinshū suitable for all classes of people. Once in Hawai'i, the tree received a solid graft of a universal Buddhism, and this branch spread its shade beyond Japanese class structure and reached out to ethnic Caucasians. The success of that graft, however, was threatened by an older, well-developed branch that came with the tree. Japanese nationalism had long been grafted onto the bodhi tree in Japan, and while it was allowed to flourish in Hawai'i—the first generation were, after all, loyal subjects of the emperor, and many from the second generation maintained similar loyalties—Buddhist leaders like Imamura felt a tremendous pressure from the American community to prune the branch, or even to sever it completely so that it could be replaced by American nationalism.

The sap of family Buddhism keeping the tree in good health was mostly taken for granted as custom and did not elicit the public attention that the branches of nationalism did. Many eyes watched to see if Imamura would replace the branch of Japanese nationalism with an American one, and add the branch of universal Buddhism to complement the budding egalitarian Buddhism already on the tree. The horticultural challenge was intricate. He had to prune the political species of Japanese nationalism, graft in its place another political species from a different country, also graft a philosophical species of universal Buddhism, and continue to nurture the rootstock bearing the double helix of family religion and Japanese ethnicity. Imamura went about his work carefully—transplanting, pruning, and grafting, all the while making sure that cross-pollination would not take place, that nothing genetically new would be produced. Each branch retained its own identity and could be removed or added without changing the double helix of the stock. This strategy worked exceedingly well, and thus Imamura avoided the dangers of cross-pollination that had destroyed Kagahi before him.

GRAFTING UNIVERSAL BUDDHISM

In 1918 Imamura's architectural dream came true with the completion of the Honpa Honganji main temple. Designed by two American architects working under the close guidance of Imamura, the temple departed radically from Japanese styles and featured an international combination of Indian and Western exterior forms. The roofline no longer had gently curving slopes, but dramatic circles stacked to form stupas topped by rings of Indian cosmology. It was important for the temple not to look Japanese so that it could take its proud position in an American city without being out of place. Young people should be proud of its international appearance and not shamed by an ethnically circumscribed building. Although the stupa forms were certainly foreign, they resembled domes, and the front roof structure was supported by a series of massive Roman Tuscan columns. At the dedication ceremony, Imamura declared that "true religion ought to rise above and be applicable to any country and nationality and so assimilate with every state and nation."[14]

Had he stopped there, Imamura could be seen as a cross-breeder of hybrids. But he went on to add that "the final object of the Hongwanji mission's idea is to plant the gospel of Buddha Amida in the true spirit of every nation in every corner of the world" (Imamura 1918, 54). This was triumphalism at its missionary best and once again restricted his universal Buddhism to his own sectarian gospel. Imamura saw no need to modify his Shinshū faith through hybridization and was satisfied that his purebred religion was suitable for the entire world because it was the universal truth. If anything, states and nations *should* be changed by assimilating Shinshū. While in his actual work he did little to convert Christians, his stated ideals were imbued with the spirit of a missionary seeking to win the world over to his faith.

The theme of sectarian universalism was repeated by many of Imamura's colleagues. Writing at his request, Tsunoda Ryūsaku, an educator in Hawai'i who would later do much to shape Asian studies in America while teaching at Columbia University and directing its East Asian Library, wrote *The Essence of Japanese Buddhism,* "in order to inform the white circles of essential features of Buddha's teaching and bring them to the right understanding of it."[15] In his preface to the book, Imamura explained that "in the teaching of St. Shinran, the central idea is to induce all nations and all races on the earth, with no regard to their color and rank, to unite in the work of forming one large family, with our Buddha Amida as their universal parent."[16] After explaining the basic tenets of Indian Buddhism, Tsunoda argued that the Buddha taught both a religion of the "emphatic nay," which promoted the ascetic rejection of desires, and the way of the "emphatic yea," in which all beings are buddhas with nothing to reject or negate.[17] In Japan the emphatic yea was perfected by Shinran, who affirmed that all people, regardless of gender, status, ethnicity, or nationality, are saved by the grace of Amida. Christians have wrongly accused Shinshū of teaching "national prejudice and bigoted patriotism," but "the teaching of Amida's salvation is far from being national or racial in its essence." "Not only are Shinshuists free from racial or national prejudices, but they are also free from petty hatred of sectarianism" (Imamura 1918, 64–65). Shinran transformed the "emphatic yea" into the "Absolute Yea" (ibid., 82).

Writing in 1918, Ōtani Kōmyō (1885–1961), a high-ranking Honpa Honganji official who had studied in Europe and America, reminded his readers that Imamura was remarkable not only for establishing and spreading Shinshū in Hawai'i, but for "propagating the path of true peace to all the peoples of the world." The highest good, he explained, is to strive for an equality shared by all peoples of the world, not just those from individual homes, certain societies, particular nations, or specific ethnic groups. He recalled his visit to Hawai'i and the speeches he gave in which he discussed these ideas and the essentials required for good relations between Japan and America: "I remember saying that the spiritual foundation for this exists only in the sacred sphere of [Amida's] selected vow."[18]

Takakusu Junjirō (1866–1945), the eminent Indologist and Buddhist scholar, looked upon Hawai'i as the place where the ocean currents from the East and West mix and provide sustenance for "international fish" (*kokusaiteki gyozoku*). For Takakusu, the teaching of Buddhist egalitarianism goes back to India, where the Buddha transformed a religion for aristocrats into one for ordinary people. That egalitarianism made its way to Japan, where Prince Shōtoku promoted it as the basis for culture. Shinran then perfected the teaching of equality that the Buddha and Shōtoku Taishi could not realize themselves, and it is therefore not surprising that Shinran should be called "the avatar of egalitarianism."[19]

The idea of a sectarian universalism is conceptually problematic if it must combine the particular and the general with the internal consistency of a hybrid; but seen as a doctrinally conceived universal Buddhism grafted onto the stem of sectarian family religion, the combination preserves the separate and even contradictory identities of the parts. Amida was thus made to reign over all peoples and nations at the same time that Amida remained a family deity (*ujigami*). The branch of universalism was promoted with such vigor that it even came close to overwhelming the rest of the tree. If through the lens of assimilation theories Buddhism in Hawai'i appears to be Americanized or westernized it is because this branch alone dominates the view. The overspreading branch was so commanding that there were some who came close to advocating that the sectarian trunk of family religion itself be pruned away from the branch of universal Buddhism.

Ernest Hunt (1876–1967) was a British merchant-marine seaman who had converted to Buddhism in his travels throughout Asia. Hunt arrived in Hawai'i in 1915 and worked in the offices of several sugar plantations before Imamura recruited him and his wife, Dorothy, for the Honpa Honganji English Department, which was established in 1921; it had initially been run by M. T. Kirby, a former cowboy and lumberjack convert who loved to strut about in his Buddhist robes delivering tirades against Christianity, which he was fond of saying should be taken "*cum grano salis*" (with a grain of salt). Of questionable sanity, Kirby left the islands after "more than five years of irreparable disservice to Buddhism in Hawai'i," sparing everyone, Buddhists and Christians alike, more sermons such as "Did Jesus Really Live?"[20] Well-read and a gentleman, Hunt was a welcome relief. In a move that would be unthinkable today, Imamura ordained Hunt and his wife in 1924, and as Buddhist ministers the couple contributed to the Buddhist movement in extraordinary ways. Inducted into the Honpa Honganji, they were nevertheless like lemons on a lime tree, devoid of Japanese ancestral religion.

What they really espoused was Theravada Buddhism. Hunt held the degree of Bachelor of Dharma issued by the Burma Buddhist Mission in Rangoon. A popular preacher, he toured temples throughout the islands, and older nisei today still remember his sermons delivered in English, their own native tongue. His message centered on moral lessons drawn from the teaching of karma, the Four Noble Truths, and the Eightfold Path. His was a Buddhist humanism in which Shakyamuni was a wise teacher but not a god, and the Dharma was about love, charity, kindness, respect, service, gratitude, and poise.[21] Hunt wrote English hymns (Skt: *gathas*), English services, textbooks, pamphlets, and a catechism for Buddhist Sunday schools. As early as 1900 two Caucasian women had founded the Children's Church, which later became the Honpa Hongwanji Sunday School, and the Hunts worked tirelessly to develop such schools. Their influence reached beyond the

Honpa Honganji, and by 1931 there were 12,800 children studying in 125 Sunday schools throughout the islands.[22] He was also a leader of the Young Buddhist Association, the Y.B.A., which was patterned after the Y.M.C.A. Working with Imamura within the Honpa Honganji, Hunt developed a basic Buddhism promoted as a nonsectarian, nonethnic, and universal religion.

In 1929, the Chinese Buddhist reformer Taixu (also Tai Hsü; (1890–1947) visited Hawai'i and met with Imamura and Hunt about establishing a Hawaiian branch of his International Buddhist Institute (I.B.I.). Based at the Honpa Honganji, the I.B.I. set out to propagate Buddhism in English, foster cooperation among all sects, banish war, promote peace, foster international-mindedness, and work for social good.[23] On the issue of sectarianism, Hunt went beyond Imamura's call for cooperation and advocated the elimination of traditional divisions, expressing his "fervent desire" to abolish "the heresy of separateness now prevailing among Buddhists of Honolulu" and to replace it with "the fundamental and ethical teaching" of basic Buddhism.[24] Hunt did not share in Imamura's Shinshū triumphalism, and for him "the Teaching of Amitabha means the divine character and continued power of the Buddha to lead all people, who follow the Teachings and repeat His Holy Name, to Nirvana."[25] His *Catechism for Buddhist Sunday Schools* does not mention Shinran at all.

In 1930 the I.B.I sponsored an international Buddhist youth conference, which was attended by 170 delegates from the U.S. mainland, Hawai'i, Canada, China, Japan, Korea, Thailand, India, and Burma. The participants discussed two pressing issues: how to propagate Buddhism among young people everywhere in the world and how to eliminate sectarian divisions. The conference passed a resolution naming Hawai'i as the "nucleus from which nonsectarian Buddhism, adapted to Western countries, may be spread to Pacific countries." This high ideal was never realized, but the conference marked the high point of the movement to create an international Buddhism.

On December 22, 1932, Hunt and Imamura sat in the bishop's office discussing plans. Imamura abruptly excused himself and walked to his nearby residence. Alerted by the hysterical cries of a temple member, Hunt rushed to Imamura's home to find him dead of a heart attack. The loss was felt far beyond the Honpa Honganji, and American leaders as well as Japanese mourned his passing at his funeral attended by more than three thousand people. Imamura was replaced by an interim bishop who neither opposed nor actively helped the I.B.I., and Hunt continued the work that he and Imamura had begun, attracting an increasing number of members. By 1935, despite Imamura's death, the I.B.I. had become a territory-wide association, winning the acclaim of local and international Buddhists.

Nineteen thirty-five was also the year in which a new bishop arrived from Japan. A staunch nationalist and ardent Shinshū Buddhist, Bishop Kuchiba Gikyō was opposed to Hunt's nonsectarian international Buddhism. Kuchiba was distressed that Japanese in Hawai'i professed a Buddhism that "follows the stream of Japanese Buddhism [but] is not Japanese Buddhism."[26] Dissolving the English Department, he fired Hunt. Though I.B.I. activities continued on an ad hoc basis, the institute was permanently damaged. In one swift stroke, Kuchiba lopped international Buddhism from the Shinshū tree. While there was a resurgence of Japanese nationalism in the late 1930s, that branch of the tree was also pruned, more slowly and with greater difficulty. The six-colored international Buddhist flag designed in 1889 in Sri Lanka had been a popular accouterment at Buddhist functions, but it passed into disuse. So too did the Japanese flag.

PRUNING JAPANESE NATIONALISM AND GRAFTING AMERICAN PATRIOTISM

As attested to in any number of photographs, a standard feature of temple celebrations in the prewar period was the posting of the American and Japanese flags, often with their standards crossing each other. Like other immigrant groups, the Japanese in Hawai'i held double loyalties, one prevailing over the other according to the individual or the occasion. Few questioned the need to Americanize, but Americanization had at least two distinct components, one political, the other cultural. The political aspect, expressed as loyalty, was not an easy issue to resolve, but it was far simpler than the question of cultural allegiance.

As one trained in a Buddhist institution that had close ties to Japanese nationalism and the emperor system,[27] Imamura was a typical Japanese nationalist at the time of his arrival in Hawai'i but quickly realized that those born there could never be Japanese loyalists. Imamura became an outstanding leader in the Americanization movement in its political component and is remembered for this more than for any other aspect of his career. Aware that many of the laborers were making Hawai'i their permanent home, and that their children were American citizens (or at least held dual citizenship), Imamura declared his stand very clearly in 1931:

> I take here the liberty of announcing in no ambiguous terms that our mission as a whole advocates Americanizing the people of this territory in every possible way. I, more than anyone else, am aware of my incompetency in carrying on this work. Born as a Japanese, brought up as a

Japanese, I am a Japanese through and through. Whatever honest intention and pure motive I may have, this sense of incompetency has always kept me from pushing to the front as an active participant in this work of Americanization. But it was our mission that extended its ready hand when the local Y.M.C.A. asked us to co-operate in the proposed citizenship educational campaign. It was our mission that published, when [the First World] war broke, a reprint of the five great state papers of American history with a Japanese version, in order to inform our public of the true idea and principle of the great Democracy. In the Food Conservation Campaign, in the Red Cross movement, our mission was second to none in doing its very best. In saying all of this I am perfectly aware that our mission has done nothing more than the level best of honest men. Strange to say, however, our mission, during its existence of twenty years in this territory, has often been accused of strong autocratic or anti-American tendency. Let our accusers have their day. I have no mind to say anything against them. Our record is our best defense.[28]

Despite his own sense of not being a truly cultural citizen, Imamura unequivocally advocated loyalty and patriotism to America. He knew that his job was not to convert Americans to Buddhism, but to transform Japanese Buddhists into Americans.

Political identity is easier to negotiate and transfer than cultural self-definition, and Imamura knew that good cultural Japanese can also be politically loyal Americans. He condemned what he called the "fifty-fifty" spirit of dividing political loyalties between two countries. There must be only one national allegiance, and the second generation of Japanese in Hawai'i should commit themselves totally to America. "The first of the evil tendencies which one cannot fail to observe in the immigrant community is the lack of single-minded loyalty, the prevalence of that 'fifty-fifty' spirit" (Imamura 1931, 9). Aware that Japanese parents would "feel lonesome" if their children exercised their right to become American citizens, he instructed his ministers to "give them solace. Tell them that good parents must think more of the future of their children than their own. To give in this Life is to receive in another." Ministers must teach parents how to obtain proper birth certificates for their children, encourage them to send their children to public schools, and interest them in participating in Americanization programs. "Get a right understanding of TRUE Americanism. This is essential to the work of a Buddhist priest in the Hawaiian Islands" (ibid., 22–23).

While critics continued to charge that Buddhism was anti-American, Imamura was content to let the record show that the temples had pruned the bodhi tree of Japanese nationalism. To it were grafted citizenship campaigns, Red Cross volunteerism, and active support for America's war effort. The tree spoke for itself and was there for all to see. Removing Japanese nationalism was easy enough, but despite the clarity and sincerity of his Americanism, splinters still remained. For all of his vaunted Americanism, Imamura was still "Japanese through and through" and could not free himself from the very "fifty-fifty" spirit he condemned.

The problem was not political but philosophical and cultural. In a short essay published in a widely distributed bilingual pamphlet, Imamura began by asserting the absolute compatibility between Buddhism and democracy. "Democracy according to the Buddhist Viewpoint" was written in 1918 and begins with a heartfelt lament about the horrors of the First World War. The central issue of that war, as he saw it, was the battle between democracy and autocracy. Buddhism was clearly on the side of democracy, being in "perfect harmony" with it, and "in fact, whatever democracy there is in the East, it derives its power and support from Buddhism." The Buddhist teaching of nonduality is philosophically consonant with democratic principles of equality, and as the "rational culmination of the Buddhist teachings," Shinshū Buddhism holds to the social ideal of universal brotherhood. Modern democracy in practice, however, is filled with contradictions created by those who espouse the ideal but fail to live up to it. "To take away all such contradictions, to open the way unobstructed for the advance of democratic ideals . . . this is the proclamation of Buddhism to all the modern advocates of democracy." Buddhism can transform imperfect practice into a perfect democracy.[29]

Buddhist nonduality, however, is double-edged. Just as it eliminates inequality between all people, so does it dissolve any antagonism between democracy and autocracy.

> Therefore, our solemn conviction gained in the light of the Buddha is this: If autocracy has no absolute value, neither has democracy. If democracy is right, why should not autocracy be right also? We Buddhists believe that in this world as well as in the ideal world of Amida there are no absolutely determined values or particular things that cannot be reduced to some other terms, and therefore that autocracy does not unconditionally exclude democracy, nor does democracy autocracy, they are after all two aspects of a thing which is in itself above such opposites (Y. Imamura 1918, 26–27).

In addition to asserting a profound dualism between the truth of nonmultiplicity and the falsity of plurality, the Buddhist teaching of nonduality also posits the simultaneous existence of both (*ni funi*, two but not two). It can, on the one hand, be exemplified by the image of the pot that melts away all distinctions, or it can be likened to a salad of discrete but equal parts. Or, to use Imamura's own horticultural language of flowers:

> In the Land of Purity all flowers are blooming in profusion, each in its own individual magnificence. Why can we not in this world of ours make all forms of government flourish each with its special characteristic advantages? Cannot autocracy prosper side by side with democracy? Indeed, democracy is autocracy popularised, and autocracy is democracy consolidated (ibid., 28).

Imamura concluded with a plea for a multicultural diversity that would prevent America from trying to change Japan's preference for autocracy, just as it would keep Japan from forcing America to abandon its democracy. Buddhism, then, does not justify democracy by rejecting autocracy, but "in the great Ocean of Love and Mercy of Amitabha Buddha" embraces our "individual and national differences." Insisting on preserving separate genetic identities, Imamura rejected hybridization as a function of the Buddhist temples.

Hybridization in the melting pot is the proper work of the public schools, and should be supported there. "Public instruction was there of course, and it was doing highly credible work for the 'melting pot.' As an instrument of teaching the duties of American citizenship, the public schools of this territory command the respect of the right-thinking residents."[30] The temple schools had the different task of preserving the rootstock of family heritage. Public education cannot and should not instill knowledge of this heritage. The primary identity of the children was based in the family: "children are members of the family before they belong to the community." Buddhist temples preserve a religion for Japanese family ancestry; only secondarily is it for the community at large.

Imamura thus had it both ways. On the one hand, political loyalty was relatively easy to transfer from the emperor to the president, from autocracy to democracy, and immigrants should free themselves from the "fifty-fifty" spirit; on the other hand, the philosophy of Buddhist nonduality embraced both in a hundred-hundred totality that did not require any side to compromise its integrity. Likewise in the cultural sphere, family heritage must be taught and preserved by keeping it out of the melting pot. Nurtured in the garden of the temples and its private schools, family religion was pruned of Japanese nationalism and received grafts of American nationalism and democracy. Understood horticulturally, the single tree can been seen in its genetically different parts, and Imamura's affirmation of its American and Japanese distinctions made sense; but from a more common viewpoint that expects only assimilation or hybridization, "Imamura's position at best seemed full of contradictions or, at worst, just so much double talk."[31]

Christian rivals attacked Imamura's double talk and proclaimed the advantages of an exclusive identity between Americanism and Christianity: only a Christian could be a good American. Christians rejected the fifty-fifty spirit in a way that Imamura, despite his claims about doing the same, could not. As long as it defined itself in ancestral terms, Buddhism was inextricably tied to being Japanese. Those who converted to Christianity—and many did—severed that tie, but Imamura knew that the Buddhist–Japanese cultural equation could be maintained at the same time that Japanese nationalism could be pruned and replaced by American patriotism. And it worked: nisei Buddhist soldiers died for America as willingly as did Christian servicemen and were buried with Buddhist rites that confirmed forever their ancestral place and identity.

Once the issue of loyalty was settled through the Second World War, the branch of Americanism could be taken for granted, and even forgotten, as Japanese Americans found the same shade in more easily accessible places like the public schools, the military, business, and government. Few congregated under the branch of Americanism growing in the temple yards, but many still gathered for ancestral rites performed in the familiar shade of the maturing bodhi tree. They also went to the temples as loyal Americans to enjoy the shade cast by the branch that used to be Japanese nationalism, now flourishing as cultural nostalgia for things Japanese and a yearning for a spiritual homeland (furusato). They celebrated their heritage—and continue to do so—with a deep sense of gratitude to predecessors and ancestors, expressed by the phrase okagesama de, which in arboreal terms means that they were who they were "because I stand in your shade."

Although civic identity was produced by Americanization, nostalgia for the spiritual homeland, moving in the opposite direction, manifested itself as increasing Japanization. This is clearly seen in the history of the Shinshū hymns or gathas. In 1924 Ernest and Dorothy Hunt published Vade Mecum, a collection of hymns they wrote with several other Caucasian Buddhists. The songs were nonsectarian, espoused the ideals of Theravada Buddhism, and did not sing the praises of Shinshū teachings. But the songbook blended well with Imamura's international interests, and it was used extensively in Shinshū services. The influence of the Vade Mecum and its general Buddhist principles survives in the current hymnal, but the intervening editions of 1939, 1962, and 1990 steadily increased the number of hymns that were translations from the Japanese or espoused the virtues of Shinran, the teachings of Shinshū, and Japan. The pruning and grafting of hymns from one edition to the next produced an increasingly sectarian body of songs that shifts attention from Shakyamuni to Amida, from India to Japan, and from general Buddhism to Shinshū. To the ordinary worshiper, for whom Shakyamuni, the Buddha, and Amida blur into one loving deity, it may not matter, for they all offer the same pietism that satisfies the longing for a spiritual home. Still, Japan looms large in the 1990 edition, and the universal virtues of the original *Vade Mecum* are rooted in moral abstractions, not a homeland, so it is not surprising that the hymns were shorn of an earlier, nearly exclusively, Western version of Buddhism in favor of one that is more Japanese.[32] In a similar reference to the mother country, modern temple architecture has reinstated the graceful slope of the Japanese roof.

CONCLUSION: THE ARCHITECTURE OF THE TREE

Pruned of Japanese nationalism and universal Buddhism, the trunk of family religion still remains, with a mostly unused branch of American patriotism and a popular outgrowth of cultural and spiritual nostalgia. The architecture of the main temple is also emblematic: the exterior facade is international, the outer sanctuary (*gejin*) of pews American, and the inner altar (*naijin*) purely Japanese. Thus, the external architecture, the branches of the tree, and the outer sanctuary all have been altered from what is Japanese in Japan, but the inner core remains the same. The Amida statue, a priceless treasure from medieval Japan, and the inner altar could be transported back to Japan and easily placed in any Shinshū temple. The double helix of Amida and ancestry has never changed.

Under the leadership of assimilation theorist Romanzo Adams, University of Hawai'i sociology students such as Katsumi Onishi predicted the development of a new Buddhism in 1937, but nothing that is new at the inner core has emerged. Onishi wrote that second-generation Buddhists are "breathing new life and vigor into the Hongwanji, freeing it from the shackles of narrow sectarianism, creating and evolving a new Buddhism, peculiar and native to Hawai'i."[33] Had he been right, a hybrid Hawaiian Buddhism would have emerged, but no such creature exists. The temples are solidly sectarian, the members are almost exclusively of Japanese ancestry, and the important rituals, abbreviated in length, are still unchanged in essence. Hybridization has not taken place.

The resistance of Japanese Buddhism to change at the center is also apparent among Japanese Brazilians. Writing in this volume, Cristina Rocha (Chap. 6) documents the popularity of Zen Buddhism among non-Japanese Brazilians, but their Zen was imported from hybrid Zen sources in America and Europe, not from the ethnic Japanese Zen community that has long been in Brazil. Despite their remarkable successes in adopting new host cultures as their own, the Japanese immigrant communities in Brazil and Hawai'i have preserved forms of traditional Buddhism as ancestral religions. Peter Clarke, however, points out in his essay (Chap. 5) that Soka Gakkai, with its strategy of inclusive pluralism, may be the exception to this exclusive pattern. For the most part, however, the self-imposed isolation of traditional Japanese Buddhist groups has prevented them from exerting a significant influence outside of their ethnic boundaries. Assimilation at the political and cultural surfaces is visible, but the rootstock remains largely uncompromised.

The political graftings in Hawai'i have either died or lost their immediate significance. Once ubiquitous, the flags are all gone. The international Buddhist flag is nowhere to be seen, the Japanese flag is no longer flown, and even the Stars and Stripes hardly makes an appearance. Political branches were easily added and just as easily removed since those surface manipulations did not involve any change in the core. In contrast to Japanese Buddhist missionaries in Hawai'i, Japanese colonial Buddhists in Korea, China, and Taiwan carried out the political task of transforming non-Japanese colonial subjects into imperial loyalists (kōminka), and many Buddhist ministers served both in Hawai'i and the colonies. Isobe Hosen, the first bishop of the Sōtō Mission in Hawai'i, also established important temples in Korea. For the Japanese Buddhist priests in Korea, however, "what really was at stake was not the spread of Buddhist teachings, but the thought and behavior of the Korean people, which were to be made compatible with the cause of Japanese colonialism."[34] Buddhist teachings and ritual did not really apply to Koreans because they were of different ancestry. In Korea, Isobe did religious work with the ethnic Japanese residents and carried out political and cultural tasks with the Koreans. Japanese Buddhist ministers in the colonies were charged with the duty of assimilating their subjects into the colonial melting pot, not the spiritual crucible of Japanese ancestral religion. The task for the ministers in Hawai'i was to assimilate their Japanese members into the American political and social melting pot without allowing cross-breeding to take place at the religious core. In both places, hybridization was allowed and even encouraged at the political, social, doctrinal, and philosophical levels, but not at the rootstock of family religion.

Imamura did reach out to a few non-Japanese and bring them into the fold. Unlike the Koreans, who were kept out of the religious arena entirely, Ernest Shinkaku Hunt would seem to have been assimilated into the core. Was he a rare case of religious hybridization? He was ordained a priest, wore the robes, wrote *gathas*, propagated teachings, conducted worship services, and preached sermons. The key question, however, must be asked of the inner sanctum of ancestral ritual: did he perform funerals? There is as yet no evidence that he did.

Notes

An early version of this paper was presented at the Buddhist Studies Workshop at Princeton University in April 2000. I am indebted to Stephen Teiser for arranging my visit and to faculty and students who commented on my paper.

1. Alfred Bloom, "Buddhist Dimensions of Japanese Ethnic Identity," lecture at Japanese Cultural Center of Hawai'i, February 12, 2000.

2. The Shingon Mission of Hawai'i, for example, celebrated its centennial in 2002 and called for the internationalization of Shingon Buddhism for the next one hundred years.

3. This is the term used by Benedict Anderson to describe conversion, an impulse that is foreign to nationalism. Benedict Anderson, *Imagined Communities: Reflections on the Origin and Spread of Nationalism*, rev. ed. (London and New York: Verso, 1998), 14–15.

4. See Ian Reader and George J. Tanabe, Jr., *Practically Religious: Worldly Benefits and the Common Religion of Japan* (Honolulu: University of Hawai'i Press, 1998).

5. While the histories of Japanese Buddhist sects in Hawai'i are not the same, the case of Honpa Honganji lends itself best to analysis. With an orthodoxy that rejects magic and superstition, Honpa Honganji is anomalous in important doctrinal and ritual ways, but its practices and beliefs about the family and the ancestors is emblematic of the funeral Buddhism *(sōshiki Bukkyō)* that is the common ground for most sects.

6. A certain Reverend Tsunemitsu believed that this was the reason for Kagahi's belief. Ruth M. Tabrah, "A Grateful Past, A Promising Future," in *A Grateful Past, A Promising Future: The First 100 Years of Honpa Hongwanji in Hawai'i*, ed. Centennial Publication Committee (Honolulu: Honpa Hongwanji Mission of Hawai'i, 1989), 9.

7. This account of Kagahi's mission is based on Louise H. Hunter, *Buddhism in Hawai'i: Its Impact on a Yankee Community* (Honolulu: University of Hawai'i Press, 1971), 32–45.

8. Imamura Emyō, *Hawai kaikyō shi* (Honolulu: Hawai kaikyō kyōmusho, 1918), 25.

9. Cited by George Y. Yamamoto, *The Origin of Buddhism in Hawai'i* (Honolulu: Y.B.A, 1976), 1–2. The need for funeral specialists is also noted by Inoue Nobutaka, *Umi o wattata Nihon shūkyō* (Tokyo: Kōbundō, 1985), 12.

10. Imamura, *Hawai kaikyō shi*, 26.

11. Emyō Imamura, Introduction to Riusaku Tsunoda, *The Essence of Japanese Buddhism* (Honolulu: The Advertiser, 1914), 5.

12. Imamura, *Hawai kaikyō shi*, 28.

13. Ōtani Kōmyō, "Preface," in ibid., 15.

14. Cited by Tabrah, A Grateful Past, 54.

15. Riusaku Tsunoda, The Essence of Japanese Buddhism (Honolulu: The Advertiser, 1914), 9.

16. Yemyo Imamura, "Introduction," in ibid., 7.

17. Tsunoda, The Essence of Japanese Buddhism, 25–31.

18. Ōtani Kōmyō, "Preface" in Emyō, Hawai kaikyō shi, 13–14.

19. Takakusu Junjirō, "Preface" to Emyō, Hawai kaikyō shi, 23–29. Egalitarian Buddhism is a common characterization that can also be found, for example, in Walpola Rahula, What the Buddha Taught (New York: Grove, 1962), and G. Malalasekera and K. N. Jayatilleke, Buddhism and the Race Question (Paris: UNESCO, 1958).

20. Hunter, Buddhism in Hawai'i, 133, 152–153.

21. Ernest Shinkaku Hunt, Buddhist Sermons (Honolulu: Takiko Ichinose, 1955).

22. Hunter, Buddhism in Hawai'i, 165.

23. Yemyo Imamura, A Short History of the Hongwanji Buddhist Mission in Hawai'i (Honolulu: Hongwanji Buddhist Mission, 1931), 17–18.

24. Ernest Hunt, Vade Mecum: A Book containing an Order of Ceremonies for Use in Buddhist Temples Together with Gathas expressing the Teaching of the Buddha (Honolulu: International Buddhist Institute, 1932).

25. Ernest Hunt, Catechism for Buddhist Sunday Schools (Honolulu: International Buddhist Institute, 1946), article 94.

26. Hunter, Buddhism in Hawai'i, 171.

27. The intricate relationship between nationalism and religion in Japan has been well documented. See, for example, Helen Hardacre, Shintō and the State, 1869–1988 (Princeton, N.J.: Princeton University Press, 1989); Brian Victoria, Zen at War (New York: Weatherhill, 1998); James Heisig and John Maraldo, eds. Rude Awakenings: Zen, the Kyoto School, and the Question of Nationalism (Honolulu: University of Hawai'i Press, 1995); Robert Sharf, "The Zen of Japanese Nationalism," in Curators of the Buddha, ed. Donald Lopez (Chicago: University of Chicago Press, 1995); Nam-lin Hur, "The Sōtō Sect and Japanese Military Imperialism in Korea," Japanese Journal of Religious Studies 26, nos. 1–2 (Spring 1999): 107–134; Christopher Ives, "The Mobilization of Doctrine: Buddhist Contributions to Imperial Ideology," Japanese Journal of Religious Studies 26, nos. 1–2 (Spring 1999): 83–106.

28. Imamura, A Short History, 7.

29. Y. Imamura, Democracy according to the Buddhist Viewpoint (Honolulu: Publishing Bureau of the Hongwanji Mission, 1918), 5–20.

30. Imamura, A Short History, 4.

31. Hunter, *Buddhism in Hawai'i*, 98.

32. For a detailed account of the development of the Shinshū hymns in Hawai'i, see my "Glorious Gathas: Americanization and Japanization in Honganji Hymns," in *Engaged Pure Land Buddhism: Essays in Honor of Professor Alfred Bloom,* ed. Kenneth K. Tanaka and Eisho Nasu (Berkeley, Calif.: Wisdom Ocean, 1998), 221–237.

33. Katsumi Onishi, "The Second Generation Japanese and the Hongwanji," *Social Process in Hawai'i* 3 (May 1937), 48.

34. Nam-lin Hur, "The Sōtō Sect and Japanese Military Imperialism in Korea," 120.

4   Hiding in Plain Sight: The Invisibility of the Shingon Mission to the United States

Richard K. Payne

While Tibetan Buddhism has entered into the mainstream of American popular religious culture since its introduction in the 1960s, another tantric Buddhist tradition has remained effectively invisible. Despite having been in the United States for over a century, Shingon Buddhism remains almost entirely unknown to American converts to Buddhism and even to the overwhelming majority of scholars of either Buddhism or American religion.[1] Even beyond the narrow provincialism of American academe, Shingon as well as the other immigrant forms of Buddhism are also not to be seen on the "international mediascape" of Buddhism. This essay seeks to answer the question of why one tantric Buddhist tradition should have become an icon of popular culture while another remains an obscure oddity. My thesis is that one of the important factors creating this discrepancy is the conflict between the romantic presumptions of American popular religious culture, which desired mimetic union with Buddhism as the idealized and exotic Other, and the desire of the Japanese-American community to accommodate to the dominant religious culture. This thesis will be tested against a possible counterexample, the apparent success of Zen, which is as much a cultural icon as Tibetan Buddhism and draws the same kind of attention from the media. This discussion highlights the utility of the categories of immigrant and convert Buddhisms as a preliminary distinction toward more fully nuanced analyses.

Focusing on the ways in which different missionaries have responded to their new environment, we find an interplay between three different concerns in the transmission of Buddhism.[2] These concerns, to be seen in all of the chapters included in this book, are: conservationist, in which missionaries and congregations attempt to retain what they perceive to be essential to their faith; propagationist, in which missionaries attempt to draw in new disciples, revitalize existing adherents, or simply retain current members, by emphasizing the uniqueness and the superiority of what they have to offer over what is available in the surrounding community; and accommodationist-assimilationist, in which missionaries and congregations attempt to bring their own tradition into better consonance with the surrounding society. Interestingly, efforts to "modernize" Buddhism can be seen to address all of these concerns. Drawing a cognitive distinction between accommodation and assimilation, this chapter focuses on the way in which American romantic values have made the Buddhism espoused by immigrants invisible. At the same time, it also gives some attention to the interplay between the dynamic of propagating Buddhism, which utilized the romantic values in American religious culture, and the modernizing dynamic of some of the other Buddhist missionary activities.

Piaget's terminology for describing childhood development distinguishes between assimilation and accommodation. These psychological categories can be adapted as a heuristically useful sociocognitive distinction to examine the difference between the popularity of the Tibetan forms of tantric Buddhism and the invisibility of the Japanese forms.[3] "Assimilation" is used here to identify the process by which new information is made to fit into existing cognitive categories. "Accommodation," on the other hand, identifies the formation of a new category in light of new information and is much the same as the dynamic referred to by Tanabe (Chap. 3) as "acculturation." These two dynamics—assimilation and accommodation—simplify the complex social and historical actualities and, it should be noted, are not mutually exclusive.[4] In attempting to identify a general social pattern, however, such simplification is necessary. Complex as all sociohistorical processes are, it is the contention of this essay that assimilation and accommodation contribute to our understanding of contrasting dynamics of religious change.

Other factors that also played a role in the development of Buddhist churches in America but would require separate analysis include economic differences; the specifically ethnic character of the Shingon as well as many of the other Japanese-American Buddhist churches; and the modernizing, reformist intent of those Tibetans who migrated to Western countries. Both economically and institutionally there is a significant difference between the pattern of immigration and that of exile. Where the Japanese-American Buddhist churches were established within the context of immigrant communities that could provide economic support, Tibetan teachers usually came to the United States as individuals and had to establish convert communities for their own support. Likewise, Tibetan teachers in exile were largely dependent upon their own authority, whereas the immigrant temples maintained institutional affiliation with their head temples in Japan, depending upon an external source of institutional authority. The founding orientation of the Japanese-American Buddhist churches toward immigrant communities gave them a markedly ethnic character, one that can appear totally impenetrable even to interested and sympathetic outsiders. This ethnic insularity was very strongly reinforced by the events of World War II when, rejected by the dominant society, the Japanese community turned inward and was largely alienated from the rest of the society.

Finally, those Tibetans who chose to leave their South Asian exile and seek to establish themselves in the West adopted the orientation of Buddhist modernism, including a psychologistic interpretation of Buddhism.[5] Though not a unified movement as such, the nineteenth and early twentieth centuries saw several similar responses to the challenge of Christian evangelism by Buddhists in various Asian countries. These reformers sought to represent Buddhism as a modern religion that could relate on the basis of equality with other "world religions." It is also characterized by an emphasis on the ethical, rational, and psychological character of Buddhist teachings, and by the creation of lay associations.[6] Although it is unknown inside Tibet per se, Tibetan teachers in exile—particularly the Dalai Lama—have adopted this modernist stance.[7]

Just as Buddhist modernism has been employed in the representation of Tibetan Buddhism to the West, so some Zen teachers who came to the West from Japan shared this modernizing approach (see Rocha, Chap. 6). However, because the Shingon church in the United States was established to serve immigrant communities and functioned as a center of ethnic identity, the missionaries who founded it would have had no motivation to re-create Shingon along the lines of Buddhist modernism.

Other chapters in this book address these issues for other Buddhist schools elsewhere in the world, and they are not without relevance to Buddhism in the United States (see Rocha on the importance of economic class, Tanabe on ethnic insularity, and Kemper and LeVine on modernization). Acknowledging the importance of these other factors, this essay focuses on the way in which the religious culture of the United States made Shingon invisible. By employing the concepts of assimilation and accommodation, we can restate the thesis of this essay: the mismatch between the Japanese-American attempt to accommodate to American religious culture and the tendency of the romantic presumptions of American religious culture to assimilate Buddhism into its own conception of the exotic Other led to the invisibility of the Shingon tradition in the United States. This mismatch precluded the immigrant-based churches of Japanese Buddhism such as Shingon from appealing to the romantic mimetic impulse within a powerful segment of American religious seekers—that is, their desire to become the exotic Other.

SHINGON AND ITS MISSION TO THE UNITED STATES

Shingon Buddhism is the Japanese form of the Vajrayana tradition, and was established in Japan by Kukai at the beginning of the ninth century. Shingon practitioners trace their lineage back to the teachings of the Dharmakaya Buddha, Mahavairocana Tathagata (*Dainichi Nyorai*). According to his autobiography, Kukai traveled to China specifically to study the esoteric teachings. There he received initiation into a dual lineage that brought together two sets of ritual practices, mandalas, and texts. The primary textual basis for the tradition are the Mahavairocana (*Dainichi kyo*) and the Vajrashekhara (*Kongo cho gyo*) scriptures.[8] Though Western scholarship is only starting to discern the formative role of esoteric Buddhism in East Asia, Shingon ritual practices and conceptual schemes molded the development of Japanese religions for a millennium.

The official Shingon mission to the United States began in 1909. In October of that year, the Reverend Shutai Aoyama left Japan for the United States with the intent of providing religious services to the immigrant Japanese community. Shortly after his arrival in San Francisco, however, he fell ill and his medical expenses entirely depleted his resources. Lacking any other means of supporting himself, he worked as a farm laborer for three years. Eventually, in 1912 he arrived in Los Angeles, where one of the leaders of the local Japanese community encouraged him to establish a temple. Thus, it was not until January 1913 that a Shingon temple was opened on a temporary basis in a house rented for the purpose.[9]

The temple was established as an O *Daishi kyokai*, that is, a church devoted to Kukai, whose posthumous title is Kobo Daishi, meaning "the Great Teacher who is an Ocean of Wisdom." The official name of the temple was the Los Angeles Daishi Church. The centrality of devotion to the founder is common in Japanese Buddhism,[10] and for the Shingon tradition devotion to Kukai is one of the unifying threads that distinguishes it from other forms of Vajrayana Buddhism, many of which have strains of devotionalism focused on their own founders.[11]

Shingon was established in Hawai'i in a very different fashion, but one that itself emphasizes an important aspect of the religious needs of an immigrant community—healing. In 1902 a layman, Hogen Yujiri, established himself in a "preaching hall" in Lahaina. He claimed that he had been "miraculously cured of an eye disease through the limitless compassion of Kobo Daishi."[12] On the island of Kauai, another layman, Kodo Yamamoto, worked together with other devotees to recreate in miniature the pilgrimage route of Shikoku Island.[13] Here also there were reports of miraculous cures, and additional Shingon temples headed by lay practitioners were established in Waimea, Hilo, and Honolulu.

The lay practitioners were untrained in Shingon practice, having only a superficial grasp of doctrinal understandings behind the ritual forms. Competition between lay practitioners and the disdain of other Buddhist professionals led to a view of Shingon as a corrupt and unorthodox form of Buddhism. Eventually this came to the attention of Shingon authorities, and a priest, Eikaku Seki, was sent to investigate the situation in the islands. After completing his investigation the Reverend Seki established an official branch of Kongobuji, the head temple of the Koyasan branch of Shingon, in Honolulu. By 1926, when Honpa Honganji—then the largest Buddhist denomination—had seventy-one temples and mission stations, there were twenty-five Shingon temples in the islands.[14]

Institutional development of the church took two forms: the reproduction of services within the temple based upon the Japanese model of temple organization and the adoption of services based on the model of American church organization. Exemplary of the former are funeral and memorial services and the Fujin-kai (women's auxiliary), while the formulation of a Shingon wedding ceremony and the institutionalization of their own Boy Scout troop exemplify the latter.

Because the performance of funerals has been fundamental to Buddhist institutions in Japan, perhaps the most symbolically dramatic instance of the expansion of religious services provided by the church was the first funeral service to be held at the Los Angeles Daishi Church. This was conducted for Shigeru Koyama, who died on November 7, 1913, at the age of twenty-seven.[15] Because most immigrants were young, such funeral services were rare. More commonly the church was asked to perform memorial services on the event of the death of a parent in Japan. With the epidemic of Spanish influenza of 1918, however, the number of funeral services increased.

As in most Japanese-American Buddhist temples, the Los Angeles Daishi Church's Fujin-kai served as one of the key organizations within the temple. As well as other fund-raising activities, the Fujin-kai is commonly responsible for providing food at any public event sponsored by the temple. In the case of the Los Angeles Daishi Church, however, one of its main activities highlights the continuing identification of the immigrant Japanese community with Japan. This took the form of hosting sailors from Japanese navy ships when these came to Los Angeles. Between 1934 and 1939 eleven ships visited Los Angeles, and their crews were entertained by the Fujin-kai. These services were acknowledged by Japan's minister of navy, and the ministry donated an oil painting to the temple in 1939. Later in that same year the ground-breaking ceremony for a new temple building was moved up by two days in order to coincide with the arrival of the Japanese Navy Special Service Vessel *Shiriya*.[16] As tensions between the United States and Japan grew in the subsequent year, the propriety of continuing to welcome sailors became an issue within the temple. No definite decision was reached, however, prior to the beginning of the war.

Accommodation to the religious culture of the United States is evident in the request for a Buddhist wedding ceremony. In Japan, the division of religious labors was such that Buddhist priests were almost exclusively concerned with funeral and memorial services. The creation of a Shingon wedding ceremony gives us a glimpse of the complex religiocultural situation of the immigrant Japanese community in the first quarter of the twentieth century. Although at this distance we cannot discern the specific religious motivations of the participants in the creation of this novel ritual in American Shingon, we can use it as a focal point around which the complexities come into view.

Throughout the nineteenth century, marriage ceremonies in Japan were normally domestic affairs officiated over by members of the household. The only religious aspect was the presentation of the in-marrying spouse to the ancestors— present within the household in the form of their memorial tablets (J. *ihai*) on the Buddhist altar (J. *butsudan*) or ancestor shelf (J. *senzodana*). Toward the end of the nineteenth century, however, some lay Buddhist groups in Japan began to perform Buddhist wedding ceremonies, perhaps under the influence of Christian missionary activity. According to Richard Jaffe, "what is probably the first Japanese Buddhist wedding ceremony" was written by Tanaka Chigaku, the founder of the Nichirenist lay association Rengekai, in 1887.[17] According to Tanaka's own report, his Buddhist wedding ceremony proved popular and was soon copied in the Jodo Shinshu and Zen sects.[18]

Widely publicized, the marriage of the crown prince in a Shinto shrine in 1900 appears to have had a great effect on the general populace's expectations of what should comprise a proper wedding.[19] This novelty caught on quickly, gaining the patina of ancient custom in the process. It seems reasonable to assume that by 1918 Japanese immigrants to the United States would have been exposed to this idea that a wedding service is primarily a religious affair within Japanese religious culture itself, whether considered to be specifically Shinto or Buddhist.[20]

Living in the religious milieu of Christian America would have strongly reinforced this reconceptualization of weddings as religious in two ways: the longstanding Christian tradition of weddings as sacramental and the understanding that, as exclusive institutions, all churches are expected to provide a full range of religious services for their adherents. Thus it was that Jutaro Narumi, one of the church leaders, asked the Reverend Aoyama to perform the wedding ceremony for his marriage to Yoneko Tsukada, which took place on June 25, 1918.[21] This required that the Reverend Aoyama create an entirely new ceremony, as according to the temple history: "Japanese Buddhist priests normally concern themselves only in funeral or memorial services, and do not officiate a wedding ceremony. Therefore, there was no program for a wedding ceremony in the Daishi Church."[22]

Thus, changes to religious culture in Japan, particularly the creation of religious wedding ceremonies—both Buddhist and Shinto—and the expectations created by American church practices, began to transform the religious life of the Shingon church in the United States.

Boy Scout Troop 79 (later renamed Troop 379) was established by the Reverend Kitagawa in 1931.[23] He saw it as a means of providing a positive response to the Great Depression which had begun two years earlier. And, as with present-day Chinese Buddhist Master Xingyun (see Chandler, Chap. 7), it was also a means of instilling a set of positive values—ethics, responsibility, discipline—shared by both the Japanese community and the wider society, as well as being an organization that rejected racial discrimination and prejudice.

According to the temple history, Troop 379, particularly the Drum and Bugle Corps, worked very hard to excel. Their success is indicated by the fact that it was the only Boy Scout Troop to be invited in its entirety to attend the Jamboree commemorating the twenty-fifth anniversary of the Boy Scouts hosted by President Roosevelt in 1935. After the troop had completed all their arrangements for the trip to Washington, D.C., including fund-raising, the jamboree was canceled due to an outbreak of polio. To avoid their having to abandon their plans entirely, the Japanese ambassador in Washington arranged for the troop to receive a special invitation to visit the White House. They brought with them a photograph album of Japan's national treasures as a gift from Kongobuji to President Roosevelt. The president's schedule precluded their being able to make the presentation directly, however. Like the Fujin-kai's greeting of Japanese sailors, the intervention of the Japanese ambassador on behalf of the temple's Boy Scout Troop indicates the continuing identification with Japan.

It was in this same year that Kongobuji, head temple of the Chuin ryu lineage located on Mount Koya, raised the status of the Los Angeles Daishi Church. The church now became a branch of Kongobuji, and its name was changed to Koyasan Beikoku Betsuin Temple. The title of "betsuin" marks the status of being a direct branch of the head temple. "Beikoku" is an older Japanese term referring to the United States and literally means "rice country," an allusion to the prosperity promised to immigrants by labor contractors.

Since 1929 there had been discussion about the need for a larger temple. However, after being raised to the status of betsuin, plans for establishing a new temple building advanced rapidly. In 1936, the decision was taken to pursue the acquisition of property on East First Street in Los Angeles, in the heart of the Japanese section of town. This initiated a cycle of planning and fund-raising, and the property was purchased in July 1937. At this time it was against the law for noncitizens to own real estate, so the purchase was made in the names of one son each of Tomozu Tomio and Zenzaburo Yamamoto, two of the organizers of the building effort. As the design of the building developed over the next two years, so did the estimated costs—from a total of $40,000 to $64,000. However, the committee persevered in their efforts, overcoming the difficulties of fund-raising and seeing the project through to its completion. Contributions from Kongobuji included a cash contribution of $3,000 and twelve logs of Koya cypress, considered the highest-quality building material, for use as columns of the new building. Individual donations amounting to about $400 were also collected from Shingon priests in Japan. As mentioned above, groundbreaking for construction was held on November 17, 1939, and the temple was completed on August 21, 1940. In this we can see the continuing ties to the head church in Japan.

Just over a year later, the attack on Pearl Harbor precipitated the declaration of war between Japan and the United States and the relocation of Japanese Americans—whether citizens of the United States or not—to concentration camps away from the coast. As a leader of the Japanese community, the Reverend Takahashi was one of the first arrested. This left the Reverend Sogabe, who had only recently been posted to Los Angeles, in charge. Sogabe made the temple buildings available to members of the community as a place to store their belongings during their absence, and when he was ordered to leave as well, closed up the temple buildings.

For two and a half years, the priests did their best to minister to the Shingon community, which was now diffused through the ten relocation centers: Topaz, Poston, Gila, Granada, Heart Mountain, Minedoca, Tule Lake, Jerome, Rohwer, and Manzanar. Assisted by lay leaders in these camps, by correspondence, and by occasional opportunities to visit among camps, the temple maintained religious services. At the end of the war the Japanese returned from the camps only to find themselves displaced from their homes. Again, under the guidance of Sogabe, who had been allowed to return prior to the actual cessation of conflict, the temple became a refuge, providing temporary housing. As with other Japanese-American Buddhist denominations, the wartime relocation left their members more spread out over the United States than previously.

After all of these difficulties, Los Angeles County added a final insult by claiming that the temple was in arrears on its property taxes to the amount of $5,000. The county's claim was that the temple had ceased to operate as a religious institution, serving instead first as storage for members' belongings and then as a hostel. Other Buddhist temples in the same situation sought relief in the courts, but lost their suits. The Shingon temple was finally able to pay off this debt when in 1957 it received funds from the Wartime Evacuation Compensation Bill.

The temple celebrated its fiftieth anniversary in 1962. At that time efforts were under way to improve the qualifications of priests to provide religious services in English. Four priests pursued advanced degrees. These included Yoshito S. Hakeda, who published translations of key works for the study of Shingon Buddhism,[24] Shunsho Terakawa, who taught philosophy and religion at San Jose State University for many years, and Taisen Miyata, who is currently bishop at the Koyasan Beikoku Betsuin Temple.

ACCOMMODATION TO THE PROTESTANT NORMS OF AMERICAN RELIGIOUS CULTURE

In the early part of the twentieth century, Japanese Buddhist denominations in the United States experienced a significant loss of membership to Protestant Christian churches, particularly the Methodist. Active evangelism on the part of the Protestants, together with a desire on the part of Japanese to blend into American society, were significant factors contributing to this shift in religious affiliation. Japanese-American Buddhist organizations responded by adapting their liturgical practices so as to appear closer to the normative model of American Protestantism, in some cases building on adaptations that had already been initiated by modernizers in Japan. For example, both Shin (a Japanese Pure Land denomination, see Tanabe, Chap. 3) and Shingon churches hold Sunday services, with the congregation (usually referred to by the Sanskrit term "sangha") seated in pews, listening to organ music, singing hymns set to Western musical forms, and in some cases listening to choirs. At the center of the Sunday liturgy is a Dharma talk, or sermon. While many Buddhist churches retained traditional altars, some "modernized," adopting very spare altars highly reminiscent of the Puritan model of church as courtroom.

Institutionally, many Buddhist churches also developed their social role as community centers, simultaneously accommodating aspects of American culture while seeking to preserve their Japanese heritage. Basketball leagues, for example, were sponsored alongside more traditionally Japanese cultural activities such as judo, kendo, or flower arranging. In many communities the largest public activity of the temple is the midsummer O Bon festival. This festival, celebrating the ancestors, provides an opportunity for annual fund-raising by selling teriyaki chicken and sushi alongside hamburgers and corn on the cob. In some circles one can hear rather disdainful comments regarding Japanese-American Buddhist temples because of their function as community centers. The disparaging tone of these comments—made by both insiders and outsiders—implicitly accepts the this-worldly versus other-worldly dualism which pervades American religious culture. The presence of activities judged to be this-worldly is equated with the absence of an other-worldly, or spiritual, orientation. Not only is the application of this dualistic preconception problematic for the Buddhist tradition, but the attitude fails to recognize the pivotal role that temples played in creating a sense of community for the immigrants. It was not simply a matter of being a community center, but of creating a community by providing it with a center.

Accommodation, however, did not extend as deeply into the liturgical realm as is sometimes assumed, particularly when one considers the modernizing efforts of someone like Dharmapala (see Kemper, Chap. 1). One of the few scholars in the contemporary study of American Buddhism even to note the existence of Shingon in the United States is Charles Prebish. Some aspects of his brief comments do, however, misrepresent the actual situation of Shingon in America. While it is accurate to say that the Koyasan Buddhist Temple follows the Buddhist Churches of America's[25] "pattern of holding a Sunday service, maintaining a Sunday-school program, and serving as a community center for its adherents," it is inaccurate and misleading to claim that for "the most part, the use of mantras and mudras has been eliminated from the practice."[26]

On the contrary, the ordinary lay adherent would in the course of an English-language Shingon service recite many mantra. The order of service for English-language Shingon services is adoration, repentance, Three Refuges, confirmation of commitment to the Triple Jewel, Ten Precepts, aspiration for awakening (Skt. *bodhicitta*), pledge, recitation of the Heart Sutra, recitation of the mantras of the thirteen Buddhas, recitation of the light mantra, recitation of the guru mantra, universal prayer (transfer of merits), and concluding adoration.[27] In addition to the liturgical acts specifically identified as mantra recitation, several of the others also include mantra. The claim that mudra as well as mantra have been *eliminated* points to a further confusion. It seems to imply that performance of mudra and recitation of mantra by lay adherents are the norm for Shingon services in Japan. My own observations of Japanese Shingon services across the span of a quarter-century indicate that lay adherents very rarely recite mantra and are even less likely to perform mudra. Generally, as seems also to be the case in many other Buddhist traditions in Japan, the only activity undertaken by lay adherents in the course of a service is the offering of incense. The inclusion of mantra recitation by lay adherents as a part of the order of service for Shingon in America appears to be part of the accommodation to the model of religious services as found in American religious culture. Without proper initiation, however, lay adherents would not be taught to perform the mudra, which constitutes the priest's role in the service.

Central to the idea of Shingon as an "esoteric" tradition is the role played by initiation. Initiation is felt to be necessary because Shingon practices are efficacious and powerful, and it is necessary to protect them from individuals who might misuse the powers inherent in those practices and would thereby endanger both themselves and others. Thus, mudras are the special province of the priests and are often performed secretly, under the concealment of their robes.[28] This distinction is not one that originated in the adaptation to the religious culture of the United States but is also found in contemporary Shingon temples in Japan. Indeed, it is implied by the fact that descriptions of the mudras are not to be found in the earliest translations of tantric texts into Chinese. It is the mudras that are considered to activate the mantras, thus while the mantras could be recorded, the mudras were to be directly transmitted from teacher to disciple. The adaptation to mainstream Protestant norms is substantial enough, however, that even those Americans whose interests led them to investigate a wide variety of esoteric traditions did not find the Shingon tradition appealing enough to pursue.[29]

ROMANTICISM, MIMESIS, AND THE
DESIRE FOR THE EXOTIC OTHER

As an identifiable movement, the origin of romanticism has been traced to the eighteenth century.[30] Although largely concerned with aesthetics—art and poetry—it was also very influential as a religious and philosophic orientation, as well as having social and political consequences.[31] To greatly simplify two complex phases in the history of European thought, romanticism was in large part a reaction to the Enlightenment, which had valued reason and order, emphasizing instead emotion and spontaneity. The idea that "authentic" religiosity is rooted in the emotions and is manifested by a childlike naïveté and spontaneity are romantic conceptions of religion that continue into the present. While romanticism in general is characterized by the emotions of nostalgia, longing, and alienation from one's natal society, its mimetic impulse is key to understanding the reception of Buddhism in the West.

The mimetic impulse[32] is not by any means unique to the romantics.[33] Mimesis is used in Shingon—and tantric Buddhist ritual generally—when the practitioner identifies with the deity evoked.[34] Indeed, all of Buddhist meditation practice might be interpreted as a kind of mimesis—you have to practice what the Buddha practiced in order to become a buddha. For the romantics, however, the mimetic impulse was informed by their social alienation, which directed them toward Asia, and by their preconceptions regarding religion. While they sought fulfillment in the object of their mimetic desire, their appropriation of Buddhism was a form of assimilation—of incorporating Buddhism into their own preconceptions regarding religion. Of course, not all converts to Buddhism were motivated primarily by mimetic desire or have not grown into a deeper appreciation of the actualities of Buddhist practice. However, romantic mimesis is central to the formation of popular conceptions of Buddhism and other Asian religions within American religious culture, including the marginalization of traditions that did not fit into the preconceptions of romanticism.[35]

The mimetic impulse can be described as the desire to obtain the power of the Other, not by conquest, but by becoming that Other.[36] In the case of Tibetan Buddhism, Donald Lopez has noted that "Tibet operates as a constituent of a romanticism in which the Orient is not debased but exalted as a surrogate self endowed with all that the West wants."[37] The romantics located that powerful Other in Asia and marked it as the exotic. This is so central to the development of romanticism that Edward Said has summarized Raymond Schwab's *La Renaissance orientale* as asserting that "Romanticism cannot be understood unless some account is taken of the great textual and linguistic discoveries made about the Orient during the late eighteenth and early nineteenth centuries."[38]

These discoveries also influenced the way in which the American variant of romanticism, transcendentalism, developed.[39] Arthur Versluis has demonstrated the pivotal role of Asian religions in the early formation of transcendentalism, especially in the works of Ralph Waldo Emerson and Henry David Thoreau, who are considered to be the most important figures in the movement's establishment. According to Versluis, "neither Emerson nor Thoreau would have written the same works had they not read Hindu and Buddhist scriptures."[40] Although later transcendentalist authors did not read widely in Asian religions, they did continue to develop ideas, such as the one that a "universal religion" was already emerging in their own day, that set the stage for New Thought in the late nineteenth century and New Age religiosity in the late twentieth.[41]

One of the origins of mimetic desire is Hegel, who framed the structures of thought within which and against which romanticism developed. Hegel placed mimesis at the heart of his epistemology—the truest knowing comes by becoming the other.[42] The fuller this identification, the more adequate the knowledge. The romantics transformed this from an epistemology into a doctrine that one's full potential was to be achieved by a sudden, transformative experience, or religious insight. Such central Buddhist concepts as merit making (Kemper, Chap. 1) and the path structure would not fit within this naturalized, individualistic romantic anthropology.[43]

For Romanticism, mimetic desire is directed toward the idealized Oriental Other, who is perceived as having qualities such as tranquility, wisdom, and purity, which one can only acquire for oneself by ceasing to be oneself and becoming the Other. Through a variety of vehicles—clothing, habits, food, objets d'art— one attempts to mold oneself into the image of the idealized Other. Some forms of Buddhism, such as Foguang Shan, have purposely played up to the appeal of the exotic (Chandler, Chap. 7), while others, such as the Jōdo Shinshū temples of Hawai'i, have attempted to further Americanize themselves in order to keep later generations of Japanese Americans as members—a strategy that is the mirror image of the appeal to the exotic (Tanabe, Chap. 3). However, the romantic desire to become the exotic Other finds little of appeal in those forms of Japanese Buddhism that sought to accommodate themselves to mainstream American religious culture.

The transmission of romantic attitudes and values from the romantics per se into the religious culture of twentieth-century America was mediated by a set of individuals whose purposes were distinct enough that they have been called "neoromantics." It is these neoromantics who are most responsible for creating the current liberal understanding of religion, an understanding based on their "assertions of religious experience as an autonomous, irreducible and universal intuition or feeling of the Infinite, of human cultural expressions as the medium through which divine revelation is mediated, and of the various religions of the world as the positive forms in which the essence of religion manifests itself."[44]

Consequently, the romantic attitudes that came to pervade American religious culture in the twentieth century are not simply identical with the aesthetic movement of the late eighteenth and early nineteenth centuries. Most important, the rise of modernism, with its emphasis on quantification, and the socioeconomic correlate of modernism—industrialism—created in the twentieth century an intellectual climate radically different from that of the nineteenth. However, although no longer an identifiable movement among intellectual elites whose creativity was expressed and whose attitudes were frequently communicated through the medium of poetry, nineteenth-century romanticism lingers on in what by now have become fragmentary presumptions about human existence, social relations, and the world in which we live. Being unexamined, these presumptions were in some ways even more deeply influential in the twentieth century and are in the present than they were when they were the topic of discussion and disagreement. It is the presumptive character of these beliefs and attitudes that has allowed them to mold the Buddhism perceived by the West into a reflection of these very same beliefs and attitudes.

Indicative of the extent to which romantic values and preconceptions came
to inform the Western apprehension of Buddhism is the way in which those values
and preconceptions were themselves rhetorically employed to assert the superiority of "Eastern thought" over "Western." One of the best-known figures in the
transmission of Buddhism to the West is D. T. Suzuki. As a member of the Kyoto
school, his way of presenting Zen Buddhism was itself deeply informed by romanticism.[45] This romanticization would seem to have been an important factor in
Suzuki's international success as a promoter of Zen (Rocha, Chap. 6). The romantic basis of his approach is evident in what may be his most frequently reprinted
essays, "Lectures on Zen Buddhism."[46] In the first of these lectures, Suzuki asserts
the superiority of the "East" over the "West." Taking one poem each by Bashō and
Tennyson, he develops a simplistic comparison between East and West. Suzuki asserts that Eastern thought, which he characterizes as mystical and "antescientific,"
is superior to Western thought, which he characterizes as analytical and "scientific."[47] He structures the comparison in such a fashion as to lead the reader to value
East over West. It is ironic, however, that he does so by appealing to romantic,
that is, Western, values. The romantic mimetic ideal of mystic unity is deployed
by Suzuki in a rhetoric of reversal in which the supposedly mystical thinking of
"the Oriental," which in the hands of Euro-American imperialists had served as
a rationalization for colonialism, is now given positive valence and returned as a
critique of the colonizer.

ZEN: A COUNTEREXAMPLE?

The popular reception of Zen, being so similar to that of Tibetan Buddhism, would
seem at first sight to be a counterexample disproving the thesis proposed here. Zen
could look like a counterexample because of the failure of the following argument
by analogy:

> Shingon and Zen are alike in that both are forms of Japanese Buddhism
> found in the United States.
> Due to the dynamics of romantic mimesis, Shingon is invisible.
> Therefore, Zen should be subject to the same dynamics and be invisible as
> well.

However, Zen is as widely known—as much a cultural icon—as Tibetan Buddhism,
seeming to indicate that something other than the dynamics of romantic mimesis
has made Shingon invisible.

It is, however, important to distinguish between convert Zen and immigrant Zen.[48] The Zen of the immigrant Japanese-American communities remains just as invisible on the American religious landscape as Shingon or Shin.[49] What is known so widely is convert Zen. This is due at least in part to the internationalizing project of such figures as D. T. Suzuki, who, along with Alan Watts, actively worked to popularize Zen in the West.

One of the clearest instances of the importance of this distinction between immigrant and convert Zen can be seen in the way in which Zen is represented in the media. The media has demonstrated a consistent tendency to focus all of its attention—whether sympathetic or hostile—on convert Zen, as if it were newsworthy because it is some kind of anomalous phenomenon.[50] The version of convert Zen popularized in the media is itself informed by the romantic and modernist religious assumptions shared both by many converts themselves and by the members of the media interviewing them, as well as by the modernizing Buddhist leaders most able to articulately present Buddhism to a Western public. In this way, although there is wide public recognition of Zen, it is not the Zen of the immigrant communities. The vastly greater media attention devoted to convert Buddhism— whether Zen or Tibetan Buddhism—seems to mirror with profound irony the idea that spiritual conversion to Christianity by Orientals is analogous to cultural conversion, and that this is the normative direction of religiocultural movement.

The equivalence between religious conversion and cultural conversion is found, for example, in the merging of the interests of Christian missionaries and sociologists in the first quarter of the twentieth century.[51] While spiritual conversion to Christianity and adoption of American culture by Orientals were what the missionaries desired, the idea of white Americans converting to Buddhism seems to pose a threat to implicit assumptions that cultural conversion ought to be only toward American culture, a progress toward the presumptively superior. While much of the media attention has been sympathetic, the very fact that the focus is on those who convert to Buddhism is reminiscent of the fear felt by members of the British Empire in the eighteenth century that white men were in danger of "going native," and the loathing felt toward those who were thought to have done so.

CONCLUSION

It is important that we reflect critically on the romantic presumptions that inform the popular religious culture of America. On the one hand these presumptions have structured Buddhism as it is known in the West; at the same time, they also marginalize to the point of invisibility much, if not most, of the actual historical tradition of Buddhism.

It seems to be a regular feature of the American assimilation of Buddhism that the exotic is mistaken for the authentic. The contrast between the evident appeal of the exotic of Tibetan monks dressed in traditional robes and the accommodationist stance of Japanese priests dressed in business suits exemplifies this conflation of authenticity and the exotic. The concept of authenticity itself needs to be understood as a rhetorical strategy, deployed to support assertions of superiority. In the case of the movement of Buddhism into the religious culture of the United States, however, the appeal of the exotic extends beyond its apparent validation of authenticity. Historically, of course, concern with the exotic Other was by no means limited to the idealized version embraced by romanticism. The Oriental as "the ultimate symbol of exotic difference"[52] drew not only the positive attention of the romantics and neoromantics, but also the negative reaction of rejecting the exotic Other described so powerfully in the critiques of Orientalism.

For the mimetic desire of romanticism, the Buddhist as exotic Other provides the sense of authentic access to the "sacred wisdom of the East"—itself a Western construct—that was thought to be the corrective to the problems of one's own society. Japanese-American Buddhists who were themselves motivated to accommodate to the norms of American popular religious culture could not serve as that exotic Other. In addition, the missionary mandate of the Japanese-Buddhist churches established in the first half of the twentieth century was to serve an immigrant community, not to convert new members. Hence, despite Japanese-American Buddhist sanghas having been a part of the American religious milieu for over a century, even today they remain largely invisible.

Notes

1. A review of recent publications on Buddhism in America reveals several books claiming to make various kinds of comprehensive statements, but with only minor exceptions these include no mention of Shingon. Al Rapaport and Brian D. Hotchkiss, eds., *Buddhism in America* (Rutland, Vermont, Boston, and Tokyo: Charles E. Tuttle, 1998); the record of "the landmark Buddhism in America Conference (Boston, January 17–19, 1997)"; Richard Hughes Seager, *Buddhism in America* (New York: Columbia University Press, 1999); Charles S. Prebish and Kenneth K. Tanaka, eds., *The Faces of Buddhism in America* (Berkeley, Los Angeles, and London: University of California Press, 1998); Duncan Ryuken Williams and Christopher S. Queen, eds., *American Buddhism: Methods and Findings in Recent Scholarship* (Richmond, Eng.: Curzon, 1999); and James William Coleman, *The New Buddhism: The Western Tranformation of an Ancient Tradition* (Oxford: Oxford University Press, 2001)—all

include no reference to Shingon. In keeping with his topic, Thomas A. Tweed, *The American Encounter with Buddhism, 1844–1912: Victorian Culture and the Limits of Dissent* (Bloomington: Indiana University Press, 1992), makes several references to Shingon in relation to the Victorians Ernest Fenollosa and William Sturgis Bigelow, both of whom studied Shingon and Tendai in Japan, but does not discuss the presence of immigrant Buddhists in the United States. Rick Fields, *How the Swans Came to the Lake: A Narrative History of Buddhism in America*, 3d ed. (Boston: Shambhala, 1992), makes passing reference to Shingon, though, as he shares the concern of most of the studies with the development of convert Buddhism, his work pays scant attention to immigrant Buddhism. Similarly, the intentions of Coleman, *New Buddhism*, and Stephen Batchelor, *The Awakening of the West: The Encounter of Buddhism and Western Culture* (Berkeley: Parallax, 1994), are not to be comprehensive and also pay scant attention to immigrant Buddhism, giving no mention to Shingon. Though not mentioning Shingon, an important study that gives thorough attention to immigrant Buddhists in Canada is Janet McLellan, *Many Petals of the Lotus: Five Asian Buddhist Communities in Toronto* (Toronto: University of Toronto Press, 1999). The new, popular work by Diana L. Eck, *A New Religious America: How a "Christian Country" Has Become the World's Most Religiously Diverse Nation* (New York: Harper San Francisco, 2001), has the benefit of treating immigrant Buddhism seriously but does not mention Shingon per se. The only recent work that gives any serious attention to Shingon is the brief treatment found in Charles Prebish, *Luminous Passage: The Practice and Study of Buddhism in America* (Berkeley and Los Angeles: University of California Press, 1999). In the study of American religion, immigrant forms of Asian religions are typically marginalized in two ways. First, as discussed more fully later in this essay, there is a strong tendency to attend exclusively to converts, who are more easily accessible than the immigrant communities. The second marginalizing tendency is to focus on the changes in the immigration laws in the mid-1960s, a time when some immigrant churches had already been established for over half a century.

2. It has become something of a commonplace to identify two forms of Buddhism when discussing Buddhist missionary activity in the West. One of the ways these two are differentiated is between immigrant and convert Buddhism. However, as Jan Nattier has suggested, the actuality is more complex, and the "notion of 'two Buddhisms' . . . is clearly inadequate." Jan Nattier, "Who Is a Buddhist? Charting the Landscape of Buddhist America," in *Faces of Buddhism*, ed. Prebish and Tanaka, 189.

3. Harvey Aronson, "Is Buddhism Psychology?" lecture presented at the Institute of Buddhist Studies, Berkeley, California, October 18, 2000.

4. Although employing a different terminology—that of assimilation and ethnic retention—Lon Kurashige has called the opposition of the two a "false dichotomy." Lon Kurashige, *Japanese American Celebration and Conflict: A History of Ethnic Identity and Festival in Los Angeles, 1934–1990* (Berkeley and Los Angeles: University of California Press, 2002), xiii. Matthew Kapstein has noted a similar complexity in the case of the introduction of Buddhism to Tibet: "the Tibetan Buddhist tradition was not, for all its conservatism, a static replication of Indian antiquity, nor, in its dynamic aspects, was it the product of deliberate contrivance on the part of Tibetans motivated to construct a uniquely Tibetan form of

Buddhism." Matthew T. Kapstein, *The Tibetan Assimilation of Buddhism: Conversion, Contestation, and Memory* (Oxford: Oxford University Press, 2000), 4.

5. Gay Watson, *The Resonance of Emptiness: A Buddhist Inspiration for a Contemporary Psychotherapy* (London: Curzon, 1998), 1–6.

6. Heinz Bechert, *Buddhismus, Staat, und Gesellschaft in den Ländern des Theravada-Buddhismus*, 3 vols. (Frankfurt am Main and Berlin: Alfred Metzner Verlag, 1996), 1:37–108; Don A. Pittman, *Toward a Modern Chinese Buddhism: Taixu's Reforms* (Honolulu: University of Hawai'i Press, 2001); Gabriele Goldfuss, *Vers un Bouddhisme du XXe Siècle: Yang Wenhui (1837–1911), Réformateur Laïque et Imprimeur* (Paris: Collège de France, Institut des Hautes Études Chinoises, 2001); and Peter A. Jackson, *Buddhadasa: Theravada Buddhism and Modernist Reform in Thailand*, 2d ed. (Chiang Mai, Thailand: Silkworm Books, 2003).

7. Donald S. Lopez, Jr., *Prisoners of Shangri-La: Tibetan Buddhism and the West* (Chicago: University of Chicago Press, 1998), 184–186. One of the earliest Tibetans to actively pursue a modernization was Gendün Chöpel (1903–1951). See Thupten Jinpa, "Science as an Ally or a Rival Philosophy? Tibetan Buddhist Thinkers' Engagement with Modern Science," in *Buddhism and Science: Breaking New Ground*, ed. B. Alan Wallace (New York: Columbia University Press, 2003); and Elke Hessel, *Die Welt hat mich trunken gemacht: Die Lebensgeschichte des Amdo Gendün Chöpel* (Berlin: Theseus Verlag, 2000).

8. See Ryuichi Abé, *The Weaving of Mantra: Kukai and the Construction of Esoteric Buddhist Discourse* (New York: Columbia University Press, 1999); Stanley Weinstein, "Aristocratic Buddhism," in *The Cambridge History of Japan, Vol. 2: Heian Japan*, ed. Donald H. Shively and William H. McCullough (Cambridge: Cambridge University Press, 1999), 449–516; and *A History of Japanese Religion*, ed. Kazuo Kasahara (Tokyo: Kosei Publishing, 2001), 98–113.

9. Katsuichi Kazahaya, *Koyasan Beikoku Betsuin Goju nen shi (Koyasan Buddhist Temple, 1912–1962)* (Los Angeles: Koyasan Beikoku Betsuin, 1974), 115–118.

10. Masao Fujii, "Founder Worship in Kamakura Buddhism," in *Religion and the Family in East Asia*, ed. George A. DeVos and Takao Sofue, reprint (Berkeley and Los Angeles: University of California Press, 1986 [1984]), 155–167.

11. See James Burnell Robinson, "The Lives of Indian Buddhist Saints: Biography, Hagiography and Myth," in *Tibetan Literature: Studies in Genre*, ed. José Ignacio Cabezón and Roger R. Jackson (Ithaca, N.Y.: Snow Lion, 1996), 57–69; and Eva M. Dargyay, *The Rise of Esoteric Buddhism in Tibet* (Delhi: Motilal Banarsidass, 1977).

12. Louise H. Hunter, *Buddhism in Hawai'i: Its Impact on a Yankee Community* (Honolulu: University of Hawai'i Press, 1971), 101.

13. In 1979 I visited this miniature reproduction of the Shikoku pilgrimage. By that time it had fallen into disrepair and seemed to no longer attract any visitors. Only shells of the shrines were left, with no statues or other iconographic representations. Located on private property just off the main road, there was no sign to indicate its presence, and only if one

had information as to its whereabouts, such as I received from the local Shingon priest, would one be able to find it.

14. Hunter, *Buddhism in Hawai'i*, 151. The statistical significance of such a relatively large number of temples in Hawai'i in the early part of the twentieth century is also reflected in the religious demographics of mid-century Japan. In 1972, Japan's Agency for Cultural Affairs reported that Shingon claimed the third largest number of adherents of all Buddhist sects in Japan, following only the Nichiren and Pure Land sects. Agency for Cultural Affairs, *Japanese Religion: A Survey* (Tokyo: Kodansha International, 1972), 239.

15. Katsuichi Kazahaya, *Koyasan Beikoku Betsuin Goju nen shi (Koyasan Buddhist Temple, 1912–1962)* (Los Angeles: Koyasan Beikoku Betsuin, 1974), 122.

16. Ibid., 163.

17. Richard M. Jaffe, *Neither Monk Nor Layman: Clerical Marriage in Modern Japanese Buddhism* (Princeton, N.J.: Princeton University Press, 2001), 169. See also Richard Jaffe, "The Buddhist Cleric as Japanese Subject: Buddhism and the Household Registration System," in *New Directions in the Study of Meiji Japan*, ed. Helen Hardacre and Adam L. Kern (Leiden: Brill, 1997), 506–530.

18. Jaffe, *Neither Monk Nor Layman*, 172.

19. Robert J. Smith, "Wedding and Funeral Ritual: Analysing a moving target," in *Ceremony and Ritual in Japan: Religious Practices in an Industrialized Society*, ed. Jan van Bremen and D. P. Martinez (London: Routledge, 1995), 28.

20. For wedding ceremonies in contemporary Japan, see Michael Jeremy and M. E. Robinson, *Ceremony and Symbolism in the Japanese Home* (Honolulu: University of Hawai'i Press, 1989).

21. Kazahaya, *Koyasan Beikoku Betsuin*, 123.

22. Ibid. While it is possible that Japanese Shingon had—like Shin and Zen—created a Buddhist wedding ceremony, it seems unlikely. This becomes clear when we consider that the Reverend Aoyama, despite "having entered the monastic life" at age six, graduated with honors from Koyasan University, having been an instructor at Sanboin Temple, Kyoto, and head priest at his home temple before entering into missionary service (ibid., 115), did not know of any Shingon wedding ceremony.

23. Ibid., 136.

24. Yoshito S. Hakeda, trans., *The Awakening of Faith* (New York: Columbia University Press, 1967), and Hakeda, ed. and trans., *Kukai: Major Works* (New York: Columbia University Press, 1972).

25. The Buddhist Churches of America represent the Jodo Shin tradition of Honpa Honganji in the United States. See also Tanabe, Chapter 3, in this volume.

26. Prebish, *Luminous Passage*, 26.

27. Koyasan Shingonshu Kyogakubu, *Shingon Buddhist Service Book* (Koyasan, Japan: Koyasan Shingonshu, 1975); Seytsu Takahashi, ed., *Raihai Seiten* (Los Angeles: Koyasan Buddhist Temple, 1972); Yusei Arai, *Shingon Esoteric Buddhism: A Handbook for Followers*, trans., George Tanabe, Seicho Asahi, and Shoken Harada; and Eijun Eidson, ed., Koyasan: *Koyasan Shingon Mission/Kongobuji* (Fresno, Calif.: Shingon Buddhist International Institute, 1997).

28. The term "priest" is the most appropriate English rendering of the Japanese *ajari*, which derives from the Sanskrit *acarya*. As the tradition is primarily concerned with the performance of ritual, it seems in some ways analogous to the sacramental Catholic tradition.

29. Tweed, *American Encounter with Buddhism*, 50–60.

30. Kenneth Clark, *The Romantic Rebellion: Romantic versus Classical Art* (New York: Harper and Row, 1973), 19. Clark, an art historian, identifies Edmund Burke's "A Philosophical Enquiry into the Sublime and Beautiful" (1757) as the first philosophic statement of the movement.

31. On the political consequences of romanticism, see Isaiah Berlin, "The Romantic Revolution: A Crisis in the History of Modern Thought," in Isaiah Berlin, *The Sense of Reality: Studies in Ideas and Their History*, ed. Henry Hardy (New York: Farrar, Straus and Giroux, 1996).

32. Charles Hallisey has used the phrase "intercultural mimesis" to refer to the way in which Buddhists effected the Victorian representation of Buddhism, e.g., in the work of Rhys-Davids. Charles Hallisey, "Roads Taken and Not Taken in the Study of Theravada Buddhism," in *Curators of the Buddha: The Study of Buddhism under Colonialism*, ed. Donald S. Lopez, Jr. (Chicago: University of Chicago Press, 1995). See also Peter van der Veer, *Imperial Encounters: Religion and Modernity in India and Britain* (Princeton, N.J.: Princeton University Press, 2001). Richard King has also used the concept of mimesis in relation to Asian religions, discussing counter-hegemonic strategies, drawing a distinction "between *re-presentative* mimesis (that is, merely re-presenting or mirroring the hegemonic stereotype)—an act that involves conformity to the cultural stereotype—and *parodic* mimesis (undoing by overdoing)." Richard King, *Orientalism and Religion: Postcolonial Theory, India and "The Mystic East"* (London: Routledge, 1999), 203.

33. Karl F. Morrison, *The Mimetic Tradition of Reform in the West* (Princeton, N.J.: Princeton University Press, 1982).

34. See Richard K. Payne, "Realizing Inherent Enlightenment: Ritual and Self-Transformation in Shingon Buddhism," in *Religious and Social Ritual: Interdisciplinary Explorations*, ed. Michael B. Aune and Valerie D. Marinis (Albany: State University of New York Press, 1996).

35. Two sets of beliefs and attitudes related to romanticism are primitivism and perennialism. Primitivism is the idea that modern society is responsible for all of the ills that plague humans, and that in the past, or among present-day primitives, these problems are absent. Primitives are seen as spontaneous, motivated by their emotions, and inherently honor-

able—an idealization that is extended to women and children. Perennialism is the contemporary expression of the Neoplatonic notion that there is a single truth, which is at the same time the source of ethics and real existence. It is most commonly expressed in the metaphor that different religions form different paths to the top of the same mountain. Extended consideration of these two important topics would take us too far afield at this time.

36. On the connection between mimesis, desire—and seduction, see Gunter Gebauer and Christoph Wulf, *Mimesis: Culture, Art, Society,* trans. Don Reneau (Berkeley and Los Angeles: University of California Press, 1995), 211–216.

37. Lopez, *Prisoners of Shangri-La,* 202. While Tibet itself could be the object of romantic mimetic desire, once Japan had taken the road to an aggressive policy of nationalism in the Meiji era and modernization, it could no longer be the object of romantic fantasies.

38. Hallisey, "Roads Taken and Not Taken," 32; see also Edward W. Said, "Introduction," in Raymond Schwab, *The Oriental Renaissance: Europe's Rediscovery of India and the East, 1680–1880,* trans. Gene Patterson-Black and Victor Reinking (New York: Columbia University Press, 1984), xix.

39. Louis Menand, *The Metaphysical Club: A Story of Ideas in America* (New York: Farrar, Straus and Giroux, 2001), 248.

40. Arthur Versluis, *American Transcendentalism and Asian Religions* (Oxford: Oxford University Press, 1993), 305.

41. For an example of the treatment of Buddhism in New Age thought, see Wouter J. Hanegraaff, *New Age Religion and Western Culture: Esotericism in the Mirror of Secular Thought* (Albany: State University of New York Press, 1998), 191–193.

42. Michael Taussig, *Mimesis and Alterity: A Particular History of the Senses* (London: Routledge, 1992), 36. It is this mimetic epistemology, further developed by Dilthey's distinction between explanation and understanding and by Husserl's phenomenological methodology, that has become so influential in the study of religion under the notion that through empathy or intuition one can oneself constructively reexperience the religious experience of the other.

43. Suzanne R. Kirschner, *The Religious and Romantic Origins of Psychoanalysis: Individuation and Integration in Post-Freudian Theory* (Cambridge: Cambridge University Press, 1996).

44. Arthur McCalla, "Romanticism," in *Guide to the Study of Religion,* ed. Willi Braun and Russell T. McCutcheon (London: Cassell, 2000), 378.

45. Robert Sharf, "The Zen of Japanese Nationalism," in *Curators of the Buddha: The Study of Buddhism under Colonialism,* ed. Donald S. Lopez, Jr. (Chicago: University of Chicago Press, 1995), "Whose Zen? Zen Nationalism Reconsidered," in *Rude Awakenings: Zen, the Kyoto School, and the Question of Nationalism,* ed. James W. Heisig and John C. Maraldo (Honolulu: University of Hawai'i Press, 1995); and "Buddhist Modernism and the Rhetoric

of Meditative Experience," *Numen: International Review for the History of Religions* 42, no. 3 (October 1995).

46. D. T. Suzuki, "Lectures on Zen Buddhism," in D. T. Suzuki, Erich Fromm, and Richard De Martino, *Zen Buddhism and Psychoanalysis* (New York: Grove, 1963).

47. Ibid., 5, 10.

48. My thanks to Robert Bellah for raising the question and to George Tanabe for suggesting the importance of the difference between the two forms of Zen.

49. It has been suggested that one of the important differences between Zen and Shingon is the relatively greater freedom Zen priests had from control by central authorities in Japan, particularly the freedom to conduct local ordinations that were recognized by Japan. (My thanks to one of the anonymous reviewers for bringing this issue to my attention.) This is very suggestive but, as with other dynamics, cannot be entirely separated from the context of romanticist religious culture as an independent variable. For example, not all Zen priests exercised such freedom equally. While Suzuki Shunryu established the San Francisco Zen Center on his own, this only happened after he broke with the Zen temple that brought him to the United States, which, as a primarily immigrant temple, did not want him being so involved with Anglo-Americans. The freedom to conduct initiations and ordinations locally seems to have been instrumental in creating a convert community, but the interest in conversion existed only against the background of an already romanticized version of Buddhism.

50. This focus is evident even in the media coverage of Eck's recent work, *A New Religious America*. While itself noteworthy for providing a very balanced treatment, the media attention has continued to focus on converts to Eastern religions, rather than on the long-term presence of immigrant communities.

51. Henry Yu, *Thinking Orientals: Migration, Contact, and Exoticism in Modern America* (Oxford: Oxford University Press, 2001), 65.

52. Ibid., 63.

5 Globalization and the Pursuit of a Shared Understanding of the Absolute: The Case of Soka Gakkai in Brazil

Peter B. Clarke

This chapter considers the development within the Nichiren Buddhist movement Soka Gakkai (Value Creation Society) of a new interpretation and application of its criteria for distinguishing "real" from "provisional" Buddhism and for distinguishing religions of the "inner way" *(naido)* from those of the "outer way" *(gedo)*. In this presentation it is suggested that Soka Gakkai's expansion outside Japan, and more generally the East, in pursuit of its global mission, beginning with Brazil in 1960, has acted as a catalyst in this development. It has precipitated a change to a more inclusive, less oppositional understanding of and approach to other forms of Buddhism and other religions, in particular Christianity in its Brazilian, Catholic form and African-Brazilian religion. This change, which came with expansion overseas, is sometimes seen essentially as the substitution of *shoju* or peaceful co-existence with other religions and philosophies for *shakabuku*, a strategy of evangelization that aimed at destroying the truth claims and undermining some of the core values they espoused.[1] It is suggested here that what has developed in the Brazilian context is more than mere coexistence but something approaching a revolution in the way Brazilian members of Soka Gakkai, at least, think about and interact with other religions. While they continue to be persuaded that Soka Gakkai provides the effective spiritual means to transform the world,[2] other means are not rejected out of hand. A culture of experimentation has gradually taken over from one of exclusive emphasis on the unique merits of the movement's own spiritual technologies to bring about the desired human revolution.

In the 1950s, during the presidency of Toda Josei (1900–1958), Soka Gakkai became fixated with questions of religious orthodoxy and with the establishment of criteria for the purpose of differentiating between "inner" and "outer" forms of religion and "real" and "provisional" forms of Buddhism. All forms of Buddhism, with the exception of Nichiren Buddhism, were classified as provisional or low-grade Buddhism, including the Jōdo or Pure Land sects. Even within the Nichiren tradition a distinction was made between Soka Gakkai, which claimed to be the purest form of Nichiren Buddhism, and the other Lotus Scripture *(Hoke-kyo)* based sects.[3] Among other religions classified as outer and low-grade were Shinto and

Christianity, the latter being placed on a par with the Jodo-shu and Jodo Shinshu schools of Pure Land Buddhism.

As will be seen, several of the same principles that the movement used in the 1950s, and for much of its history in Brazil, to distinguish between real and provisional Buddhism and inner and outer forms of religion are now increasingly interpreted and applied in an inclusive as opposed to an exclusive sense. Moreover, fundamental beliefs held by other religions, such as belief in God, once considered to be fundamentally contrary to Soka Gakkai's teachings, are no longer characterized as "unscientific" doctrines that relegate those faiths that espouse them to the category of low-grade, outer forms of religion. On the contrary, a strategy of reflexive syncretism is now encouraged, at least in Brazil, which seeks to find parallels between these beliefs and those of Soka Gakkai.

There are, it should be mentioned, limits to the amount of doctrinal accommodation this more inclusive brand of Soka Gakkai found in Brazil is prepared to accept, and these limits are not always determined by the leadership. One such is the notion of a personal God who intervenes in human affairs and is responsible for all that happens. Brazilian members who are interviewed stress that this concept has to be refuted, albeit with sensitivity and respect, as it undermines a fundamental principle in Soka Gakkai that every individual is responsible for her/his own actions. On the other hand, members are open to, and even suggest to potential recruits, the existence of parallels between fundamental Buddhist ideas and the notion of God as Creator. In discussions with members in the state of Bahia in northeastern Brazil—a state still deeply influenced by a tense intermixture of Catholicism, popular religion, various forms of African-Brazilian religion, and Spiritualism, and unaware of basic Buddhist beliefs—this notion was frequently juxtaposed with the movement's mantra "Nam-myoho-Rengekyo" (I put my faith in the wonderful Lotus Scripture).

For the purpose of illustrating the above-mentioned developments in Soka Gakkai teachings on and attitudes toward other religions, this chapter is divided into three main sections. The first focuses on Soka Gakkai teachings on the truth claims and status of Buddhism and other religions, and for this I am heavily indebted to research carried out by Professor Kamstra (1989),[4] in which he examined the content of the Canon of Shakabuku (Shakabuku kyoten), which the then president of the movement Toda Josei had compiled in 1954, and the revised version of this canon completed in 1969.[5] The second section outlines the steps taken by Soka Gakkai to move from an ethnic Japanese-based religion to a universal Buddhist humanist movement in Brazil and shows how dependent, for a decade and more, Soka Gakkai International Brazil's (BSGI) views on "inner" and "outer"—

or true and false—forms of religions were on the Canon of Shakabuku, particularly the 1954 version.

The third part of the chapter, in addressing the changing response of Soka Gakkai to other religions, and in particular Roman Catholicism in Brazil, covers some of the same ground as a previous publication.[6] It is based on my fieldwork in Brazil, carried out over almost twenty years, on the change in Japanese new religions (shinshukyo) in that country from ethnic to universal religions. As this third section makes clear, Weber's idea of elective affinity inevitably came into play as BSGI underwent a process of universalization. This change in the ethnic composition of the membership, and the increasingly poor response from the wider society where religious mixing is normative, put pressure on BSGI to alter, albeit not in every respect radically, its perspectives on and attitudes toward other religions and also its rules governing its own members' participation in these religions.

Readers might want to note here for comparative purposes how different movements in different cultural and religious contexts have developed similar ideas and adopted similar strategies to those of Soka Gakkai in their attempts to adapt. Particularly relevant and interesting is Rocha's chapter on Zen in Brazil, which like Soka Gakkai is increasingly unconcerned about denominational boundaries. Other interesting comparisons can be drawn between Soka Gakkai and the Taiwanese Compassion Relief Foundation (see Huang, Chap. 8 in this volume), both of which place great stress on grassroots support and lay witnessing. There are also interesting differences between Soka Gakkai and several other movements discussed in this book, including the former's commitment to the idea that Buddhism is not only Japanese but is for all, a position that contrasts with that taken by other Japanese Buddhists groups in, for example, Hawai'i (see Tanabe, Chap. 3).

SOKA GAKKAI, BUDDHISM, AND OTHER RELIGIONS

Under the leadership (1944–1958) of Toda Josei (1900–1958), Soka Gakkai was turned into a well-organized, efficiently administered, and highly separatist, if not fundamentalist, Buddhist movement. The content of the Soka Gakkai canon (Shakubuku kyoten), which is based on the Nichiren Buddhist kyohan (4),[7] in its 1954 form approved by Toda, reflects its exclusive approach to other Buddhist schools and to other religions.[8] The ultimate purpose of the canon was the crushing (shakabuku) of all forms of Buddhism and all other religions whose teachings and practices failed to meet the criteria established for true Buddhism or true religion.

As Kamstra points out, the canon divides religions into two kinds: those of the "outer way" (gedo) and those of the "inner way" (naido), placing in the latter

category the superior religions and the superior form of Buddhism, the Mahayana tradition.[9] While the canon affirms that Mahayana Buddhism is superior to
Hinayana Buddhism, it differentiates between *real* and *provisional* forms of the
former kind. It claims that certain schools, including the esoteric Shingon School,
have not understood the true meaning of Buddhism and, therefore, what they
teach is only *provisional*. Among the criteria used to distinguish real from provisional Mahayana Buddhism, the most important one is the Lotus Scripture, which
Toda discovered in prison in 1944 and which from then on supplied him with
the meaning of life.[10] According to the 1954 version of the Soka Gakkai canon,
real Mahayana Buddhism consists in adhering to the doctrines of the Lotus Scripture, which are made complete by the teachings of Nichiren and the recitation
of the previously mentioned mantra devised by him—"I put my faith in the wonderful Lotus Scripture" *(Nam-myoho-Rengekyo)*. In practice this meant that only
Nichiren-derived sects were authentically Buddhist, and the most authentic of
these was Nichiren Shoshu.[11]

On the matter of 'true' and 'false' religion, the canon asserts that all religions
with the exception of Buddhism are false. Buddhism, it stresses, is scientific, and
this makes it true, a claim that we will see repeated in *Brasil Seikyo*, the movement's Brazilian newspaper. Furthermore, Buddhism is construed as relevant, in
ways that Christianity and other religions are not, to the modern world, where
scientific understanding prevails. Christianity is thus inferior to "real" Buddhism
and similar to the low-grade type of religion that is Amida Buddhism, which is dismissed as *untrue* on the ground that it is based on an empty fable of the Western
Pure Land (Kamstra 1989, 42).

Of core Christian beliefs, beliefs that are almost universally accepted in Brazil
without being questioned, the canon is equally dismissive, describing the resurrection of Jesus, his virgin birth, and his ascension as fables. Moreover, it emphasizes
that Christianity has no logical, scientific explanation to offer for the healing and
other miracles attributed to Jesus. Buddhism, on the other hand, does possess an
explanation for certain kinds of healing in the law of cause and effect (Kamstra
1989, 42). Core Christian teachings are said to fail the ultimate test of a truth claim
by contradicting what are called "the laws of the science of the universe" (Kamstra 1989, 41). Among the examples given are the resurrection of Jesus and the
immaculate conception of Mary, Brazil's most popular saint. On the latter miracle
the canon states: "No matter from what angle one looks at it . . . the conception
of a virgin is contrary to the laws of the science of the universe. It is absolutely
impossible that a virgin can become pregnant without a human father . . ." (Kamstra 1989, 41). As to the empirical basis for an even more fundamental Christian

belief, the resurrection of Jesus, this was not a miraculous event but the result of the imaginings of the people in an abnormal state (Kamstra 1989, 41).

Also rejected is belief in the notion of a creator God. On this point the canon affirms that "All living and dead beings of the universe without any distinction were not made by some other being. We received our lives from our parents and we were not made by God or by the Buddha . . ." (Kamstra 1989, 41). The notion of God as spirit is also regarded as ill conceived, for all beings possess both body and soul. A spirit separated from matter cannot exist (Kamstra 1989, 42). All the qualities attributed to God by theists are in reality human qualities, for there is no other law than that of cause and effect, and no such being as an absolute God.

As was previously suggested, the intention here is to make Soka Gakkai stand apart as the most genuine and authentic form of Buddhism, and of religion. The canon seeks, therefore, to exclude all other forms of Buddhism and of religion by relegating them to the category of *outer* or *provisional* or *low-grade* paths. It is over and against this doctrinal and philosophical perspective and in response to other forms of Buddhism and other religions that the developments discussed in the third part of this chapter need to be assessed. But first I shall draw a brief outline of how Soka Gakkai opened up ethnically in Brazil—an opening up that had a considerable bearing on the more recent process of opening up doctrinally and in terms of its rules relating to membership.

FROM ETHNIC TO UNIVERSAL RELIGION

Officially founded as a lay Buddhist organization in 1937 and named Soka Kyoiku Gakkei (System of Value Creating Education), later changed to Soka Gakkai (Institute of Creative Values), SGI began its global mission in earnest with its establishment of a branch in Brazil in 1960 by the newly appointed president of the movement, Ikeda Daisaku (1928–). At the time, its membership was composed entirely of Japanese nationals or Japanese Brazilians. This was also the case with every other Japanese religion in Brazil.[12]

Brazil contains the largest population of Japanese descent in the world outside Japan, and this clearly provided a source of converts for the Japanese new religions in Brazil seeking to expand beyond the shores of Japan. This ready-made pool of converts was also in some respects counterproductive for some of these movements and for the older schools of Buddhism, including the Pure Land and Zen schools, by giving these religions the appearance of being exclusively for Japanese people or people of Japanese descent. The following brief account of how this large immigrant presence came to be will highlight the changing attitudes of the Japanese immigrants toward religion and will focus on the dynamics of the development among them of Japanese new religions, including Soka Gakkai.

In modern times large-scale Japanese emigration started with the Meiji Restoration in 1868. No more than a trickle until 1885, it gathered momentum from then onward, and by 1963 a total of around one million had emigrated.[13] The largest number of emigrants was eventually to settle in Manchuria, followed by Brazil, Hawai'i, mainland United States, Southeast Asia, Australasia, Canada, Peru, Mexico, and Colombia. The search for a livelihood was the principal motivation for emigration to the Americas, but not the only one. In other instances, such as Manchuria, demographic, political, and strategic factors became important.

Beginning in 1908, with the demand for labor principally for the São Paulo coffee plantations, Japanese outward emigration to Brazil continued with several interruptions until the early years of World War II. By 1941 an estimated 234,000 Japanese emigrants had arrived in Brazil.[14] At the time of writing there are approximately one million three hundred thousand citizens of Japanese origin and/or descent in Brazil, the majority of whom are settled in São Paulo and elsewhere in the south of Brazil, including Rio de Janeiro and Paraná, with only a few isolated communities in the north of the country, such as Tomé D' Açu in the state of Pará.

If the concerns, preoccupations, and lifestyles of the immigrants as described by the historians of Japanese immigration to Brazil—including Saito and Handa, both Japanese immigrants themselves—can be used as a rough guide to the norm, then the first generation of Japanese in Brazil expressed little interest in religious matters, leaving them in the hands of the family back home.[15] Almost all were committed to returning home and believed that if they were unlucky enough to die abroad before this could be arranged then their souls would find their own way back to Japan. Pre–World War II Japanese immigrants in Brazil spoke of death there as "death in a foreign land" (morte aldeia) or as the "death of a visitor" (morte do visitante).[16] The fact that the departing soul was leaving kin behind in Brazil did not pose a problem, for it was believed to be simply going on ahead to the common ancestral homeland.

Immigrants, then, made no provisions for the teaching of religion of any kind. Their schools provided no religious education as such, the emphasis being placed on the Imperial Rescript on Education proclaimed in 1890 and on filial piety to the emperor, which it was designed to cultivate. A picture of the emperor occupied the center wall of the school entrance, and all communal meeting places and school assemblies focused attention on him and on the imperial ancestors only. As to religious ceremonies and rituals, so little was known about them that it often proved difficult to find anyone well versed enough in the relevant Buddhist scriptures to recite those appropriate to burial ceremonies. For these and other rites of passage, immigrants were served by "monks made on the spot" (*bonzos feitos na hora*, or substitute monks). Moreover, the ancestral tablets were rarely if ever cared for and were usually consigned to the corner of the bedroom of the head of the household, where they simply gathered dust.

Little attended to, Japanese religions abroad, both old and new, were thus, until the late 1960s, essentially ethnic religions. Isolated as they were in their colonies in Brazil, the Japanese experienced little contact with the rest of society except by means of the Catholic Church, which made baptism a condition of entering its much sought-after schools. Some of the Japanese who "converted," were later to reconvert after a fashion by joining a Japanese new religion. One interviewee, a second-generation immigrant from that still very Japanese town of Suzano east of the city of São Paulo, informed me that he always felt himself to be a Buddhist and knew he would remain a Buddhist despite the pressure from Catholicism at school.[17] Such people have found in Soka Gakkai and other new Buddhist movements present in Brazil a way of returning to Buddhism in a modern, practical, and relevant form, in contrast to the Buddhism of their parents, the older Buddhist traditions, which were perceived to focus on death and funeral rites.

A major shift in outlook among the Japanese immigrants in Brazil was already evident by the end of World War II. By then, some had begun to consider Brazil their home, and by the late 1950s the idea of returning home to Japan had lost much of its force. It was greatly weakened by the numbers of Japanese who had gone back to Japan either immediately before or immediately after World War II, only to find that life there was too rigid and restrictive compared with their Brazilian experience, leading many of them to retrace their steps. Their children's poor knowledge of Japanese and the inevitable educational problems this would entail also greatly influenced the older generation of immigrants to accept Brazil as their permanent home, the place where they would die and become, in their turn, ancestors (*senzo*).

This opting for Brazil and the kinds of domestic and lifestyle changes that accompanied it gave religion greater importance and significance in the life of the Japanese immigrant, and this in turn impacted on the understanding and interpretation of belief and practice, widening both their application and their scope. For example, protector deities of the land and the people (*ujigami*), once confined in terms of their influence and power to the Japanese immigrant community, began to be promoted by their 'natural' devotees as the deities, not just of the Japanese in Brazil, but of all the country's inhabitants. The most typical of Shinto shrines in Brazil today, the Great Shinto Shrine of Brazil, the Dwelling of the Myriad Deities

(*Kaminoya Yaoyorozu Kyo*), established in 1966 by the now nonagenarian Suzuko Morishita, daughter of a Shinto ascetic (*gyoja*), stresses the universal character of the Japanese sun goddess Amaterasu, commenting that in the afterlife there will be "no nationalities, only people."[18] This Shinto shrine, like other Shinto shrines in Brazil, tends to be inclusive at the margins, so to speak, incorporating elements of Catholic, African-Brazilian, and Amerindian iconography in the outer shrines beyond the main sanctuary. The inner sanctum, on the other hand, remains a perfect replica of the Grand Shrine of Ise Jingu in Mie Prefecture southwest of Nara, where the inner sanctuary (*naiku*) is dedicated to Amaterasu.

Soka Gakkai broke out of its ethnic mold in Brazil at different speeds, making headway faster in São Paulo and in the south generally than elsewhere in the country. In the state of Bahia, in the northeast, it was started in 1958 by a Japanese immigrant family, the Kominatus, who farmed on the Japanese Colônia da Mata de São João, 100 kilometers south of the capital city, Salvador. Mrs. Kominatu in particular devoted herself to aggressive evangelism (*shakabuku*) among the Japanese immigrants in São João da Mata, and it was only in the late 1960s that non-Japanese Brazilians joined the movement. Even with this change in ethnic composition, the ceremonies remained entirely in Japanese. In Bahia there was general hostility toward Japanese ways and an almost complete lack of information for those who wanted to improve their understanding of Japanese culture. One of the first non-Japanese Brazilians to join BSGI recalled that all that she could find as sources of information were a few of President Ikeda's discourses that had been translated into Portuguese, and it was through reading these she came to admire him "as a complete philosopher."[19] Ikeda's stature as a philosopher and teacher in Bahia is high. Though few revere him as a prophet or savior with supernatural powers, he is widely regarded as a great and wise man. One senior member of BSGI in Salvador placed him alongside President Mandela and former President Gorbachev as one of the three most important personalities of the twentieth century.[20]

By the beginning of 1999 there were 823 BSGI families in Salvador itself and 8,000 in the northeast of Brazil as a whole. This growth has been achieved without salaried staff and without any full-time administrators. All events, including ceremonies, study group (*zadankai*) sessions, seminars on Buddhism, and youth activities are organized by volunteers. The entirely voluntary character of the enterprise generates an atmosphere of authenticity in the main center (*kankai*), which is situated in the district of Tororo, close to the center of Salvador. Participants seem not only to hold genuinely to their beliefs but to be tightly held by them. Those who attend the ceremonies are not comfortably off. Few have cars and many will have taken up to half an hour or more to walk to the center. The director, who displays a clear grasp of Nichiren Buddhist principles and is obviously widely read in general philosophy and psychology, came from a poor family background in the interior (sertão) of Bahia, where there was no opportunity to attend school. This he did after marrying and moving to the city of Salvador in 1966. Makiguchi's stress on education was of great importance in attracting him to the movement.

Although not affluent, members are generally not from the most materially deprived sections of society. Like Brazil's evangelical Protestants, BSGI members dress modestly and neatly. In other respects, however, they are unlike Protestants. They are less judgmental about matters relating to private morality, going to the beach, smoking, drinking alcohol, dancing, and participating in profane festivals such as Carnival. In this respect they resemble Catholics rather than evangelical Protestants. Nevertheless, BSGI in Bahia is not seen as an easy option; members confess to being challenged by the movement to realize their own potential. During a certificate-awarding ceremony on December 2, 1998, mothers with children who had completed courses on Buddhism expressed great satisfaction and pride in their achievement—in which the 120 others present shared—when presented with their diplomas, the first public affirmation of their abilities they had ever received.

What is most noticeable in Bahia and further distinguishes this branch from BSGI in São Paulo is the repeated emphasis in interviews, seminars, and sermons on the social dimension of Nichiren Buddhism. In this it echoes liberation theology discourse, though the philosophical paradigms of analysis in the two cases differ greatly. Rather than emphasizing the inner transformations or the material rewards that have been achieved through chanting, BSGI members in Salvador are much more likely to point to the social improvements that have been made in a particular community where chanting has been introduced. Tenement blocks and even whole neighborhoods, once known as socially unfriendly and dangerous, are said to have seen a marked improvement in interpersonal relationships since the practice of chanting began.

To return to the theme of the movement's transformation from ethnic to "universal" religion in Brazil, the success of this process had much to do with the translation of Soka Gakkai's philosophy and teachings into Portuguese. Also crucial was the role of leadership both at the center and on the spot. Where the center has been flexible and has allowed for local initiatives there has usually been rapid progress in Brazil. This has been the experience of both House of Growth (Seicho no Ie) and Church of World Messianity (Sekai Kyusei Kyo) in Brazil and is increasingly a feature of the BSGI leadership (Clarke 2000b).[21] BSGI membership in Brazil is estimated at 150,000, more than 80 percent of whom are of non-Japanese origin. Most are residents of the city and/or state of São Paulo.

From a global perspective, BSGI is not only the largest branch of SGI in Latin America, but anywhere in the world outside Japan. Greater success might have been expected in the more secular and pluralist contexts of western Europe and North America than in Brazil, which, despite what has already been referred to as the explosion of Protestantism there since the 1960s,[22] remains a predominantly Catholic country. There are no obvious reasons, therefore, why BSGI should continue to make steady progress in contemporary Brazil, where a highly charged, dynamic, renewed Catholicism is reaching out to millions in many different religious traditions and particularly to those in the neo-Pentecostalist churches, with which it is in strong competition.[23]

CONTINUITY AND CHANGE

Among the reasons for entertaining substantial doubts concerning Soka Gakkai's prospects, particularly in the less cosmopolitan centers of the north and northeast of Brazil, is the apparent discontinuity between its own teachings and practices and the religious culture of Brazil. This, following Stark,[24] should constitute a major obstacle to the success of religion in a foreign environment, although ever-increasing cultural globalization is likely to render this proposition less meaningful. If the 1954 canon and even the revised 1969 version are taken as guides, the ideological and liturgical divide between BSGI and Catholicism is great. As we have seen, the canon is explicit in stating that there is no place for belief in a personal God and in the resurrection of Jesus, or for the veneration of Mary, the mother of Jesus, pilgrimages to whose many shrines and belief in whose countless miracles have become integral elements of Brazilian religious culture.

Ikeda was clearly aware when he launched the Brazilian district of Soka Gakkai that the theological and cultural distance between Nichiren Buddhism and Latin-based Catholic Christianity was a potential obstacle to his movement's development in their country. He likened his pioneering journey to Brazil in October 1960 to that of the first Catholic missionaries to Japan in the sixteenth century: it was a voyage into unknown territory, without any knowledge of the culture, customs, and language of the people he was seeking to convert.[25] Brazil, Ikeda insisted, was to play the lead role in the movement's global strategy. It had been entrusted, he announced, with the mission of proclaiming Nichiren Buddhism not only throughout Latin America but throughout the world.[26]

Ikeda's concerns and his global ambitions notwithstanding, there is abundant evidence that the Canon of Shakabuku greatly influenced BSGI thinking on and attitudes toward other Buddhist groups and toward Catholicism in Brazil until well into the 1970s. From then until the early 1990s, BSGI seems to have simultaneously pursued a mixed strategy of *shakabuku*, or aggressive evangelism, which sought the "crushing" of other religions, and *shoju*, or coexistence, which was the approach counseled by President Ikeda in 1964 for all countries outside Japan. With regard to African-Brazilian religions and Spiritualism, the strategy was outright *shakabuku* until the mid- to late 1990s. This aggressive missionizing notwithstanding, BSGI adopted from the outset what might be termed a "politically correct" attitude to Catholicism in public, acknowledging that it constituted an integral part of Brazilian religious and cultural life.

This politically correct approach is evident in BSGI's weekly journal *Brasil Seikyo*, which carried articles on how Soka Gakkai's members should relate to Catholicism, one of which, written by Mr. Saito, the then executive director of the movement in Brazil, is worth commenting on at some length. With the title "Let Us Be Useful to Brazil" (*Sejamos úteis ao Brasil*), the article emphasized that Nichiren Buddhism was the only legitimate and authentic form of Buddhism and the religion that would save humanity, for it was the "most correct and marvelous of all religions" (*a mais correta e maravilhosa religião entre as demais*).[27] This truth, the article continued, was to be believed and spread with conviction and energy, but without belittling other religions. Moreover, followers were informed that *hobobarai* (essentially, the duty of converts to destroy all other objects of worship in their homes) was not to be practiced in Brazil for the time being. This meant that those who possessed them were dispensed from the duty to remove non-Nichiren images and icons from their person or homes; nor was this to be demanded of new converts. Such objects could be kept, members were advised, until such time as through the practice of Nichiren Buddhism they acquired their own copy of the object of worship, the sacred scroll or *Gohonzon* inscribed by the monk and founder of Nichiren Buddhism, Nichiren Daishonin (1222–1282).[28]

BSGI placed other limits on exclusivity, granting members the freedom to associate with Catholics and even to participate in certain of their ceremonies. Thus, if asked by a parent or a friend to attend a baptism or one of the other rites of passage in a Catholic church, members should do so without any fear, for "it would be worse for us to belittle them by not going."[29] This sensitivity to Catholic feeling and culture was motivated by more than pragmatism. It was also based on the firm belief and confidence in the unique power and efficacy of BSGI's own practice to protect its members from any dangerous influences that contact with

Catholicism, or any other religion, might bring with it and, at the same time, on the notion of a clear separation between the religious and other spheres of life.

Such an outlook allowed for considerable interaction in various spheres of life with Catholics, including the important sphere of education. Members were advised not to worry about their children's attendance of Catholic schools, "because this has nothing to do with religion," and, even if difficulties over faith were to arise, the pupils would be protected by the invincible power of the *gohonzon*, or object of worship.[30]

These concessions to religious, social, and educational mixing notwithstanding, at no time were theological boundaries blurred. In the following year another article in *Brasil Seikyo* spelled out the criteria according to which the authenticity of other religions should be assessed.[31] There were three tests of authenticity, readers were informed: one was the proof from literature, a second was the theoretical proof, and the third proof was derived from experience. The first—the proof from literature—was to be found in the writings (*gosho*) of Nichiren Daishonin, which were described as impeccably logical, rational, scientific, and relevant to the modern world. The second was a logical consequence of the first, in that Nichiren Daishonin's teachings provided both a totally comprehensive and appropriate philosophy for the modern world compared with Christianity, which, because it was based on miracles, was irrelevant to contemporary life. The proof from experience (*prova real*) derived, it was explained, from the principle that belief can either benefit or harm the believer. Nichiren Buddhism's greatest benefit, it was claimed, was the attainment of complete happiness through practice in this life. Readers were not to concern themselves with a detailed investigation and analysis of the scriptures to confirm all of this, for the most intricate details of true Buddhism, they were informed, were incorporated in the *gohonzon*, just as the "principles of electricity were incorporated in the various appliances."[32]

In the 1960s, 1970s, and 1980s, BSGI put a great deal of effort into demonstrating the compatibility between modern scientific thought and Buddhism. *Brasil Seikyo* carried article after article on Buddhism and contemporary science, including features illustrating the complete harmony between the former and the theory of relativity.[33] Another article elaborated on the theory of evolution to demonstrate the agreement between the Buddhist understanding of the origins of human life and that of modern science in this area as well, and how Christian theology was incapable of grappling with this "supremely important issue raised by biology."[34]

BSGI's approach not only to Catholicism but also to other religions, including the increasingly popular African-Brazilian religion and Spiritism, had begun to undergo a profound change by the early 1990s, so much so that by the middle years of that decade its views on and attitude toward other religions were almost unrecognizable when compared with those that prevailed in the 1960s. By the middle of the 1990s the movement had effected a significant shift in strategy during a period of some thirty-five years from *shakabuku*, the "crushing" or tearing apart of other religions, to *shakabuku-shoju*, "crushing" tempered by coexistence, to qualified engagement with the beliefs and philosophy of other religions and the acceptance of the principle of multiple membership. Thus, this once doctrinally exclusive movement had become inclusive to the extent that it had not only begun to tolerate but also to accept in principle religious diversity within its own ranks and multiple memberships. New recruits were no longer required to reject their previous religion. As Rocha has shown in her study of Zen in Brazil (Chap. 6), a similar attitude to denominational boundaries is also present in that movement. "Formerly," it was explained by the present BSGI leadership, "there was a lot of this but now it is over. Attending Church or Umbanda or a Spiritualist session is a decision for the individual."[35] The leadership had come to accept that those interested in joining Soka Gakkai would decide for themselves what to believe, for "everyone has enough intelligence to know what is best for them."[36] This outlook allows BSGI to compete on more favorable terms with other Japanese new religions in Brazil, and in particular with House of Growth (*Seicho no Ie*) and the Church of World Messianity (*Sekai Kyusei Kyo*), both of which have much larger memberships.[37]

The more inclusive approach of BSGI is not simply pragmatism on the part of a minority movement in a dominant religious culture characterized by tolerance and openness or in a world of keen competition with other alternative religions, spiritualities, and philosophies, including Japanese new religions. It is also an expression of BSGI's desire to proclaim its newfound identity as a universal humanist philosophy, an identity that obliges it to demonstrate to its ethnically varied membership and to potential members from a variety of other faiths that it not only has the capacity to engage in dialogue with them but also to offer them something new, an approach once regarded as distinctive of other Japanese new religions in Brazil, and in particular of *Seicho no Ie* (House of Growth).

Many of the young who are joining BSGI while at university are attracted by its ecological and human rights programs, which have moved to center stage, creating an image of the movement in Brazil as a radical, humanist philosophy derived from Buddhism rather than a religion per se. Members themselves stress that BSGI is more than a religion or, as one adept from Rio de Janeiro commented: "It is not a religion for the sake of being a religion" (*"Não é religião por ser religião"*). For members, the ultimate test of whether BSGI is a religion or not is the impact it makes on individuals and society; if it fails to change people and their environment, then it is not, informants stress, a religion.

CONCLUSIONS

Although its goal is world transformation, BSGI is no longer preoccupied with converting everyone. To shape the thinking and attitude of a substantial minority of the inhabitants of Brazil is its goal, not the conversion of all. The outlook and behavior of such a minority, it is believed, will have a profound and lasting impact on the rest of the population. Meanwhile, given its new, more inclusive attitude to other religions, all those for whom belief in God, Jesus, Mary, and the miraculous is important can continue on in that vein, even inside BSGI. The movement's tendency to be tolerant of diversity in matters of belief and belonging will not diminish the crucial importance it attaches to the power of its faith in the Lotus Scripture and its mantra, described by former president Toda Josei as a never-failing machine that produces happiness.[38]

SGI's global ambitions and the success achieved by BSGI in becoming a multiethnic movement made up of members from diverse religious backgrounds have resulted in the adoption of a strategy of reflexive syncretism, a strategy also used by Zen in Brazil (see Rocha, Chap. 6) and in certain Theravadin Buddhist contexts in Sri Lanka (see Kemper, Chap. 1). The most striking outcome in the case of BSGI has been the abandonment of a previously widely espoused ideology of exclusion based on the evaluation and assessment of beliefs according to the movement's own criteria regarding what constitutes the inner or outer way of religion, or the real and provisional path of Buddhism. This chapter has attempted to chart the course that led to the abandonment of this culture of exclusion in favor of one of inclusion, in which the beliefs held by others are no longer evaluated and assessed using the criteria found in the Canon of Shakabuku and accordingly relegated to the category of outer paths, or lower-grade religions. A more likely outcome is the suggestion that, providing the belief in self-responsibility is not endangered, a mutually beneficial discussion can be had on the similarities between, for example, the belief in God as Creator, a notion rejected in the canon, and the power of "Nam-myoho-Rengekyo."

The developments discussed here may appear to be pragmatic responses designed to facilitate expansion on the part of Soka Gakkai. Indeed, all ecumenical dialog may be construed in this way and labeled euphemistically in academic circles as reflexive syncretism. It is my view, however, that this local micropursuit of a shared understanding of the Absolute reflects—fundamentalist reactions notwithstanding—what is also occurring much more widely and even at the macro or global level. It mirrors what many new forms of religion or spirituality, whatever their leadership may intend, are searching for, perhaps unconsciously, and that is to be independent of the confines of traditionally imposed definitions and ways of approaching the sacred—insisted upon by missionaries in the past who often had the protection, if not the support, of a particular colonial power—in a manner not dissimilar to the search for a consciousness beyond the nation-state, beyond land or territory.

Notes

1. Jacob H. Kamstra, "Changes in Buddhist Attitudes towards Other Religions: The Case of the Soka Gakkai," in *Zeitschrift für Missionwissenschaft und Religionswissenschaft* (Münster: Verlag Ascendorff, 1989), 56.

2. I prefer to describe Soka Gakkai as a world-transforming movement rather than use the term "world-affirming movement," suggested by Roy Wallis in *The Elementary Forms of the New Religious Life* (London: Routledge and Kegan Paul, 1984).

3. Kamstra suggests that the distinction among Nichiren groups was based on the division of the Lotus Scripture (*Hoke-kyo*) into two sections of fourteen chapters. The first is the footprint gate (*shakumon*) and the lesser of the two, for in it the Buddha did not reveal his eternal nature; and the second, to which only Nichiren sects belong, is known as the main gate (*hammon*), in which that nature was revealed. Further, the claim was made that the Nichiren sects became the only authentic ones by following Nichiren Daishonin's instructions and adding the mantra "*Nam-myoho-Rengekyo*" to the second section of the Lotus Scripture. As for Soka Gakkai's position of preeminence among Nichiren groups, this is based on its claim that its teachings alone correspond fully with those of Nichiren. Kamstra, "Changes in Buddhist Attitudes," 34.

4. Ibid., 28–61.

5. To avoid any misunderstanding that might lead people to believe that the full content of the Canon of Shakabuku is a Soka Gakkai creation, it is important to note that it is actually an explanation, with certain reformulations and additions, of the *Kyohan* (see n. 7 below) of the Nichiren Shoshu School.

6. Peter B. Clarke, "Buddhist Humanism and Catholic Culture in Brazil," in *Global Citizens: The Soka Gakkai Buddhist Movement in the World*, ed. David Machacek and Bryan Wilson (Oxford: Oxford University Press, 2000), 326–348.

7. *Kyohan* is a critical classification and evaluation of the doctrines of the Buddhist and non-Buddhist religious groups of East Asia.

8. Kamstra, "Changes in Buddhist Attitudes," 28–61.

9. Ibid.

10. Kiyoaki Murata, *Japan's New Buddhism: An Objective Account of Soka Gakkai* (New York and Tokyo: Weatherhill, 1971), 89.

11. See note 3 above.

12. Peter B. Clarke, "Japanese New Religions in Brazil: From Ethnic to Universal Religions," in *New Religious Movements: Challenge and Response,* ed. Bryan R Wilson and Jamie Cresswell (London: Routledge, 1999), 197–209.

13. Teijiro Suzuki, *The Japanese Immigrant in Brazil,* vol. 2 (Tokyo: Tokyo University Press, 1969), 14.

14. Ibid.

15. Hiroshi Saito, *O Japonês no Brasil* (São Paulo: Editora Sociológica e Política, 1961); and Tomoo Handa, *Memórias de Um Immigrante Japonês no Brasil* (São Paulo: Editora T. A. Queiroz/Centro de Estudos Nipo-Brasileiros, 1980).

16. Takashi Maeyama, "Japanese Religions in Southern Brazil: Change and Syncretism," *Latin American Studies* 6 (1983): 181–238.

17. Interview, São Paulo, December 1997.

18. Interview, Aruja, August 1994.

19. Interview, Salvador, Bahia, December 1998.

20. Interview, Salvador, Bahia, December 1998.

21. Peter Clarke, "Success and Failure: Japanese New Religions Abroad," in *Japanese New Religions in Global Perspective,* ed. Peter B. Clarke (London: Curzon, 2000), 272–311.

22. David Martin, *Tongues of Fire* (Oxford: Blackwell, 1990).

23. Clarke, "Success and Failure."

24. Rodney Stark, "Why Religious Movements Succeed or Fail: A Revised General Model," *Journal of Contemporary Religion* 11, no. 2 (May 1996): 133–147.

25. Daisaku Ikeda, *Nova Revolução Humana* (São Paulo: Editora Brasil Seikyo, 1994), 181.

26. Ibid., 191.

27. *Brasil Seikyo,* April 15, 1966, 3.

28. *Gohonzon* is the sacred scroll inscribed by Nichiren Daishonin and the object of worship. The *gongyo* ritual, consisting of the chanting of two chapters of the Lotus Scripture, is usually performed twice a day in front of the *gohonzon*.

29. *Brasil Seikyo,* April 15, 1966, 3.

30. Ibid.

31. *Brasil Seikyo,* November 11, 1967, 3.

32. Ibid.

33. *Brasil Seikyo,* March 30, 1968, 3.

34. *Brasil Seikyo.*

35. Interview, Soka Gakkai headquarters, São Paulo, November 1998.

36. Interview, Soka Gakkai headquarters, São Paulo, November 1998.

37. Clarke, "Success and Failure."

38. Murata, *Japan's New Buddhism,* 107.

6

Being a Zen Buddhist Brazilian: Juggling Multiple Religious Identities in the Land of Catholicism

Cristina Rocha

BUSSHINJI TEMPLE, MARCH 2000

The room is teeming with excitement. Folding chairs are arranged in rows. Japanese men wearing suits and ties are sitting in the front rows and Japanese women are at the back, as is appropriate in Japanese culture, where men take precedence. In the middle rows, there are many T-shirted non-Japanese Brazilians, men and women mixed, as befits their culture. This is the forty-seventh General Assembly of the Sōtō Zen Buddhist Community of South America (Comunidade Budista Sōtō Zenshū da América do Sul), and, as usual, it is taking place in the basement of Busshinji (Buddha Heart-Mind Temple) in São Paulo city. There are about 115 people present, most of them non-Japanese Brazilians and Japanese descendents; very few are part of the old, first-generation Japanese community.

Tension is in the air because this morning elections are taking place. Two congregations are vying to run Busshinji's administration—one composed of the old, traditional, Japanese board, the other composed of their descendents who align with the non-Japanese Brazilians. To aggravate matters, after a five-year hiatus, a new *sōkan* has just arrived from Japan.[1] In the interim, this position was filled by the missionary in charge of Busshinji, a non-Japanese Brazilian woman, Coen Souza, who trained under the Zen master (*rōshi*) Maezumi at the Zen Center of Los Angeles (ZCLA) for three years and then in Japan for a further twelve years.[2] Although Coen is a non-Japanese Brazilian nun, she had slowly gained acceptance among the Japanese community because she worked hard to preserve the rituals the Japanese community expects to be performed. Speaking both Japanese and Portuguese fluently, she was a successful intermediary between the Japanese and Brazilian communities. Paradoxically, her success was also the source of tension. From 1995 (the year she was appointed) until 2000 (the year she lost her position in the temple), Coen increasingly attracted Brazilians of non-Japanese ancestry and began to conduct most of the temple's activities in Portuguese. On that very morning, she had reluctantly consented to run for the presidency of the Japanese descendents' faction. Because of the growth in the number of non-Japanese Brazilian adherents under Coen's missionary work, this congregation had succeeded in gaining control of the temple in 1998, when both groups disputed elections for the first time. Now, with the presence of an "authentic" Japanese missionary (the *sōkan*) to oversee the elections, would the coalition of non-Japanese Brazilian and young Japanese descendents still prevail?

The new *sōkan* starts his speech, and his tone is conciliatory: "In the past five years, when there was no *sōkan* in Latin America, the number of adherents of the Sōtō Zenshū increased, thanks to teacher (sensei) Coen's work. There are many Zen groups in the U.S.A., France, and Spain, and they speak many languages other than Japanese. Therefore, it is only natural that conflicts arise. But these conflicts are not necessarily negative. Let's think of conflicts as an opportunity for growth. . . ."

Yet the general mood is not one of appeasement and the old disputes for power are pervasive. Halfway through the assembly, following a series of speeches by former members of the 1998–2000 administration, a Japanese man suddenly stands up and bursts into Japanese. He is obviously upset. Many non-Japanese Brazilians call out angrily that he should be speaking Portuguese, but he resists. One Japanese descendent aligned with the non-Japanese Brazilian side shouts that they are in Brazil and should therefore speak Portuguese. Commotion takes over the room, only to be settled after some time, when a translator offers his services. It turns out that the Japanese was a member of the administration prior to 1998. He wanted to speak directly to the *sōkan* and to the fellow Japanese present so that his words would not be misinterpreted. His speech is cut short, and he goes back to his seat. The assembly proceeds with only minor incidents, and in the end a new board comprised of the Japanese descendents (aligned with the non-Japanese Brazilians) is elected. The morning is coming to a close, and everyone stands up to prepare the room for the big lunch that is ahead. *Feijoada* (a typical Brazilian dish purportedly originating from the food of slaves and consisting of black beans, meat, rice, oranges, and vegetables) is served alongside sushi and Japanese green tea. Forks, knives, and chopsticks rest on the table—an appropriate set of utensils for the ever-present contentions that Japanese, Japanese-Brazilians, and non-Japanese Brazilians undergo at Busshinji.

In this chapter, I will shed light on how these two distinct congregations have laid claim to Busshinji temple in São Paulo city. I shall argue that the conflicts over the "authenticity" of Zen stem from the different modes of religious practice. On the one hand, for the first-generation Japanese, religious identity is expressive of their ethnic identity; on the other hand, non-Japanese Brazilians use Zen Buddhism as a marker of social distinction.[3] After presenting an overview of the arrival of Zen in Brazil, identifying its demographics and adherents, I will proceed to map the Brazilian religious landscape in order to show how established religions in Brazil have creolized Zen Buddhism. I contend that converts use a Brazilian religious "grammar" as a matrix for new Buddhist "vocabulary," and that the process has facilitated the spread of Buddhism in the country.

AUTHENTICITY OR INNOVATION?

An occasion such as an election is a very telling situation. It is a time when sides are clearly taken and decisions are made about who will hold power and for what purpose. Moreover, such an event works as a metaphor for what is really at stake—in this case, ethnic resistance against the surrounding society and the religious identity of both groups. For many Japanese (issei) and some second-generation Japanese-Brazilians (nisei), it is evident that theirs is the "authentic" Zen, since they were the ones who brought Zen Buddhism to Brazil. For them, "true" Zen is comprised of "masses" (as the members call the rituals, appropriating the Catholic word), namely, funerals and rites for the worship of ancestors. Ethnic boundaries are more clearly marked in situations where an individual or group is faced with the "other." For diasporic communities surrounded by a diverse population, these boundaries have to be constructed, policed, and reinforced, so that the ethnic identity of the community may be preserved.[4] Religion can provide a strong bond with the past and the homeland. The competition for authenticity described in the above narrative shows that, by preserving some Japanese cultural traits (among them language and religion), the Japanese-Brazilian immigrant community sought to maintain its ethnic identity as distinct from other Brazilians.[5]

On the other side of this dispute for authenticity are the non-Japanese Brazilians and some Japanese-Brazilians. For them, Zen Buddhism relies mainly on meditation (zazen) as a way of experiencing enlightenment. Invoking the Buddha Shakyamuni's meditation practice and subsequent enlightenment, as well as Dōgen's assertion that Zen is basically about meditation, they regard devotional practices and worship of ancestors as not authentic Zen Buddhism.[6] This kind of conflict between motivations, practice, and aspirations has occurred in other Buddhist centers in the West.[7]

THE ARRIVAL OF BUDDHISM IN BRAZIL

Buddhism was introduced into Brazil by Japanese immigrants who first arrived in 1908 at the port of Santos, in the state of São Paulo.[8] These immigrants worked mainly in coffee plantations and had hoped to return to Japan as soon as they accumulated enough savings. The maintenance of their culture, language, religion, and beliefs was considered crucial. However, with the Japanese defeat in World War II, the immigrants had to give up their dream of returning to their home country, prompting them to request missionaries from Japan to preach in their new homeland. Until then, apart from a few independent missionaries, there were no Japanese religious organizations in Brazil that would officiate at the death of an immigrant.[9]

Zengenji, the first Sōtō Zen Buddhist temple in Brazil, was built in the early 1950s in Moji das Cruzes, a town in the outskirts of São Paulo City. In 1955, Busshinji was established in São Paulo City as the headquarters of the Sōtō Zen School in South America. These two temples, along with a temple in Rolāndia, in the state of Paraná, have catered for three hundred Japanese-Brazilian families over the past four decades.

Buddhism was also introduced to Brazil by non-Japanese Brazilian intellectuals who imported European literature on Buddhism at the beginning of the twentieth century. The Buddhist Society of Brazil (Sociedade Budista do Brasil) was founded in 1923 by Theosophists in Rio de Janeiro but was soon dissolved. In 1955, Murillo Nunes de Azevedo reestablished it. Azevedo was deeply influenced by the ideas of the Theosophical Society, where he had acted as president of the Brazilian chapter for nine years.[10] As professor at the Pontifical Catholic University in Rio de Janeiro, Azevedo taught philosophy of the Far East and organized a collection of translations called *Luz da Ásia* (Light of Asia) for Civilização Brasileira, a well-known publishing house in Brazil. In this collection, he published twenty books dedicated to Eastern philosophies. Among them was D. T. Suzuki's *Introduction to Zen Buddhism*, which Azevedo had translated into Portuguese in 1961. This book was fundamental to the spread of Zen Buddhist ideas in Brazil and was frequently cited in the interviews that I conducted among Zen practitioners in the late 1990s in Brazil.

Azevedo and other intellectuals followed a similar path. Their initial encounter with Buddhism and Zen was through imported literature (European and North American), which then led them to seek a place to practice; they found it in Busshinji in São Paulo. In order to cater to the demands of Brazilians of non-Japanese origin, in 1961 Ryōhan Shingū, the *sōkan* in charge at the time, created a Zen meditation group (*zazenkai*) that met every Saturday. His interpreter was Ricardo Gonçalves, a history professor from the prestigious University of São Paulo. In making Zen accessible to Brazilians, Gonçalves helped to break down the language barrier that had been the main obstacle to the proselytization of Buddhism in Brazil.[11] Until very recently, when Brazilians of non-Japanese descent sought association with other Japanese Buddhist schools, they were redirected to Busshinji, because "they speak Portuguese there, and it is the place for non-Japanese Brazilians," as some non-Japanese adherents told me. The diminishing numbers of Japanese-Brazilian members (a similar phenomenon pointed out by Tanabe, Chap. 3), along with the growth in Buddhism in the past decade, have prompted many Japanese Buddhist schools to make room for non-Japanese Brazilians. Indeed, a Jōdo Shinshū temple in Brasília has introduced meditation sessions in order to attract this new clientele.[12]

BUDDHISM IN NUMBERS

Since 1976, as many as twenty-six Zen centers have been established for and by non-Japanese Brazilians in Brazil. Unlike Busshinji, they do not have Japanese immigrant adherents and so their practice is based on meditation. Statistics available on religion from the 2000 census show that, at that time, the Brazilian population of 170 million people was comprised of 74 percent Roman Catholics (125 million), 15.5 percent Evangelicals (26 million, including traditional Evangelicals and Pentecostals), 7.3 percent of no religion (12.3 million), 1.4 percent Spiritists (2.3 million), 0.14 percent Buddhists (245,000), 0.06 percent Jews (101,000), 0.04 percent esoteric religions (67,200), 0.03 percent Afro-Brazilian religions (51,000), 0.01 percent Muslims (18,500), and, finally, 0.06 percent indigenous religions (10,700).[13] It is worth comparing these figures with those of the 1991 census. While those who identified as Catholics decreased by 10 percent since 1991 (83.8 percent in 1991), there was an increase in other categories: evangelicalism (9.1 percent in 1991), no religion (4.8 percent in 1991), and Spiritists (1.2 percent in 1991).

As the statistics show, the great majority of Brazilians still come from Catholic families. What these figures do not show is the movement from one religion to another, multiple religious affiliations, as well as the combination of elements of different traditions, which is commonplace in Brazil. Many Brazilians either practice more than one religion at the same time or convert from one religion to another. Indeed, according to the Brazilian sociologist Reginaldo Prandi, one-quarter of the Brazilian adult population has converted to a religion different from the one they were born into.[14]

A survey I conducted among Zen practitioners in the cities of São Paulo, Rio de Janeiro, Ouro Preto, and Porto Alegre in 1998 and 1999 corroborates this fact. Out of a total of eighty respondents, the majority (sixty-six) came from Catholic families. The remaining fourteen respondents were equally distributed among

Jewish, Spiritist, Evangelical, Protestant, the Church of World Messianity (Sekkai Kyūsei Kyō, a Japanese New Religious Movement [NRM]), and nonreligious backgrounds.

Of the eighty respondents practicing Zen Buddhism, twenty had moved from the religion of their upbringing to other religions before adopting Zen Buddhism. Many (nine) had been affiliated with Spiritism, but the majority also combined the religion of their upbringing with other religions, such as Protestantism, Theosophy, Rosicrucianism, the Church of World Messianity, Daoism, Nichiren Buddhism, Tibetan Buddhism, and nonreligious backgrounds. Eleven of these twenty "migrants" still practiced other religions while regularly practicing Zen meditation at their Zen center or temple.

Finally, when asked if they considered themselves to be Buddhists, thirty-eight respondents said "yes," while eleven answered "not yet," "sort of," or "almost." This is a hard question for Brazilians, as they consider Zen Buddhism and Buddhism in general mostly as a philosophy rather than a religion (see Clarke, Chap. 5). One respondent gave a very revealing response: "If one who practices zazen is considered Buddhist, then I am a Buddhist." The "not yet" Buddhists could be classified as "sympathizers," a term Thomas Tweed has used for "those who have some sympathy for a religion but do not embrace it exclusively or fully. When asked, they would not identify themselves as Buddhists. They would say they are Methodists, or Jewish, or unaffiliated."[15]

WHO ARE THESE COSMOPOLITAN ZEN BUDDHIST BRAZILIANS?

The interviews I conducted with non-Japanese Brazilian practitioners showed that their interest in Zen Buddhism was mediated by the United States, through the media, books on Zen,[16] movies,[17] and travel. The word "Zen" is fashionable in the West: one sees Zen perfume, shops, beauty parlors, restaurants, magazine articles, and architecture. In Brazil it is a common occurrence to call someone "Zen," meaning very peaceful, collected, and tranquil. The word "Zen" usually appears in the title of newspaper and magazine articles that report on a range of alternative religions and practices, such as other Buddhist schools, yoga, Tai Chi Tchuan, and meditation. Furthermore, Zen has a positive image in the country; it is associated with refinement, minimalism, nontension, nonanxiety, exquisite beauty, and exoticism. Indeed, the word "Zen" appears almost daily in the trendy social column of *Folha de São Paulo*, one of the leading newspapers in Brazil.

Moreover, all of the people interviewed described their first contact with Zen as being through books. The United States is an ample source of ideas on Zen for various reasons. First, English is more accessible to Brazilians than Japanese. Indeed, most of the books on Zen available in Portuguese had first been translated into English. Moreover, because these practitioners come from the intellectual upper-middle class and are educated liberal professionals, many of them are able to read the books in English before they are translated. Some buy books on Zen via the Internet and/or subscribe to American Buddhist magazines, such as *Tricycle*. This is a very different constituency from that of Sōka Gakkai, which appeals to lower-middle classes (Chap. 5).

In the late 1990s, web sites of Buddhist texts translated from English into Portuguese by Brazilian Buddhists began to appear. The two visits by His Holiness the Dalai Lama to Brazil (1992 and 1999) were highly publicized in the media, and translations into Portuguese of his talks are on web sites as well. His books have been translated into Portuguese, and *The Art of Happiness: A Handbook of Living* (1999) was number one on a best-sellers' list for many months after it was published in June 2000. This book alone had sold 185,000 copies by July 2001 and became the publishing company's best seller since its establishment in 1975.[18] In August 2000, a long article in the leading newspaper *Journal do Brasil* titled "The Soft and Sweet Eastern Invasion: The Interest in Eastern Philosophy Increases and Opens a Series of New Book Releases Heralded by new Dalai Lama's Book," commented on the boom of books on Eastern philosophy, particularly Buddhism, due to the demand of readers. In addition, it reported on the growing interest in Buddhist psychology among Rio de Janeiro and São Paulo's psychoanalysts, which was also boosted by this year's release of Mark Epstein's book *Going to Pieces without Falling Apart: A Buddhist Perspective on Wholeness* (New York: Broadway Books, 1998).

The increasing number of web pages and e-mail discussion lists about Buddhism on the Internet is noteworthy.[19] It is impossible to report the current number of web pages, for new ones appear very quickly. However, e-mail discussion lists are more stable. There are five lists in Brazil, three of them dedicated to three different Buddhist schools (Theravada, Zen, and Tibetan), a general one on Buddhism, and one for discussion of scriptures and translations. An average of ten to twenty messages are posted daily on each list, and the topics discussed include vegetarianism, Catholicism and Buddhism, new books on Buddhism, interfaith dialog, reincarnation or rebirth, neophytes' doubts on behavior and doctrine, koans, announcements of retreats in Brazil and abroad, translations of scriptures and poems, and biographies of important Buddhist masters.

It is a significant fact that whereas Evangelical, Pentecostal, neo-Pentecostal, and Catholic (particularly the Charismatic) churches proselytize to Brazilian disenfranchised classes through radio and television,[20] the urban upper-middle-class and intellectual elite who are interested in Buddhism interact through a highly literate medium,[21] the Internet, forming a "cybersangha."[22] In contrast to radio and television, where there is the authority figure of the priest and no direct contact among the viewers, the cybersangha is more participatory, allowing recipients to interact and communicate with each other by posting messages. Doubts on the teachings, appropriate behavior, the differences among Buddhist schools, the history of Buddhism, and so on are answered, not by authorities on Buddhism certified by a Buddhist institution, but by the sangha itself. Moreover, anyone can construct a web site and furnish it by translating anything—from scriptures, Buddhist poems, and koans, to stories of great masters—all according to one's own personal interpretation and understanding. This is increasingly common in Brazilian cyberspace. These cybersangha features are consonant with trends of religious modernity such as an emphasis on individual quest, privatization of religion, shunning authority, and relying on experience rather than faith.[23] These are precisely the values prized by my informants when asked about the reasons for their choice of Zen Buddhism. Thus while Japanese and non-Japanese Brazilian Buddhist monks and nuns have been fundamental to the institutionalization of Buddhism in Brazil, much of the propagation of Buddhist ideas is also the result of these self-appointed speakers on its behalf.

The study of urban elite Brazilian Zen also requires an understanding of the transnational linkages that enable the white urban upper class to forge a sense of connection with their peers overseas. Such a fact creates a feeling of belonging to a subculture group that extends beyond national borders.[24] By going to retreats abroad, translating scriptures, and publishing them independently on the web, Brazilian Buddhists feel that they are part of a much larger world. Moreover, the prestige Buddhism is enjoying in the developed world also confers cultural capital upon the Brazilian urban intellectual elite, who play the role of introducing new ideas and ways of behaving into Brazil. Accordingly, I argue that being Buddhist is a way of belonging to the developed world and detaching oneself from the rest of the "backward" Brazilian population. This is something Brazilians aspire to intensely, especially because they have in the past two decades suffered considerably from the country's economic crisis, endemic corruption, inflation, and rampant crime and violence. According to the Brazilian anthropologist José Jorge Carvalho:

> Some sects have originated more due to a modernizing movement in our
> society than due to religious matters. The identity issue is crucial: to adhere
> to a certain group is to adhere to what is up-to-date, it is to be able to do

certain things which are currently prestigious. [It] is a way of connecting oneself to the meaning producing centers.[25]

In light of the transnational links between the Brazilian urban intellectual elite and their counterparts overseas through books, media, travel, movies, and the Internet, the diffusion of Zen Buddhism in Brazil could be seen as part of a "faculty club culture," a term coined by Peter Berger as one of four processes of cultural globalization. According to Berger: "[The 'faculty club culture'] is the internationalization of the Western intelligentsia, its values, and ideologies carried by foundations, academic networks, and non-governmental organizations.' Similar to 'non-Japanese Zen', the 'faculty culture club' is primarily an elite culture, which spreads its beliefs and values through some of the media of mass communication. Some examples of these values are feminism and environmentalism."[26] Indeed, many of the adherents I interviewed told me that the close relationship between Buddhism and the ecological movement, as opposed to the Catholic way of approaching nature, made them adhere to Buddhism.

Moreover, Peter Berger argues that English is the lingua franca of globalization.[27] As I mentioned before, most of the information on Zen in Brazil is conveyed through Portuguese translations of English material. For instance, when Coen sensei was the head nun of Busshinji, in her weekly lectures she used to translate passages from books in English, written either by Japanese monks while they lived in America or by American scholars. At that time, there was also a scripture study group, where one lay ordained follower translated, printed, and handed out parts of books originally written in English to be studied. In the Zen Center of Porto Alegre, many adherents are learning English to be able to speak to Moriyama rōshi without the need of a translator. Following this trend of globalization of North American Zen, some practitioners even choose to travel to Zen centers in the United States and feel that it is more in tune with their own practice than is Japanese Zen. As a result of such transnational links, developments in North American Zen are very influential in Brazilian Zen. However, the ways in which Brazilians localize Zen differ, as their own religious matrix differs from that of North Americans.

As noted earlier, the vast majority of the people interviewed were Catholics before starting to "shop around" in the religious marketplace and eventually finding Zen Buddhism. Adherents who left Catholicism and are studying Zen Buddhism explain their disenchantment with the former as based on its dogmatism, its separation from daily life, its hierarchical organization, its attitude toward nature, and its almighty God. Looking for an alternative, Catholic adherents seek their symbolic universe via something that they can construct by themselves in daily life. They are attracted to the freedom of the individual to interpret the scriptures and the possibility of practicing mindfulness in daily life, outside the temple. Notably, these are the same themes invoked by Buddhist and New Age practitioners in the United States and United Kingdom.[28]

Likewise, Zen Buddhism for Brazilians accepts pluralism and diversity. This approach to religious practice is justified through the Zen Buddhist idea of non-attachment. The famous Zen saying: "If you meet the Buddha on the road, kill the Buddha" is interpreted by practitioners as the impossibility of one religion being the permanent answer to their spiritual needs. From this perspective, a practitioner may participate in meditation both in a Tibetan Buddhist center and at a Japanese Zen center. An adherent may even become lay ordained (*ordenado leigo; jukai*)[29] and receive different Buddhist names from different lineages.[30]

Another characteristic of those who seek Zen Buddhism is that they are in search of relief from personal problems. They wish to learn about their "inner-self." Very frequently, people I interviewed said they sought Zen meditation as a way to learn about themselves. Zen meditation worked in place of psychotherapy or in conjunction with it.[31] One can appreciate how meaningful Zen Buddhism is for its adherents when one realizes that many practitioners use their leisure moments, such as weekends and holidays, to go to meditation sessions and retreats (*sesshin*). The consumption of goods is clearly evident in the sales of books, magazines, courses, retreats, seminars, clothes, and utensils for meditation, as if enlightenment (satori) itself could be reached through consumption. Carvalho has noted that

> Samadhi, enlightenment, satori appear now also as a fetish, almost as a
> commercial exhibition, as image of power, as merchandise. The possibility
> of a trance, of a touch of energy, of a hug of divine love is as desired in
> the present social context as the acquisition of a car, of an appliance, of a
> trip to a famous place. The religious advertisement [. . .] has already incor-
> porated, as any other advertisement of consumption society, the mimetic
> desire of ownership.[32]

CREOLIZING ZEN IN THE BRAZILIAN RELIGIOUS FIELD

The term "creolization" originates from the Spanish *criollo* and Portuguese *crioulo*, both derived from the Latin verb *creare* (to breed or to create). Until recently, the concept of a "creole culture" was deeply connected to the encounter of African and European culture in the Caribbean. As a result, the term was extended to en-compass the language spoken by these so-called Creole people. Such languages were the result of the superimposition of the dominant language's lexicon upon the dominated language's own syntax, grammar, and morphology. The resulting new language revealed a twofold predicament: at the same time it demonstrated that colonial peoples had yielded and adopted the dominant language by using its lexicon, it also showed that they had clung to inner forms of their own language as a matrix for this lexicon, a sign of resistance.[33]

Furthermore, contemporary scholars have detached the trope "creolization" from its Caribbean and linguistic roots and applied the term more broadly to pro-cesses of cultural encounter and exchange. Many cultural and postcolonial theo-rists have used "creolization" as a synonym for hybridity.[34] "Hybridity," however, as a metaphor for cultural contact, carries with it the predicament of its origins in bio-logical science, where it was juxtaposed to notions of racial purity.[35] Hybridity also derives from horticulture and animal-breeding practices, which in turn juxtapose it with ideas of sterility and passivity, since hybrid plants and animals do not repro-duce.[36] Notwithstanding contemporary recuperation of hybridity as a subversive practice/agency within postcolonial and cultural theory, it still has to grapple with the dilemma of the discourse of race. Creolization as an analytical trope, on the other hand, although having originated during colonial contact, carries notions of creativity, agency, and innovation on the part of the colonized.[37] Furthermore, the concept of creolization, when inflected by its linguistic facet, highlights *how* the process of continuous contact and negotiation takes place.

Nevertheless, I should mention a caveat before employing the term "creoli-zation" to analyze Brazilian Zen. As previously mentioned, the word "creole" de-rives from the Portuguese *crioulo*, which even today is a derogatory term for Afro-Brazilians in Brazil. Furthermore, the use of this concept may lead some readers to think that the history of Brazilian society is deeply connected with that of the Caribbean. Nothing could be further from the truth. In spite of these drawbacks, I believe that, in the context of an analysis of Zen Buddhism in Brazil, the trope of creolization is meaningful because it sheds light on *how* Japanese Zen has been superimposed on a Brazilian religious syntax upon arrival in the country. Unlike the Jōdo Shinshu temple in Hawai'i, where the membership is dropping due to lack of "hybridization" (see Tanabe, Chap. 3), Busshinji temple thrived in the 1990s due to Zen's popular appeal and Moriyama rōshi's and Coen sensei's flexi-bility in negotiating with Brazilian culture. During this time, even "immigrant" Zen practices such as funeral and ancestor rites became more visible, and some non-Japanese Brazilians have taken part in them. While for Payne Shingon Buddhism's invisibility in the United States derives from Americanization and lack of exoticism (Chap. 4), Busshinji is visible because it has undergone renewal, introducing Japanese architectural features that invoke exoticism while making room for non-Japanese Brazilian practices. The Brazilian media, however, is just as obsessed with "convert" Buddhism as its U.S. counterpart (as pointed out by Payne). Although it is still too early to see the results of such creolization, I would like to explore *how* this process is taking place.

Although Brazil is well known by the epithet "the world's largest Catholic nation," such a description ignores the presence of many other religions and religious practices that have been introduced and creolized in Brazil since the Portuguese arrived in 1500. During the colonial period (1500–1822), Catholicism went through a process of creolization when it encountered Afro-Brazilian traditions and indigenous religions. Popular Catholicism was created from such a convergence, adding indigenous beliefs, rituals, and devotion to saints to the formal Catholicism of the clergy and upper classes.[38]

In the nineteenth century, immigration brought German Lutherans and other traditional Protestants to Brazil. By the beginning of the twentieth century, North American Protestant missionaries were sent to Brazil and started to preach outside of the ethnic enclave. Furthermore, still in the nineteenth century, French Spiritism—which would become one of the main religions in Brazil[39]—was introduced by the Brazilian elite who were quick to adopt the then new French fashion. Spiritism or Kardecism, as it is known in Brazil due to its founder Hyppolyte Rivail's pen name, Allan Kardec (1804–1869), was itself a synthesis of many religious practices such as Catholicism, Protestantism, and occult philosophies that flourished in eighteenth- and nineteenth-century Europe, such as Swedenborgianism, Mesmerism, Rosicrucianism, Freemasonry, and Theosophy.[40] Along with Spiritism, other esoteric traditions arrived at the turn of the century to pave the way for the diffusion of Eastern philosophies in Brazil. *Círculo Esotérico da Comunhão do Pensamento* (Esoteric Association for the Communion of Thought), an association that studied and disseminated Hindu philosophy, was founded in São Paulo in 1908. Later it established a leading publishing company for esoteric and Eastern philosophical books (Editora Pensamento). In addition, the Theosophical Society was established in São Paulo City in 1919, and in Rio de Janeiro in 1923.[41]

In the early twentieth century, Umbanda emerged—a quintessential Brazilian religious creation that deployed elements of the main religious traditions of the country (Catholicism, Kardecism, Afro-Brazilian, and indigenous religions). Umbanda was created by white middle-class Spiritists attracted by the possession rituals of the Afro-Brazilian religions.[42] Since it relies on Kardecist literature, Umbanda also draws ideas from Hinduism and Buddhism (derived from the Theosophical Society), which are reinterpreted to fit the demands of Umbanda's adherents.[43]

The main contributors to the wide acceptance of the concepts of karma and reincarnation in Brazil were Kardecist Spiritism and Umbanda. At the core of Spiritist doctrine is the idea of spiritual evolution through reincarnation. Karma, and its corollary, the law of cause and effect, determine reincarnation: if one's actions in a past life were negative, one reincarnates into a life of suffering (through poverty, disease, unhappiness). By contrast, if one practiced charity in a past life (a concept Kardec drew from Christianity), one reincarnates into a life of happiness. In this context, free will plays a key role, as human beings may choose what path to take in their lives. This means that the evolution of the spirit depends solely on its own efforts.[44]

Through interviews with practitioners, reading newspaper and magazine stories on Zen, and discussions on e-mail lists, I realized that the Zen ideas of karma, rebirth, and the individual's responsibility for his own enlightenment were creolized with Spiritist concepts to bridge the gap between Brazilian culture and Zen Buddhism. However, the apparent similarity of concepts disguises deep differences, particularly in relation to key terms such as "karma" and "reincarnation" or rebirth. However, because the adherents of Spiritism are mainly white upper-middle class, which is also the main segment of society that follows Zen Buddhism, the Spiritist connotation of these concepts is very much part of how Buddhism is understood in Brazil. Here I quote two dialogs of the ubiquitous discussions that take place on the Buddhist e-mail lists on these concepts.[45] The questions exemplify how Brazilians creolize their Christian and Spiritist ideas with the novelty that Buddhism presents. The answers are given by Brazilian Buddhist students who have been studying Buddhism much longer and can therefore clarify such confusion of concepts.

> Q: Can somebody explain this to me? There is no individual soul that survives death, ok, I can believe that, but then what to do with the theory of reincarnation? (*Buddhismo-L*, July 15, 2000)
> A: The Buddhist doctrine is very different from the Kardecist one. It is impossible to reconcile the belief in spirits and Buddhist teachings. According to the *dharma*, body and mind are a unity which is undone at the time of death; hence there isn't an individual being that survives. Life continues in other beings; life is regarded as a process, not as a chain of individuals. These are seen as mere illusions. As such, there

is no reincarnation in Buddhism, but there is rebirth. (*Buddhismo-L,* July 17, 2000)

Q: In Judaism and Christianity there is guilt. Isn't it the same as negative karma? I keep hearing people telling me not to do this or that because of bad karma; this conditioning of bad and good, isn't it the same as in Judaism and Christianity? (*Zen Chung Tao,* November 9, 2000)

A: No, because in Judaism and Christianity one believes there is free will; in Buddhism we think that people act impelled by conditions (cultural, your parents, family, country) as well. Hence, there isn't an individual guilt. Karma is a much larger concept. No karma is completely individual; all actions influence the whole world. Changing karma is like steering a large ship: we need to hold the rudder for a long time until the ship's direction changes. That's why the training is long and hard. (*Zen Chung Tao,* November 10, 2000)

Another meaningful creolization takes place with Umbanda. Since Umbanda is itself an appropriation by Kardecist white Brazilians of Afro-Brazilian religions of possession, the theory of karma and reincarnation as a way of returning to earth to evolve spiritually is an essential part of it. Spirits are seen as needing to assist human beings to develop their own karma so that they too will have a better incarnation in the next life. In order to do that, they descend through mediums to help human beings, who usually seek their services to solve problems of love, work, illness, and legal difficulties.[46] There are seven lines of spirits with which to communicate. One of them is significantly called "Line of the East" or "Esoteric Umbanda."[47] Whereas in other lines mediums are possessed by indigenous, Afro-Brazilian, and African entities, in this line, Eastern entities such as "The Hindu/The Indian," "The Turk," "The Jew," "The Gypsy," "The Chinese," "The Goddess of Fortune" (sometimes interpreted as *Lakshmi*), and "Brahma" descend on mediums. Also associated with these figures is "The Buddha" who, in contrast to the other entities, is not incorporated by mediums but is exclusively associated with bringing in good fortune, happiness, and wealth. However, the images of Buddha that I found in Umbanda centers and in shops that cater for Afro-Brazilian traditions are, in fact, those of Hotei. Although originally regarded in China as the future Buddha (Maitreya), Hotei is known in Japan as one of the Seven Gods of Fortune. In Brazil, Hotei is thought of as the historical Buddha, and one can easily find small images of this fat-bellied, happy-faced Buddha in commercial outlets, coffee shops, and some homes. An informant told me that every Umbanda altar has a Buddha/Hotei, and if these altars are more elaborate, they also bear the Seven

Gods of Fortune. India and the mythic "Orient" have always fascinated Umbanda practitioners. The same informant mentioned that books by Blavatsky and Lobsang Rampa were mandatory reads for Umbanda practitioners in the 1950s and 1960s: "all these authors were a huge success. Everyone wanted to open *chakras*, talked about vibrations and so forth" (personal communication).

These examples illustrate the fact that when the first Zen texts were introduced into the country in the 1960s, Buddhist concepts had long been in the Brazilian *imaginaire*, carried by Spiritists, Umbandists, and a host of Eastern and Occultist traditions that arrived in the country from the nineteenth century onward.

ZEN AND THE NEW AGE BOOM

In the past two decades, so many New Age practices have become conspicuously present in Brazil that David Hess described the Californian New Age reality as bland compared to the Brazilian one.[48] Brazil is experiencing an expansion of alternative spiritualities among urban middle classes and elites.[49] The trend became evident in the late 1980s, when there was a remarkable increase in sales of esoteric books. By the 1990s, there was an extensive network of shops, seminars, therapies, and bookstores that catered to the demands of people who were interested in a vast range of practices and religions, such as New Age spirituality, yoga, and world religions such as Buddhism, Hinduism, and Japanese NRMs. Indeed, Robert Carpenter describes the Brazilian religious marketplace in such terms:

> [Brazil] is the home of the world's largest Catholic population, as well as to more Pentecostals, Spiritists, and adherents of traditions derived from African religions than can be found in any other country in the world. Moreover, there are more followers of the cluster of traditions known as Japanese New Religions in Brazil than in any other country outside Japan. Brazil's religious economy is unquestionably the most diversified in all of Latin America.[50]

New Age religions, such as the Rajneesh movement, are a common source of Zen adherents. The Rajneesh movement, a NRM that began in India in the early 1970s, drew on both Western and Eastern sources to form a synthesis of New Age spirituality. Bhagwan Rajneesh wrote a series of books where he analyzes and interprets Zen teachings. Most of them have been translated into Portuguese. Many adherents interviewed had been or still are his followers. Particularly in Porto Alegre, some adherents had a Buddhist name, which had been given at their lay ordination, and a Rajneesh name. The New Age boom is also responsible for a New Age University (Unipaz), which was established in Brasília, the nation's capital. Zen is taught at Unipaz, and the monastery of Morro da Vargem (in Espírito Santo state) is one of the recommended sites for students to conduct their last semester research.

Paulo Coelho, the Brazilian best-selling author who writes New Age, self-empowering and pilgrimage books, has a weekly column in *Folha de São Paulo*, where he usually writes about popular occultism, mysticism, and Buddhism. He particularly writes on Zen masters and their koans, spreading these tales to mainstream society. Likewise, the *Folha de São Paulo* web site has a link called "Tudo Bem, Tudo Zen" (Everything's alright, Everything's Zen, http://www.uol.com.br/bemzen), adopting the common usage of the word "Zen" as a synonym of peace and tranquility. In this site, many alternative practices and world religions are discussed.

The people I interviewed identified several New Age practices that they frequently associated with Zen Buddhism—practices of healing (yoga, shiatsu, *do in,* tai chi chuan, and acupuncture), eating habits (vegetarianism and macrobiotics), practices of self-understanding (many kinds of psychotherapy and astrology), martial arts (aikido, karate, and kendo), and other religions (Spiritism, African religions, Mahikari, and Rajneesh).

Let us start with healing practices. Many Brazilian adherents are first interested in shiatsu, a massage based on acupressure before getting in contact with Zen. Furthermore, meditation is closely associated with healing by the Brazilian media, particularly as a way of eschewing urban stress. For instance, the cover report of the national weekly magazine *Isto É* featured an article entitled "Meditation: How to Use This Ancient Technique to Overcome the Economic Crisis, Escape Daily Stress, Improve Your Concentration, and Make Difficult Decisions." The story reported that meditation as a technique has entered mainstream society, where instructors go to corporations, usually at lunchtime, to improve productivity.[51]

As for eating habits, there has always been a dilemma in Brazil: should Japanese food or organic, vegetarian, macrobiotic food be used in retreats *(sesshin)*? Urban Brazilians asked such a question in the 1960s and 1970s, when they started practicing Zen at Busshinji, the only temple that was open to Brazilians at the time. Because it catered mainly to the Japanese community, some Brazilian adherents got to the point of bringing their own food when going to retreats. Nowadays, after the establishment of Zen centers by non-Japanese Brazilians, fruit, brown rice, and vegetarian food are served most of the time. Vegetarianism is closely connected with Buddhism in the West. For instance, Jan Nattier describes how her Asian-American Buddhist friends felt ill at ease at a lecture by a famous Vietnamese monk because of the "not altogether friendly stares of the mostly Caucasian (and overwhelmingly vegetarian) crowd as they tried to enjoy their hot dogs and potato chips."[52] Similarly, one of the most popular topics discussed on Brazilian Buddhist e-mail lists is whether one should be vegetarian if converted to Buddhism. The same is true for the United States, as reports Richard Hayes, the moderator of *Buddha-L,* an international e-mail list.[53]

Martial arts are also very much a part of the Zen milieu. At Porto Alegre Zen Center, many adherents came from aikido classes, because their teacher has a close connection with Zen and Moriyama rōshi. Conversely, some Zen adherents started to study this martial art after meeting these aikido practitioners. Furthermore, many martial art halls (dojo) conduct Zen meditation before classes. Conversely, Busshinji temple also holds karate and kendo classes attended mainly by non-Japanese Brazilians.

Adding to such pluralization of faiths in the Brazilian religious field, Japanese NRMs such as Seichō-no-ie, Sekai Kyūsei Kyō, Brazil Sōka Gakkai International, Ōmoto, Tenrikyō, Risshō-kōseikai, Perfect Liberty Kyōdan (PL), and Seikai Mahikari Bumei Kyōdan arrived in Brazil in the 1960s and became highly successful among non-Japanese Brazilians in the following decades. For instance, in 1990, 90 percent of the followers of Seichō-no-ie, PL, and Sekai Kyūseikyō were non-Japanese Brazilians.[54]

As for the Buddhist traditions, Japanese, Tibetan, Korean, Chinese, Thai, and Singhalese Buddhist monks were increasingly present in Brazil in the 1990s. Dharma Centers (Buddhist centers managed by non-Japanese Brazilians) bring their spiritual mentors from abroad to give workshops, promote spiritual retreats, and disseminate their teachings. Many followers undertake trips to the centers where their mentors live.

I have already mentioned the conspicuous "religious migration" of Brazilians among these diverse religious traditions, and the consequent blurring of their boundaries. According to Brazilian anthropologist Roberto da Matta, Brazilians see these religious traditions as complementary, not mutually exclusive.[55] For instance, a survey conducted in 1988 showed that when Catholics who attended church once a week were asked if they believed in reincarnation, 45.9 percent said they did.[56] Since reincarnation is not part of the Catholic doctrine, one can see how permeable the borders of the Catholic world are in Brazil. Conversely, the survey also showed that 89.7 percent of the people classified as of "no religion" declared they believed in God, 55.9 percent declared they believed in heaven, and

44.1 percent believed in hell. It is clear that, the Catholic worldview has spread beyond its borders, carrying its influence even to groups that are distant from that worldview. A survey conducted by the agency Vox Populi in 1996 revealed that 59 percent of the Brazilian population believes in the existence of spirits, a concept accepted only by Spiritism and Afro-Brazilian religions such as Umbanda and Candomblé.[57] Undoubtedly, while the Catholic worldview has spread beyond its borders, the same is true for other religions in relation to Catholicism.

CONCLUSION

While the Japanese community in Brazil had to leave Buddhism behind, adopting Catholicism as a means of being accepted in the new country (much like the Japanese immigrants to the United States who converted to Christianity; Chaps. 3 and 4), many non-Japanese descent Brazilians have been adhering to Buddhism in the past years. These Zen adherents are part of the intellectual, cosmopolitan, urban elite who import Western discourse on Zen Buddhism through books, media, movies, travel, and, more recently, through the Internet. These cultural flows promote a subcultural group of Brazilian Zen adherents, who relate more easily with their peers in North America or Europe than to their fellow citizens of disenfranchised classes. Class differentiation is influential in choosing Zen—a highly literate choice indeed, as Zen literature is fundamental to their initial and sustained interest in Zen Buddhism.

While importing Buddhist concepts from metropolitan cultures overseas, Brazilians creolize it with an already pluralistic religious matrix and then propagate their interpretation of Buddhist teachings. Catholicism, Kardecist Spiritism, Afro-Brazilian religions, Japanese NRMs, and the New Age movement offer a profusion of faiths and beliefs onto which overseas Buddhist ideas can be superimposed and creolized. On the whole, already existing native religious matrices facilitated the acceptance of Buddhist concepts. Although such concepts do not necessarily have the same meaning in Brazilian culture, the slippages bridged the gap and helped to establish an understanding between the meaning-producing centers and interested Brazilians.

As a result of the diverse sources of knowledge on Zen, conflicts like the one I depicted in the opening of this chapter are ever-present. As a later development of that story, Coen sensei was dismissed from Busshinji in January 2001 and went on to establish a new temple in São Paulo City. The Japanese *sōkan* is presently the only authority at Busshinji, the Sōtō School's headquarters for South America. As a last point, I would like to note that creolization occurs also between Japanese and non-Japanese Brazilian practices. In my fieldwork I found that, whereas the Japanese superimpose Catholic terms and festivities on their Zen matrix, non-Japanese Brazilians and younger Japanese-Brazilians may ask Zen monks/nuns to conduct funerals, memorials, baby namings, and weddings. Religious boundaries are indeed very porous in Brazil.

Notes

I would like to thank Martin Baumann for giving me insightful suggestions on this essay, which is based on fieldwork conducted in Brazil in the years of 1998–1999 and 2001–2002. I used participant observation, in-depth interviews, and a survey of adherents in São Paulo, Rio de Janeiro, Pôrto Alegre, Ouro Preto, and Espírito Santo.

1. Superintendent for South America, or "bishop" as his position is referred to, the title being clear evidence of the Catholic influence that permeates Brazilian society.

2. Coen is the Portuguese spelling of her Buddhist name.

3. Pierre Bourdieu, *Distinction: A Social Critique of the Judgement of Taste* (Cambridge, Mass.: Harvard University Press, 1984).

4. Frederik Barth, *Ethnic Groups and Boundaries: The Social Organization of Cultural Difference* (London: Allen and Unwin, 1969).

5. Cristina Rocha, "Identity and Tea Ceremony in Brazil," *Japanese Studies* 19, no. 3 (1999): 287–295.

6. The Japanese monk Dōgen (1200–1253) brought the Sōtō Zen Buddhist school to Japan from China.

7. See, for example, Martin Baumann, "Creating a European Path to Nirvāṇa: Historical and Contemporary Developments of Buddhism in Europe," *Journal of Contemporary Religion* 10, no. 1 (1995): 55–70; Rick Fields, "Divided Dharma: White Buddhists, Ethnic Buddhists, and Racism," in *The Faces of Buddhism in America*, ed. Kenneth Tanaka and Charles Prebish (Berkeley: University of California Press, 1998), 196–206; Paul Numrich, *Old Wisdom in the New World: Americanization of Two Immigrant Theravada Buddhist Temples* (Knoxville: University of Tennessee Press, 1996); Charles Prebish, "Two Buddhisms Reconsidered," *Buddhist Studies Review* 10, no. 2 (1993): 187–206.

8. For a more detailed history of Japanese and Zen Buddhism in Brazil, see Cristina Rocha, "Zen Buddhism in Brazil: Japanese or Brazilian?" *Journal of Global Buddhism* 1 (2000): 31–55.

9. Jeffrey Lesser, *Negotiating National Identity: Immigrants, Minorities, and the Struggle for Ethnicity in Brazil* (Durham, N.C.: Duke University Press, 1999); Koichi Mori, "Vida Religiosa dos Japoneses e seus Descendentes Residentes no Brasil e Religiões de Origem Japonesa," in *Uma Epopéia Moderna: 80 Anos da Imigração Japonesa no Brasil*, ed. K. Wakisaka (São Paulo: Sociedade Brasileira de Cultura Japonesa, 1992), 559–601.

10. Murilo Nunes Azevedo, *O Caminho de Cada Um: O Budismo da Terra Pura* (Rio de Janeiro: Bertrand Brasil, 1996).

11. Ricardo M. Gonçalves, "O Budismo Japonês no Brasil: Reflexões de um Observador Participante," in *Sinais dos Tempos: Diversidade Religiosa no Brasil,* ed. Leila Landim (Rio de Janeiro: Instituto de Estudos da Religião, 1990), 177.

12. Regina Matsue, "O Paraíso de Amida: Três Escolas Budistas em Brasília" (M.A. thesis, University of Brasília, 1998).

13. *IBGE*, the Brazilian Institute of Geography and Statistics.

14. Reginaldo Prandi, "Religião Paga, Conversão e Serviço," in *A Realidade Social das Religiões no Brasil: Religião Sociedade e Política,* ed. Antônio Pierucci and Reginaldo Prandi (São Paulo: Hucitec, 1996), 257.

15. Thomas Tweed, "Nightstand Buddhists and Other Creatures: Sympathizers, Adherents, and the Study of Religion," in *American Buddhism, Methods and Findings in Recent Scholarship,* ed. Duncan Williams and Christopher Queen (Richmond, Eng.: Curzon, 1999), 74.

16. Many books have been translated; some of the titles are: D. T. Suzuki's *The Zen Doctrine of No Mind* and *Introduction to Zen Buddhism;* Shunryū Suzuki's *Zen Mind, Beginners' Mind;* Phillip Kapleau's *The Three Pillars of Zen;* Charlotte Joko Beck, *Nothing Special, Living Zen;* and most of the books by Thich Nhat Hahn. On the Internet site of a Brazilian bookstore in July 2002 the word "Zen" was used in forty-eight titles of books in Portuguese (http://www.livcultura.com.br).

17. The Hollywood movies *The Little Buddha, Seven Years in Tibet,* and *Kundun,* and non-Hollywood ones such as *The Cup* and *Samsāra* were very successful in Brazil. Even though they dealt with Tibetan Buddhism, they are directly associated with Buddhism itself and not specifically Tibet. Practitioners may attend various Buddhist schools at once.

18. Roberto Oliveira, "Fé de Pernas Cruzadas," *Revista da Folha,* July 15, 2001, 8–13.

19. For a bibliography on Buddhism in Brazil and a web directory of Brazilian Buddhist temples, monasteries, centers and e-mail lists, see http://sites.uol.com.br/cmrocha.

20. H. Assmann, *A Igreja Eletrônica e Seu Impacto na América Latina* (Petrópolis: Vozes, 1986).

21. The 2000 census shows that one-third of the Brazilians over ten years of age may be regarded as illiterate or "semi-illiterate," as they have not completed four years of schooling.

22. "Cybersangha" is a term coined in 1991 by Gary Ray to describe the Buddhist community online. For more on this, see Charles Prebish, *Luminous Passage: The Practice and Study of Buddhism in America* (Berkeley and Los Angeles: University of California Press, 1999).

23. Wade C. Roof, *Spiritual Supermarket: Baby Boomers and the Remaking of American Religion* (Princeton, N.J.: Princeton University Press, 1999), 46–110.

24. Ulf Hannerz, "The World in Creolisation," *Africa* 57, no. 4 (1987): 546–559.

25. José J. Carvalho, "O Encontro de Velhas e Novas Religiões: Esboço de uma Teoria dos Estilos de Espiritualidade," in *Misticismo e Novas Religiões*, ed. Alberto Moreira and Renée Zicman (Petrópolis: Vozes/UFS/IFAN, 1994), 77.

26. Peter Berger, "Four Faces of Global Culture," *The National Interest* 49 (1997): 23–29.

27. Ibid., 28–29.

28. Robert Bellah, "New Religious Consciousness and the Crisis in Modernity," in *The New Religious Consciousness*, ed. C. Glock and R. Bellah (Berkeley: University of California Press, 1976); Denise Cush, "British Buddhism and the New Age," *Journal of Contemporary Religion* 11, no. 2 (1996): 195–208.

29. *Jukai*: "granting *(ju)* the precepts *(kai)*, the ceremonial initiation into Buddhism. In this ceremony one commits oneself to be completely devoted to the three jewels and the ten main precepts." Michael Diener, Ingrid Fischer-Schreiber, and Franz-Karl Ehrhard, *The Shambhala Dictionary of Buddhism and Zen*, trans. Michael Kohn (Boston: Shambhala, 1991), s.v. *Jukai*.

30. Wilson Paranhos, *Nuvens Cristalinas em Luar de Prata* (RJ: FEEU, 1994), 155.

31. Cristina Rocha, "Zen Buddhism in Brazil."

32. José J. Carvalho, "Características do Fenômeno Religioso na Sociedade Contemporânea," in *O Impacto Da Modernidade Sobre a Religião*, ed. Maria Clara Bingemer (São Paulo: Loyola, 1992), 153.

33. E. Stoddard and G. Cornwell, "Cosmopolitan or Mongrel? Créolité, Hybridity and 'Douglarisation' in Trinidad," *European Journal of Cultural Studies* 2, no. 3 (1999): 331–353.

34. Robert Young, *Colonial Desire: Hybridity in Theory, Culture and Race* (London: Routledge, 1995); Pnina Werbner and Tariq Modood, eds., *Debating Cultural Hybridity: Multicultural Identities and the Politics of Anti-Racism* (London: Zed Books, 1997).

35. Young, *Colonial Desire*.

36. For an account of hybridity that foregrounds the possibilities of agency and reproduction of culture in the context of an analysis of Buddhism in Hawai'i see Tanabe, Chapter 3.

37. Edward Brathwaite, *The Development of Creole Society in Jamaica 1770–1820* (Oxford: Clarendon, 1971).

38. Carvalho, "O Encontro de Velhas e Novas Religiões," 74; Christian Smith and Joshua Prokopy, *Latin American Religion in Motion*, 3.

39. According to J. Carvalho, "In many aspects, the Spiritist world-view became part of the national ethos, as much as Catholicism, and more recently Protestantism"; "O Encontro de Velhas e Novas Religiões," 74.

40. David Hess, *Samba in the Night: Spiritism in Brazil* (New York: Columbia University Press,

1994); Maria Laura Viveiros de Castro Cavalcanti, "O Espiritismo," in *Sinais dos Tempos*, 147–155.

41. Carvalho, "O Encontro de Velhas e Novas Religiões," 75.

42. Lísias Negrão, "Umbanda: Entre a Cruz e a Encruzilhada," *Tempo Social, Revista de Sociologia* 5, nos. 1–2 (1994): 113–122.

43. Renato Ortiz, *A Morte Branca do Feiticeiro Negro: Umbanda e Sociedade Brasileira* (São Paulo: Brasiliense, 1999), 16–17, 69–86.

44. Cavalcanti, "O Espiritismo."

45. *Buddhismo-L* (http://www.dharmanet.com.br/listas), October 2000 and April 2001.

46. Carmen Macedo, *A Imagem do Eterno: Religiões no Brasil* (São Paulo: Moderna, 1989), 47; Negrão, "Umbanda," 116.

47. Diane Brown, *Umbanda Religion and Politics in Urban Brazil* (New York: Columbia University Press, 1994), 55–77; Macedo, *A Imagem do Eterno*, 44–46.

48. As quoted in Robert Carpenter, "Esoteric Literature as a Microcosmic Mirror of Brazil's Religious Marketplace," in *Latin American Religion in Motion*, ed. Christian Smith and Joshua Prokopy (New York: Routledge, 1999), 242.

49. Ibid., 235; José G. Magnani, *O Brasil da Nova Era* (São Paulo: Edusp, 2000); Luis Soares, "Religioso por Natureza: Cultura Alternativa e Misticismo Ecológico no Brasil," in *Sinais dos Tempos*.

50. Carpenter, "Esoteric Literature," 243.

51. *Isto É* magazine (September 1998): 87–94.

52. Jan Nattier, "Buddhism Comes to Main Street," *Wilson Quarterly* 21 (1997): 72.

53. Richard Hayes, "The Internet as a Window onto American Buddhism," in *American Buddhism: Methods and Findings in Recent Scholarship*, 174–175.

54. Robert Carpenter and Wade Roof, "The Transplanting of Seichō-no-ie from Japan to Brazil: Moving beyond the Ethnic Enclave," *Journal of Contemporary Religion* 10, no. 1 (1995): 41–53; Hideaki Matsuoka, "'Messianity Makes a Person Useful': Describing Differences in a Japanese Religion in Brazil," *Japanese Journal of Religious Studies* 28, nos. 1–2 (2001).

55. Roberto da Matta, *O Que Faz o Brazil, Brasil?* (Rio de Janeiro: Rocco, 1994), 115–116.

56. Carlos Rodrigues Brandão, "A Crise das Instituições Tradicionais Produtoras de Sentido," in *Misticismo e Novas Religiões*, 40–41.

57. *Veja* (magazine), July 26, 2000.

7 Spreading Buddha's Light: The Internationalization of Foguang Shan

Stuart Chandler

Foguang Shan (literally "Buddha's Light Mountain"), one of the most prominent Buddhist organizations in Taiwan, has over the past two decades also developed a significant network of temples around the globe. With more than 150 centers dispersed on five continents and serving hundreds of thousands of lay devotees, the Foguang "empire," as a variety of journalists and scholars have dubbed the phenomenon, is now arguably one of the most extensive and best-organized Buddhist groups in the world. There are certainly few monks who can claim to have gathered as large a sangha as has Foguang Shan's founder, Master Xingyun, who currently supervises more than thirteen hundred monastic disciples. This chapter describes the various factors that have contributed to Foguang Shan's remarkable success in transforming itself from a local institution to one of truly international magnitude. After indicating Foguang devotees' self-understanding of the historical setting of their missionary efforts, I analyze the organization's demographics and the four primary methods upon which the master and his disciples have relied to carry out their ambitious objectives: providing a cultural link to China; creating links of affinity; sparking people's curiosity; and localizing Buddhist teachings and practice. Through this discussion, the challenges inherent in the group's mission come to light, most notably the tension that arises from serving as a cultural bridge back to the homeland for the Chinese diaspora while simultaneously localizing practice to attract non-Chinese. I conclude by disclosing Master Xingyun's positive appraisal of the religious implications of globalization. For him, humankind's increasing sense of homelessness is not a negative, but rather spiritually beneficial, as it allows false divisions based upon nationality and ethnicity to attenuate, allowing people to recognize that they all share Buddha Nature. Hence, Foguang Shan provides one piece of evidence that in the postmodern world, people's primary referent for communal identity may very well increasingly revert from national to religious symbols and myths.

FROM MASTER HUISHEN TO MASTER XINGYUN

Master Xingyun first went abroad in 1963, when he joined a contingent of monks sent to India, Thailand, Malaysia, Singapore, the Philippines, Japan, and Hong Kong on a government-sponsored initiative to bolster support for the Republic of China (ROC). The beginnings of Foguang Shan's globalization are to be traced to a more recent trip: the master's visit to the United States in 1976, at which point he recognized the great potential for serving the rapidly expanding Chinese-American population. Twelve years later, Master Xingyun opened the doors of the largest Buddhist temple in the Western hemisphere. He chose to call it "Hsi Lai," which means "Coming to the West." This is a play on words, for Chinese Buddhists have long referred to Buddhism as having come from the west, namely from India.

One year after the founding of Hsi Lai, the theme of bringing the Dharma to the West gained even greater salience when Tang Degang, a historian then at New York University, gave a lecture at the Foguang Shan Buddhist Youth Academic Conference, which he billed "From Master Huishen to Master Xingyun."[1] Tang stated in his paper that during the North-South Dynasties (420–489 C.E.) the Venerable Huishen, a monk of Indian origin but living in China, sailed to America to spread the Dharma. The cleric returned to the Middle Kingdom some forty years later, presenting to the Liang emperor many gifts from the distant land, which he called Fusang. Tang cited three pieces of evidence to support his thesis. First, he quoted passages from the "Twenty-five Histories" that relate the Venerable Huishen's descriptions of his voyage and of the peoples, flora, and fauna he observed in the land he had made his home for so long. Second, the scholar noted that there are many ancient "stone anchors" (shi mao) in America with craftsmanship so Chinese in style that they must have derived from China and been brought over by the monk. Finally, Tang asserted that there are still people in Acapulco, Mexico, who are Buddhists, having received the tradition from their ancestors who had learned of the Dharma from the Indian-Chinese missionary. The Venerable Huishen's early "discovery" (faxian) of America, a full millennium before Columbus arrived, was of such historical importance to Buddhists, Chinese, and all Americans, stated Tang, that he recommended that Hsi Lai Temple build a "Master Huishen Memorial Hall."

Tang Degang was not, in fact, the first scholar to hypothesize about an early Buddhist arrival in America. This theory had been raised and debated within the European academic community during the eighteenth and nineteenth centuries.[2]

More recently, Wei Zhuxian of Taiwan National University devoted virtually his entire career to cataloging archeological, anthropological, and historical evidence for pre-Columbian contacts between Chinese and American peoples. In his opinion, Huishen represents a relatively late interaction, since a thousand years earlier Confucius had already made references to the North American hummingbird!

Whether or not Fusang was a Chinese name for the continent of America will probably never be known definitively. Most of the evidence that Tang and his predecessors cited to substantiate their claims is tentative at best. To scrutinize the soundness of the data offered, however, is to miss the point. For the Foguang community, the theory's importance lies not so much in historical validity but rather in its potential for creating a new mythology, namely, an expressive history that helps to establish the group's sense of purpose. The power of the Huishen legend arises from three elements: the portrayal of him as carrier of Chinese culture; the conviction that he successfully planted the seed of the Dharma on American shores; and the transnational profile he is given. We shall return to each of these components as we discuss Foguang Shan's missionary work not only in America, but around the world.

THE PERIMETERS OF FOGUANG SHAN'S GLOBALIZATION

Master Xingyun has been remarkably successful in planting Foguang centers around the world. In less than a decade Foguang Shan went from having virtually no overseas branches to embracing nearly one hundred. As of the year 1998, the headquarters oversaw 95 temples, Pure Land meditation centers, and lecture halls from Tokyo to Paris, Sydney to São Paulo: 27 in Asia, excluding the ROC (8 in Japan; 7 in the Philippines and Malaysia; 2 in Hong Kong; and 1 each in Thailand, Singapore, and Korea); 13 in the South Pacific (10 in Australia, 2 in New Zealand, and 1 in New Guinea); 19 in Europe (3 in the United Kingdom and Germany; 2 each in France, Spain, and Italy; and 1 each in Sweden, Netherlands, Belgium, Switzerland, Hungary, Portugal, and the Czech Republic); 7 in Africa (all in South Africa); 5 in South and Central America (2 in Brazil; 1 each in Costa Rica, Paraguay, and Argentina); and 24 in North America (19 in the United States, the rest in Canada). Master Xingyun decided to hold off on constructing new centers, so the number of Foguang temples has remained steady since 1998 and probably will continue to be so for the foreseeable future.

This network is supplemented by the Buddha's Light International Association (BLIA), the lay society founded by the master in 1992. Within five years BLIA had grown to include 110 regional chapters (*zonghui*) and local chapters (*xiehui*) worldwide: 33 in Asia (10 in India; 2 each in the ROC, Japan, Malaysia, Indonesia, and South Korea; and 1 each in Hong Kong, Macau, Brunei, Singapore, Thailand, the Philippines, Cambodia, Vietnam, Myanmar, Nepal, Bangladesh, Bhutan, and Sri Lanka); 8 in the Pacific (6 in Australia, the other 2 in New Zealand); 25 in North America (18 in the United States, 6 in Canada, and 1 in the Bahamas); 5 in Central America (1 each in Costa Rico, Mexico, El Salvador, Dominique, and Panama); 7 in South America (1 each in Brazil, Argentina, Paraguay, Chile, Uruguay, Guatemala, and Belize); 21 in Europe (3 in the United Kingdom; 2 each in Germany, Russia, and Sweden; 1 each in Belgium, Denmark, France, Switzerland, Norway, Netherlands, Spain, Hungary, Yugoslavia, Italy, Portugal, and Austria); 11 in Africa (9 in South Africa, 1 each in the Congo and Tanzania).

Foguang temples may be found virtually anywhere a relatively large expatriate population from the ROC has coalesced. The reach of BLIA is still farther, extending to areas with even small communities of Taiwan emigrants.[3] It is very difficult to determine exactly how many devotees frequent the temples or join BLIA chapters. Foguang clerics have unofficially claimed BLIA's worldwide membership to be anywhere from one million to three million. I doubt that the roster of active members (i e , those paying membership dues) has ever reached anything close to even the more modest of the two estimates, although the total number of people who participate in BLIA events in a given year probably exceeds the three million mark.

The question is, how many people are members of BLIA, how many of these live in Taiwan, and how many live abroad? Given that approximately five million people in the ROC frequent a Buddhist temple, that Foguang Shan is only one of several large Buddhist organizations, and that many of Taiwan's Buddhists do not join any of these groups, I would estimate that perhaps four to six hundred thousand people, or 8 to 12 percent of the island's Buddhists, currently align themselves with Foguang Shan as active members of BLIA.[4] The lower estimate corresponds to the number of *Awakening the World* (*Jue Shi*) magazines that were distributed each month from 1997 to 1999.

Since Foguang Shan has only fifty-seven temples in Taiwan but ninety-five overseas centers, it would appear at first that the majority of devotees live outside of the ROC, so that the total number could exceed one million. On closer inspection, it becomes clear that this is not the case. The extent to which Foguang Shan has thus far carried its banner of Humanistic Buddhism beyond the shores of Taiwan can be roughly determined by analyzing personnel distribution and temple fund-raising strategies.[5] Some Foguang overseas branch temples, such as Hsi Lai Temple (Los Angeles), Nan Tien Temple (Wollongong, Australia), and Nan Hua

Temple (Bronkhorstspruit, South Africa), are multimillion dollar structures that have become prominent landmarks and tourist attractions. Most other outposts are of much more modest scale, occupying former homes, warehouses, schools, and churches. Typically relying on a small and dispersed Chinese population, there is neither the need nor the financial resources to support ornate halls or large staffs. Hence, although international temples greatly outnumber domestic ones, they account for less than one-quarter of full-time worker assignments. Of Foguang Shan's 1,096 monastic, lay-monastic, and lay devotees who, as of August 1997, worked full-time for the organization, 434 worked at Foguang headquarters, 423 were stationed in a temple in Taiwan, and 239 were assigned abroad.[6] Overseas centers had an average of 2.5 workers, compared to an average of 7.4 for the temples in Taiwan, a finding that supports the conclusion that the devotee base is much lower elsewhere in the world than it is in the ROC.

The smaller number of devotees per monastery creates a significant financial strain. Several lay followers active in the fund-raising efforts of overseas Foguang temples confided to me that their branch would not be able to meet its bills if it were not for the generous contributions made by key donors who periodically visited from Taiwan. One nun revealed that as much as 80 percent of the funds raised at Hsi Lai derive from people who either visit from Taiwan or who, while having a second home in the Los Angeles area, still spend most of their time in the ROC (although other monastics claimed a much lower percentage). Based on these statistics and comments, I doubt that any overseas BLIA chapter, even the one in Los Angeles affiliated with Hsi Lai Temple, has a roster of over a few thousand, and those with no temple nearby generally maintain a membership of only several dozen people. BLIA therefore probably has approximately fifty to sixty thousand members whose primary residence is outside of Taiwan. The number of people who participate in BLIA-sponsored events, however, is much greater.

Although the picture I provide of the extent of Foguang Shan's global operations is not nearly so grand as that painted by Foguang devotees, one still has to be impressed by what the order has done in so brief a time, particularly when one keeps in mind that such global outreach is unprecedented in the history of Sino-Buddhism. The only Chinese Buddhist organization with a comparable global network is the Compassion Relief Foundation, which, as Julia Huang indicates (Chap. 8), has established branches in twenty-eight countries. There is one significant difference between the Foguang and Ciji strategies for international outreach: the latter opens overseas offices, not temples. In other words, no clerics have been stationed abroad. The "offices" are typically homes or rented rooms where small groups of members meet to discuss Buddhism and raise money for the headquarters' worldwide humanitarian efforts. This is not to imply that Ciji offices are any less active than are Foguang temples. As Huang observes, overseas Ciji members undertake a wide range of programs and raise considerable sums of money not only for the initiatives of the headquarters but for local philanthropic endeavors as well. Nonetheless, the lack of overseas temples and monastics has resulted in Ciji offices having a generally lower profile outside of the immediate Chinese community than do the Foguang outposts.

Foguang Shan's international network of temples not only exceeds that of other Chinese Buddhist institutions but is one of the most extensive of any Buddhist organization. Thich Nhat Hanh's Order of Interbeing has a semiformal arrangement of affiliates that by 1998 included a handful of temples and approximately three hundred "lay sanghas." The vast majority of Thich Nhat Hanh's disciples, however, remain in Plum Village, the order's headquarters in France.[7] The only other international Buddhist organization in which clerics play an important leadership role is Sangharakshita's Western Buddhist Order (WBO) and Friends of the Western Buddhist Order (FWBO), which in 1998 incorporated fifty-five city centers and fifteen retreat centers, mostly in Great Britain (where the order was founded), but also in Australia, New Zealand, Malaysia, Sri Lanka, India, Nepal, and North and South America.[8] Sangharakshita has been particularly active in India, where his efforts to carry on Ambedkar's work among Dalits is estimated to have brought several tens of thousands into the Trailoka Bauddha Mahasangha Sahayaka Gana, the Indian wing of the FWBO.[9]

Foguang Shan therefore probably has more temples and clerics around the world than any other Buddhist organization. The global profile of its lay devotee base is also among the most impressive. Having given an indication of the extent of Foguang Shan's internationalization campaign, I will now turn to consider more closely its nature. To do so, I will focus on its two main objectives: the creation for the Chinese diaspora of a bridge back to the cultural motherland; and outreach to those who are neither Chinese nor Buddhists.

CULTURE, HOME, AND LAND

It is safe to say that over 99 percent of BLIA members are ethnically Chinese. Foguang Shan's forays around the world therefore represent the globalization of a national tradition. In other words, the Foguang network is geographically international but remains almost completely associated with one cultural group and is highly focused on that group's concerns with the notion of homeland. Chinese tradition has historically been grounded in one particular setting: the Middle

Kingdom. As the number of Chinese living elsewhere in the world, even outside of Asia, has multiplied dramatically over the last half-century, organizations such as Foguang Shan have served a very important function in maintaining for their members a sense of Chinese identity. The perception that Foguang Shan is a vital carrier of traditional Chinese culture has therefore played an especially important role in attracting new devotees. To understand the dynamics of this, we must look more generally at the Foguang perspective on tradition and modernization.

The fact that Foguang Shan perpetuates certain customs and values is not in itself remarkable, since every social organ does so. Of greater note is the group's conscious promotion of itself as both fulfilling this function and simultaneously shedding those aspects of tradition regarded as encumbrances to modern life. At the same time that specific traditions identified as relatively recent deviations of Chinese Buddhism are rejected, "authentic" values of the Buddhist heritage are retained and, in fact, explicitly espoused, as are certain key virtues of the Confucian tradition.[10] Modernism and traditionalism are regarded as mutually interpenetrating and complementary. The danger, in the Foguang view, occurs when either one of these polarities eclipses the other. Within Chinese Buddhism, over-reliance on (a misunderstanding of) tradition is believed to have left the religion enervated, necessitating an aggressive modernization campaign. The problem of general Chinese society, on the other hand, is seen to be just the opposite: in the rush to modernize, people have drifted away from inherited values. This trend is traced back to the May Fourth Movement of the 1920s, when Hu Shi, Chen Duxiu, and others called for their countrymen to "overthrow" (dadao) the stultifying ritualism of "Confucius and Sons" (Kongjiadian) and to rid themselves of the otherworldly escapism of Buddhism. The Communist Party stepped up this direct assault, especially in the 1950s and 1960s.

For those under the Nationalist regime of Taiwan, the steady corrosion of tradition is attributed, not to political campaigns, but to the ubiquity of Western, especially American, influence. This foreign presence has been welcome for the most part, if for no other reason than without it the ROC could not have withstood its Communist adversaries. Hence, the "fundamentalist" vituperations against the West that have erupted in many other places around the world have found little expression among Taiwan's religious groups. Despite the lack of a strong reaction against westernization, there nonetheless has been a response to it utilizing indigenous resources. As the New Confucian Tu Wei-ming has observed, this search for roots bears a family resemblance to fundamentalism and proceeds from a critique of modernity.[11] Taiwan's "mainland complex" (dalu qingjie), to employ the term the island's media has made current to describe this pervasive heightened concern for asserting Chinese cultural continuity, derives from four factors: an underlying ambivalence about the tremendous American presence; discomfort with Taiwan's uncertain political status and future; recognition of the island's peripheral historical ties to China proper; and a sense of ever-increasing dissonance with contemporary mainland culture. Let us consider the latter two of these in more detail.

Taiwan is not the homeland for Chinese. It became a formal part of the Chinese empire and began to be settled by appreciable numbers of Fujianese and Hakka farmers in the latter half of the seventeenth century, only after the Dutch and Spanish had already briefly established outposts along its coasts.[12] From 1895 to 1945, the island was claimed by the Japanese. Taiwan is therefore geographically and historically marginal. This is compounded by a sense of exile from the heartland. The post-1949 political situation prevented most of those living outside the People's Republic of China (PRC) from even visiting until the 1980s. Since that time, sojourns for family reunions, tourism, or to conduct business have increasingly taken place. Such contact has proven bittersweet for many, however, as they often have been unprepared for the lack of resonance they have felt with their Communist countrymen. One Foguang nun who had traveled through mainland China for a year and a half in the mid-1990s while still a layperson remarked to me that she had found the experience deeply troubling for, while she loved "China the place," she could not relate to "the mentality of the people." By China the place, the young nun meant the physical sites, both of natural beauty and of historical significance, about which she had heard so much while growing up. The symbols of home are over there; and yet present realities undercut these symbols, so that this woman, like many Chinese who have visited the PRC, felt a stranger in her own land. Communist China is not home, for state socialism is believed to have deprived the populace of any appreciation for their heritage, leading many on Taiwan to see themselves as more legitimate bearers of Chinese culture. Upon returning to Taiwan, this woman had come home—yet a home in a marginal space whose oldest cultural landmarks are aboriginal, Dutch, and Portuguese. Hence, the sense of homeland has been bifurcated, home and land separated into two entities.

Foguang Shan's self-proclaimed role in protecting and perpetuating China's Buddhist (and key elements of its Confucian) heritage is one manifestation of Taiwan's search for roots. In the case of the nun just mentioned, dynamics associated with the mainland complex played not a little role in her decision to renounce under Master Xingyun. After returning to Taiwan from her journey, the young woman came upon a book by the master that so affected her that a steady stream of tears gushed down her face as she read it. "Not only the thoughts of the Master moved me," related the nun, "but the fact that here was a man from mainland China who now had struck such a deep chord with people in Taiwan. Here was my bridge." The fact that Master Xingyun originally hails from the mainland has played a vital role in his popularity, for he embodies the transferal of Chinese culture from China proper to Taiwan and the outlying diaspora.

The identity crisis felt by many in Taiwan is experienced in an even more acute form by those who have emigrated abroad, thereby leaving even the margins to enter lands with virtually no cultural connection with China. It then becomes imperative to find a means to return to one's heritage, at least to selective aspects of that heritage. Many who frequent the overseas branch temples do so, not so much as devout Buddhists, but as expatriates seeking the familiar tastes, sounds, and sights of their mother country. Weekly services, monthly retreats, and large-scale Dharma functions are religious and social events. The Chinese language schools run at many of the temples are a major drawing card. Parents regard these schools, as well as the Boy Scout troops and other Foguang children's programs, as effective means to steep their children in the ethical values and cultural legacy of what otherwise would be a far-removed birthright.

Clerics serve as important symbols for this reconstructed sense of home. Master Xingyun likes to quote the phrase "By leaving home, one gains a myriad homes." In the past, this saying pointed to the fact that all monks had the right to take up temporary lodging in any public monastery. So long as the monk had a certificate of ordination and pledged to abide by the monastery's rules, he could not be turned away. He was both homeless and yet benefited from countless abodes throughout the country.[13] For Foguang venerables, their own organization provides the myriad homes. These clerics, in turn, act as the channels to transmit traditional Chinese culture to the laity. Just as monks and nuns by leaving their biological relatives join a larger monastic family, so Foguang devotees are told that, although they may have strayed far from the Chinese homeland, through joining BLIA they have actually become part of a family that extends around the world. Each Foguang temple, as a center of Chinese culture, is home. It is not only a miniature "Pure Land" (in the sense of the Pure Lands described in Buddhist scriptures), but also a microcosmic, archetypal homeland. Mainland China may physically be situated where the Middle Kingdom once was, but the periphery is now where that kingdom's cultural legacy thrives. The geographic center has become marginal, the margins and outlying regions transformed into cultural centers. In fact, there are more than a few within the Chinese diaspora who believe that it is from these multiple centers that China's heritage can one day be reintroduced to the physical core.

ATTRACTING LOCALS AND LOCALIZING THE DHARMA

Master Xingyun very much recognizes that his overseas temples and BLIA chapters serve as cultural bridges back to China. For this very reason, he often reminds his followers that these outposts are not meant merely to be overseas Chinese associations with a Buddhist veneer. Foguang temples are to be centers of Chinese Buddhism, with the emphasis on the noun. Just as the bringing of Chinese culture was an incidental feature of the Venerable Huishen's venture to Fusang, so is it said to be a secondary aspect of Master Xingyun's vow to globalize Buddhism. For the tradition to fulfill its universal intent, the seed of the Dharma must be planted in every nation, and not just among emigrants from Buddhist countries, but among the general populace. Diaspora missions are not enough, to adopt the typology employed by Linda Learman in this book's Introduction. Foguang Shan feels called upon to energetically undertake foreign missionary work as well. The master and his disciples are still struggling with how to best accomplish this goal. Three primary methods thus far have been employed: creating links of affinity (*jieyuan*), sparking people's curiosity, and localizing Buddhist teachings and practice.

The *Foguang Encyclopedia* (*Foguang Da Cidian*) states that *jieyuan* originally referred to situations in which, "although cultivation in this life can in no way result in liberation, there is an initial point of contact for fruition some time in the future."[14] In other words, planting the seed of the Dharma in a person's consciousness usually will not lead to that person's attaining enlightenment in the present life, but such a seed of wisdom can bear fruit in a subsequent rebirth. Historically, *jieyuan* has been applied to describe those undertakings that serve to attract new devotees to Buddhism: building a temple or pagoda; donating funds; or printing scriptures, books, or tracts. In its contemporary usage, the term especially portrays any activity that establishes or strengthens a personal relationship in such a way as to spread the Dharma. *Jieyuan* relies upon and augments the spontaneous creative energy that arises through direct interaction among people. It is, one could say, a Buddhist manifestation of the Chinese proclivity to conduct affairs through personal contacts (*guanxi*), although without any of the negative connotations.

Jieyuan is regarded as an important means of attaining merit (*gongde*). The degree of merit that thereby accrues depends upon the nature of the interaction among the three components: the giver, the gift, and the recipient. The most precious gift of all is the Dharma itself, but if such a gift would not yet be appreciated by the recipient, more mundane presents will serve the purpose better. The level of merit is not determined so much by the monetary value of the gift as by its appropriateness, that is, its effectiveness in drawing the recipient to Buddhism. *Jieyuan* is often accomplished by attracting people, especially children, to Buddhist practice through distributing candies, treats, or money. This understanding emphasizes that, to plant the seed of the Dharma effectively so that it may flourish in the future, one must first create appropriate conditions (*yuan*). The goal of creating links of affinity is to instill a positive predisposition toward Buddhism so that, later, when the time is ripe, people will be that much more likely to find resonance with its teachings.

The motivation of the giver in providing the gift also affects the amount of merit gained. The purity of his or her intention is of utmost importance; he or she must have no selfish aim in establishing a relationship with the recipient. Chinese Buddhists therefore distinguish *jieyuan* from *panyuan*, which generally signifies the clinging of the wayward mind to external phenomena and, as the opposite of *jie-yuan*, refers specifically to providing favors or establishing ties with some ulterior design in mind.[15] In the unsullied giving of *jieyuan*, whether or not the recipient of the gift can assist the giver in some fashion in the future is of no concern. In fact, those who practice *jieyuan* in its highest form are said to do so with no concept of giver, recipient, or gift; all are regarded as radically interrelated aspects of ever-changing reality. According to his devotees, Master Xingyun has attained this level of compassionate wisdom.

The third element determining the amount of merit gained through *jieyuan* is the relative virtue of the recipient as this becomes manifest through his or her subsequent acts and level of cultivation. Merit is quite great, for instance, if the person eventually renounces. Significant merit may still result even if the recipient does not become a cleric, for it also compounds to the extent that the person thereafter benefits Buddhism. This is the reasoning behind Master Xingyun's emphasis on establishing ties of affinity with the elite of society, whether in the business or political worlds. When a leader becomes a Buddhist, especially an active Buddhist, others follow. If the act of *jieyuan* with a member of the elite does not lead to the person taking Triple Refuge, it may nonetheless trigger merit, for the recipient is in the position to benefit the tradition even as a non-Buddhist. A wealthy person, for instance, may donate considerable funds for a charitable drive, or a politician may help to pass legislation advantageous to the religion.

Master Xingyun has therefore long sought to create ties of affinity with political figures. He has also been remarkably successful in doing so: since the 1970s, a vast array of Taiwan's presidents, vice presidents, secretary-generals, governors, ministers, legislators, county magistrates, and city mayors have made regular pilgrimages to Foguang headquarters, especially when election season comes around. As Foguang Shan has established branch temples overseas, the master has extended this strategy, instructing disciples and BLIA leaders to seek out favorably disposed politicians and to make them well aware of the group's wealth and clout among Chinese. Such efforts of outreach have borne fruit. His Excellency Sir Clarence Seignoret, president of the Commonwealth of Dominica, joined BLIA as a non-Buddhist "friend" during the association's 1992 inaugural ceremony. One year later, Santiago Ruperez, director of the Spanish Chamber of Commerce (Spain's unofficial governmental representative to Taiwan), made the pilgrimage to Foguang Shan to take the Triple Refuge. Vice President Guadalupe Jerezano of Honduras visited the mountain in May 1995. France's President Jacques Chirac sent a letter congratulating BLIA upon the convening of its 1996 worldwide conference, which took place in Paris, and Chancellor Kohl of Germany invited two members of the Berlin chapter of BLIA to introduce the organization to him and other government officials during the Berlin International Cultural Fair in September of that year. Several Australian politicians, including Her Excellency Leneen Forde, the governor-general of Queensland, visited Chong Tien Temple of Brisbane in the spring of 1997 to allay fears in the wake of anti-Chinese sentiment sparked during the previous year's elections. Around that same time, Elizabeth Aguirre de Calderón, the first lady of the Republic of El Salvador, visited Foguang Shan.

The country in which Master Xingyun has most energetically pursued creating links of affinity with politicians is the United States. California Secretary of State March Fong Eu was invited to view the Hacienda Heights property just as construction of Hsi Lai Temple got under way. Apparently, it was she who arranged for Master Xingyun to perform purifying services to start the December 1988 session of the California legislature. Foguang literature proudly states that this was the first time a Buddhist monastic had performed this rite on government premises in the United States. (Master Xingyun later conducted such services in New York City and Chicago as well.) That same year, the mayors of Austin and Houston honored Master Xingyun as a friendship ambassador. Letters of congratulations have been sent to the temple by numerous California politicians, including Governor Pete Wilson, U.S. senator Alan Cranston, and Los Angeles mayor Tom Bradley. Over the years, politicians to visit Hsi Lai Temple have included California state senator Simon, California senate president David Roberti, U.S. congressman Mel Levine, and U.S. congressman Matthew Martinez.

The master long maintained at least nominal links with the White House. President Reagan both wired a telegram and dispatched a representative to Hsi Lai Temple in honor of its opening in 1988. The first President Bush invited Master Xingyun to his inauguration and, when the Buddha's Light International Association was founded in 1992 in Los Angeles, he sent a letter praising the group for its compassionate tenets and devotion to relieving the suffering of all beings.[16] Such contacts with the Oval Office increased and became more direct during the Clinton administration, culminating with Master Xingyun making a ten-minute "courtesy call" on Vice President Gore at the White House in March of 1996, and the vice president reciprocating by attending a banquet at Hsi Lai Temple six weeks later.

Politicians outside of Taiwan associate themselves with Master Xingyun mainly for two reasons. First, where Foguang Shan has built one of its larger branch temples, the millions of dollars spent in construction and the subsequent tourist influx are seen as a boost to the local economy. It was precisely for this reason that the business and political leaders of Wollongong, Australia, in the early 1990s sought out the master and provided land so that Foguang Shan would erect a monastery in their town. The resulting structure, Nan Tien Temple, cost US$30 million to build and has developed into one of the area's most prominent landmarks. The property for Nan Hua Temple in Bronkhorstspruit, South Africa, was acquired under similar circumstances, although the hope was not so much to attract tourism as to gain the master's assistance in encouraging devotees to establish businesses there. Second, as the master is influential in the overseas Chinese community, association with him is seen as one way to garner political support from that ethnic group. In the United States, at least, that support has been expressed directly through financial contributions. From 1993 to 1996, Foguang clerics and lay-monastics made donations of thousands of dollars to the Democratic National Committee and to the campaign war chests of such politicians as Los Angeles County Supervisor Don Knabe, California Secretary of State March Fong Eu, Congressman Patrick Kennedy, Senator Edward Kennedy, Vice President Al Gore, and President Clinton.[17]

Master Xingyun is well aware that politicians come to him mainly for money and votes. He welcomes them to do so with the idea that, even if they do not become Buddhists themselves (at least not in this lifetime), a favorable portrayal of the tradition by such leaders will encourage others to learn more about it. That Master Xingyun has hoped to rely on such a trickle-down method to promote the Dharma in countries without a Buddhist heritage is quite evident from a statement he made to a group of American scholars two months before Hsi Lai Temple's official opening. In line with the conference's topic of "Religion and Society in the Tang and Song Dynasties," the master remarked to the gathering:

> I am very interested in the theme "The Relation between Religion and Society." When religion and society have a close relationship, then religion can spread smoothly. Otherwise, it is not easy to develop. When Buddhism

spread into China, it spread from officials (*guanfang*) to the people. With this strength to promote from above to below it is easy to develop within society. When the Buddha was alive, he highly valued the thinking of the Benevolent King Who Protected the Dharma (*Renwang Hufa*). The reason why Buddhism enjoyed a golden era during the Tang and Song dynasties is that, in addition to royal patronage, there were many scholars who studied and practiced it.

Mahayana Buddhism and American society are very compatible. Buddhism is different from other religions in its lack of exclusivity, its magnanimity, and its affinity with nature. Whether or not Americans can recover the golden era of the Tang and Song dynasty Buddhism will depend upon people's efforts. If those of high status and influence support it, it will develop even faster.[18]

Master Xingyun therefore sees creating ties of affinity with politicians as an expedient means (*fangbian*) for making people in that society more favorably disposed to Buddhist teachings. In the United States, however, the strategy has backfired, at least in the short term. After it became known that the Hsi Lai banquet attended by Al Gore served as a fund-raiser for the Democratic National Committee, Master Xingyun and his disciples found themselves not only unfavorably portrayed in the media as alleged agents for Taiwan political and business interests, but even the objects of investigations by the United States Senate, House of Representatives, and Justice Department.[19] Since that time, the master and politicians (not just of the United States, but around the world) have been more wary of establishing ties with one another. Master Xingyun is now satisfied with relying on less glamorous, but also less controversial, methods of attracting non-Buddhists to the Dharma.

When a news reporter from Wollongong, Australia, asked Foguang Shan's current abbot, the Venerable Xinding, how the organization planned to spread Buddhism among non-Chinese Australians, he replied, "People will increasingly come simply through human curiosity. Seeing the beautiful temple, they will be drawn to see what goes on inside."[20] As this statement indicates, clerics believe that the very splendor of Buddhism, and the impressive way in which it is propagated by Foguang Shan, will naturally excite people's interest. Such reasoning explains why Foguang Shan has chosen to build such large, impressive structures as Hsi Lai Temple, Nan Hua Temple, and Nan Tien Temple. This mode of operation rests on the assumption that, as all people share Buddha Nature (*Foxing*), those who have proper roots will spontaneously seek out the Dharma once they have had even the slightest exposure to it. Foguang Buddhists would therefore agree with

Dharmapala's assertion that there is no need to proselytize aggressively (see Kemper, Chap. 1). Instead, Buddhists can rely on simply sparking people's curiosity so that they will on their own initiative ask about the Dharma. Such a tactic not only calls for creating impressive structures and organizing large-scale events to attract attention but also for accentuating the uniqueness of both Buddhism and Chinese culture.

In dialectical tension with the method of celebrating difference to spark curiosity is the recognition that too strong a sense of foreignness can repel people and incite prejudice. Foguang devotees from Malaysia and the Philippines say they must keep a low profile to avoid harassment. There are also significant challenges in promoting Buddhism in Africa. There, people look askance at the black robes and tonsured heads of clerics because the color black is associated with evil magical power and a person will usually only shave his or her head after the death of a parent or other close relative. Buddhist monastics are therefore vulnerable to suspicions and often the target of countermagic.[21] There have been hurdles in the United States as well. It took nearly a decade punctuated by six volatile town meetings before permission was granted for the construction of Hsi Lai Temple. Shortly after the temple was completed in 1989, the float entered by the Hsi Lai community in a local Fourth of July parade was heckled along much of the way. Only after several years of carefully cultivating good relations with neighbors and local political and religious leaders did the accusations of being a "cult" die down, although they arose once again in the aftermath of the Democratic National Committee fund-raising debacle.

To lessen tensions with the mainstream society in each country in which Foguang Shan plants one or more temples, and to smooth the transition for those attracted to the Dharma, Master Xingyun has called for the "localization" (*bentuhua*) of Buddhism. By this, he means that customs which have been generated by Buddhists in China and other cultures over the centuries may be replaced by other customs more appropriate to each new region into which the Dharma is introduced. The essential teachings remain the same, while culture-specific practices can vary. To adapt George Tanabe's horticultural metaphor, the Dharma continues as the unchanged "rootstock," although the cultural practices formerly grafted onto this stock are pruned and replaced by a new grafting.[22] The difficulty in applying this method lies in determining just where core truth ends and custom begins. In fact, the debate over the degree to which to localize touches every aspect of temple life: should Dharma functions be altered in any way? what language should be used? what kind of food should be served? what music is appropriate?

Master Xingyun believes that the people most competent to resolve these issues are natives of the respective non-Buddhist countries who have gone through intensive training in a Foguang college, preferably on the campus at the headquarters. Most ideal of all is to find such individuals who aspire to renounce. The Foguang Shan Monastic Academy has a special department to tend to the education of such candidates. As with all monastic college students, tuition, room, and board are provided free of charge. For those who come from an underprivileged background, airfare to Foguang Shan is also paid.

To date, however, Foguang Shan has not been very successful in keeping such clerics within the organization. Non-Chinese monastics typically voice two frustrations: either they find it too difficult to acclimate to Chinese customs and values or they feel that their Chinese brethren do not take them seriously. The rate of attrition is consequently very high, many leaving within a few months of matriculating in the college, others making it through the period of training but disappearing soon thereafter. Of the approximately one dozen Europeans and Americans who tonsured under Master Xingyun, only two could still be found in the Foguang Shan order as of the year 2002. Efforts in Africa and India have also had very limited success. Fewer than half of the ten young men who in 1994 became Foguang Shan's first *shramanera* from the Congo lasted through the year-long program at Nan Hua Temple Seminary, and only one continued on afterward. Staff of the Nan Hua Seminary informed me that, of the sixty-three students brought there from Tanzania and Malawi in 1998, not even a dozen remained by year's end, of whom three persevered for two years. The arrangement to bring young men and women from Ladakh, India, to Foguang Shan to be groomed as monastics has also suffered a high drop-out rate.

Although the initiative to develop a contingent of non-Chinese Foguang clerics has met with numerous setbacks, it has by no means been a complete failure and, in fact, might even be considered something of a success. As mentioned above, two Americans were still within Foguang ranks as of the year 2002, one of whom was a nun who had been with the order for over ten years, the other a monk who took full vows in Foguang Shan's ordination ceremony in Bodhgaya in 1998. Also in the Bodhgaya ordination were five men from the Congo (including a young man who in 1994 had been among the first ten to take the *shramanera* vows) and six Ladakhi women who had spent at least a year studying at Foguang Shan.[23]

The debate over the extent and ways in which to localize affects laity even more than it does clerics, especially those devotees who are either non-Chinese or ethnic Chinese who have grown up outside of China. Non-Chinese attracted to Foguang temples generally fall into two groups: Sinophiles, many of whom wish to take on a full Chinese persona, and those primarily interested in Buddhist teachings. The former have great interest in Chinese customs, ritual, and language, and therefore typically prefer to interact with the Chinese devotees rather than with any other non-Chinese who may also have become part of the community. To employ the terminology utilized by Richard Payne (Chap. 4), such neoromantics seek to have a "mimetic merger with the exotic Other." The latter have only passing interest in things Chinese and may even wish to strip the Buddhist teachings of what they see as Chinese cultural accretions. Hence, Sinophiles resist localization, the others embrace it. To again use Tanabe's metaphor, Sinophiles wish simply to tend the bodhi tree exactly as it has been transplanted from China to their particular country; "purists" hope to prune that tree of the branches that over the millennia were grafted onto the stock in the Middle Kingdom so as to return the plant to the pristine condition of the original bodhi tree as it had initially grown in India.

The localization debate is arguably most keenly felt by second- and third-generation overseas Chinese youth. During a 1997 BLIA Youth Conference that took place at Foguang headquarters, a student from Malaysia said that he and others at his temple had held some activities not considered traditionally Buddhist, and as a result they had been reprimanded by the resident monastics. He felt that the criticism was unjustified and asserted that there had to be more openness to adapting to the lifestyle of young overseas Chinese. A woman strongly disagreed, responding: "As Buddhists, we must maintain a strong line between right and wrong. Just because others do it doesn't mean that we should do it. We have to have a different standard." This interchange raises two issues. First, although the young man from Malaysia did not specify the types of activities he and his friends had held, one can assume that they were much more influenced by global pop culture than they were by the country's dominant Islamic lifestyle. This underscores the complexity of today's world, in which multiple cultural worldviews, both religious and secular, converge in nearly every society. Second, the young woman's response reminds us that, because custom is so tightly bound up with notions of morality, any change in practice is often regarded as vitiating ethical standards.

The real issue, however, is not so much one of morality as of identity. I noted earlier in this chapter that the first prong of the Foguang globalization program is to act as a bridge back to the Chinese cultural homeland. The organization's capacity to serve as a vehicle to preserve Chinese identity is directly undermined by any effort to localize practice or to harmonize it with global pop culture. These three aspects of globalization are therefore in constant tension with one another. For Foguang Shan to be able to claim to be an international operation transcending all ethnic and cultural boundaries, it must extend itself beyond its core Chinese base. To the degree that it does so, it risks ostracizing its most important source of devotees and, hence, financial support. Foguang overseas temples thus far have opted to continue to accentuate their Chinese heritage, making a few symbolic gestures toward accommodating local and global custom. Temples may provide a spoon and fork rather than chopsticks in the refectory, for instance, or clerics may shake hands with lay visitors. For the most part, however, life in the temple is essentially the same as it would be if it were located in Taiwan. In fact, non-Chinese who come to visit are frequently referred to as *laowai*, "foreigners."

These difficulties experienced by Foguang devotees in negotiating cultural boundaries point to the limitations of any language of global citizenry that implies a negation or transcendence of local ties. Exposure to the globalization of market and media forces and the setting adrift of imagined communities from their territorial anchorage interact either to multiply cultural allegiances or, as often is the case, to trigger retrenchment, that is, a reaffirmation of the primacy of one particular imagined community. Chinese Foguang devotees have mostly opted for this latter tactic as they have searched for stability in an increasingly fluid world system. Despite the predominance of this strategy, they nonetheless recognize that the global conditions of postmodernity call for an approach that better accords with the inevitable hybridity of contemporary life. The last part of this chapter will explore the Foguang Buddhist paradigm for world citizenry, one that empowers devotees not only to come to terms with the global scope of humankind's cultural hybridity but also to harness the dynamism of these conditions to further self-cultivation.

GLOBAL HOMELESSNESS

Since he retired as abbot of Foguang Shan in 1985, Master Xingyun has been said to "wander the four seas like a cloud." This is, in fact, the ideal lifestyle of all Buddhist clerics, who upon leaving home are said in the *Sutta Nipata* to become "free everywhere, at odds with none, and well content with this or that. . . ."[24] The constant movement and simple life represented by forgoing any fixed abode embody the Buddha's teaching of impermanence and his ideals of detachment and equanimity. Shakyamuni and his disciples traveled daily in search of alms, taking refuge each evening in a convenient grove or on the outskirts of some town. Only during the monsoon season did they halt their peregrinations to wait out the rains. Even in China, where monasticism has been the norm, clerics through the centuries have hoped to "travel the four quarters" (*canfang*) as symbolized by the country's four famous Buddhist pilgrimage mountains. To have an ordination certificate whose borders were embossed with the seals of China's most renowned monasteries was a source of pride, especially if one had prostrated every three steps over the course of the journey. Homelessness is not an undesirable state to be avoided or overcome. It is a religious ideal.

Until recently, only clerics enjoyed the benefits to self-cultivation afforded by long-term homelessness, and they largely enacted this lifestyle within the borders of their own country. With the development of international migration and increased global mobility, all Chinese who have departed from the homeland symbolically partake of the itinerant life. For laity, homelessness does not entail forgoing a family, but describes the physical departure from relatives and friends and the cultural distancing from Chinese society that inevitably accompany expatriate life. Foguang monastics, shifting posts of duty every three years, are the paragons of global citizenry. For them (and, mutatis mutandis, for such Sri Lankan monks as Piyadassi and Mapalagama Vipulasara who are engaged in *videshagatavima*, as described by Kemper, Chap. 1), the badge of honor is not an ordination certificate filled with the seals of temples, but a passport covered with the entry visas of various nations.

One reason the Huishen myth appeals to Foguang devotees is its transnational flavor. The Venerable Huishen, after all, was not Chinese, but rather an Indian monk who merely resided in China before moving on to spend the majority of his life in America. The designations of "Indian," "Chinese," and "American" were fleeting and secondary. Huishen was first and foremost a Buddhist. Master Xingyun similarly lacks a strong association with a particular place. He often notes that people in Taiwan refer to him as "that monk from the mainland." When he has visited the PRC, however, and when he travels abroad, people have called him "that monk from Taiwan." Master Xingyun, like the Venerable Huishen, is a monk without a home. This is not a negative, in the master's view, but a positive, for it allows him to symbolize personally the ability of Buddhism to transcend all such nationalistic designations. As he once said in an interview with me:

> I don't feel that you are Americans. I also don't feel that I am a Chinese. We are all global. We are all the same. . . . If we could join together with one another with no regard to nationality or race, it would be wonderful. So [the] global character [of Foguang Shan] doesn't simply mean building temples in various places. We want to spread peace, equality, forbearance, friendship, respect, and tolerance everywhere to everyone.

Although Master Xingyun may say that "We are all global," his call to deaccentuate national identity serves to shift a person's primary loyalty to the vehicle that allows such deemphasis to occur, namely to Buddhism. We are all global in that we all have Buddha Nature. Only to the degree that we recognize it will national and other local allegiances fade away. Such rhetoric points to what may be a growing trend in postmodernity in which the primary referent for communal identity increasingly reverts from national to religious symbols and myths. It is more than happenstance that secularization occurred during the same period as the rise of nations. Religion and nationhood are in tension with one another as contending sources of primary allegiance and identity. The attenuation of national sovereignty brought about by global capitalism has left a vacuum, one easily filled by religious traditions, since their worldviews incorporate language of both particularity and universality. Postmodernity may therefore spur people to once again more fully align themselves with reconstructed elements of premodern traditions. We see this not only in Foguang Shan devotees, but also in the interactions among Sri Lankan, Japanese, Burmese, and European Buddhists, and in the experiences of the Brazilian Zen and Soka Gakkai Buddhists (studied by Kemper, Rocha, and Clarke, respectively).

From the Foguang perspective, modern globalization is by no means antithetical to traditional Buddhist ideals or practices. Each realizes the other, as through globalization people come to realize the truth of the Mahayana Buddhist doctrines of impermanence and universal interdependence. Master Xingyun and his devotees firmly believe that the Buddha, Dharma, and sangha are not relics of the past but harbingers of postmodernity, actualizing the spiritual potential of economic, political, and cultural globalization.

Notes

An earlier version of this essay was published as "Globalizing Chinese Culture, Localizing Buddhist Teachings: The Internationalization of Foguangshan," *Journal of Global Buddhism* 3 (2002): 46–78. Most of the information for the essay was compiled through fieldwork carried out at the Foguang headquarters (Taiwan), Hsi Lai Temple (Los Angeles), Nan Tien Temple (Wollongong, Australia), Nan Hua Temple (Bronkhorstspruit, South Africa), and other Foguang branches. A total of two years of fieldwork took place over the years 1996 to 2002. Unless otherwise noted, quoted comments by Master Xingyun and his devotees represent remarks made to me during interviews or conversations.

1. Shi Xingyun, *Xingyun riji* [Xingyun's Diary], vol. 3 (Kaohsiung, Taiwan: Foguang Press, 1994), entry for January 2, 1990.

2. For a more detailed discussion of the scholarly debate concerning an early arrival in America by a Buddhist sailing from China, see Stuart Chandler, "Chinese Buddhism in America: Identity and Practice," in *The Faces of American Buddhism*, ed. Charles Prebish and Kenneth Tanaka (Berkeley and Los Angeles: University of California Press, 1998), 14–16.

3. Chinese emigrants from mainland China, Hong Kong, and Southeast Asia also frequent overseas Foguang temples and join BLIA. The moving force behind the organization's internationalization nonetheless remains expatriated ROC citizens.

4. In 1992, 4.86 million people in Taiwan indicated that they frequented Buddhist temples. Eight years later, the numbers had increased to slightly more than five million. These statistics were provided to me by the ROC Department of the Interior, Bureau of Religion, Taipei. *Awakening the World* was Foguang Shan's monthly newsletter to its devotees through the year 1999, at which point it was discontinued and replaced by the daily newspaper *Humanistic Prosperity (Renjian fu bao)*.

5. The term "Humanistic Buddhism" is the English translation of Renjian Fojiao. Master Xingyun did not coin the term "Renjian Fojiao," nor is he the only contemporary Chinese Buddhist cleric in whose lexicon it plays a central role. Master Taixu (1889–1947) was the first to employ the concept, although he usually referred to it as Rensheng Fojiao. In Taixu's opinion, Chinese Buddhism had suffered a great decline due to an overemphasis on funerary rites. He therefore devised the term "Rensheng Fojiao" to remind people that, as it is the living *(rensheng)* who are in the best position to attain enlightenment, Buddhists should devote their energies to maximizing this opportunity, both for themselves and for others. The general preference for Renjian Fojiao has come about through the work of the Venerable Yinshun (b. 1906). He preferred *"renjian"* to *"rensheng"* to give even more emphasis to the fact that Buddhist practice must occur through active participation in human society *(renjian*, or "in the human domain"). It should not be inordinately devoted to worshiping buddhas as though they were deities, a tendency that in his opinion has long plagued the Mahayana tradition. Both Master Xingyun and the Venerable Zhengyan (the founder of Taiwan's largest lay Buddhist association, Ciji) have followed Yinshun's terminology. Taiwan's most famous Chan master, the Venerable Shengyan, has preferred to maintain the wording of Rensheng Fojiao. All five of these clerics qualify "Buddhism" with adjectives approximating the English "humanistic" so as to redirect people's attention back from other realms and lifetimes to present existence in this world.

6. These numbers are based on an analysis of the worker assignments listed in *Foguang cunlin* [Foguang newsletter], no. 424 (Foguang Shan Religious Affairs Committee), August 15, 1997. By full-time workers, I mean those clerics and lay-monastics *(shigu)* who have already graduated from the monastic college and are not on some form of leave. An additional 110 monks and nuns were studying in one of Foguang Shan's seminaries. One hundred and thirty-six monastics were apparently on extended leave of absence. A "lay-monastic" has not fully renounced but has vowed to remain celibate and to live on Foguang premises for the rest of his or her life so as to devote all his or her energy to aiding the organization in spreading the Dharma.

7. Patricia Hunt-Perry and Lyn Fine, "All Buddhism Is Engaged: Thich Nhat Hanh and

the Order of Interbeing," in *Engaged Buddhism in the West,* ed. Christopher Queen (Boston: Wisdom, 2000), 45.

8. Martin Baumann, "Work as Dharma Practice: Right Livelihood Cooperatives of the FWBO," in *Engaged Buddhism in the West,* ed. Christopher Queen (Boston: Wisdom, 2000), 378.

9. Alan Sponberg, "TBMSG: A Dhamma Revolution in Contemporary India," in *Engaged Buddhism: Buddhist Liberation Movements in Asia,* ed. Christopher Queen (Albany: State University of New York Press, 1996), 73–120.

10. Master Xingyun and his disciples regard themselves as vital carriers of filial piety *(xiao)* and propriety *(li),* both traditionally closely associated with the Confucian tradition. For more on this, see chapter 8 of my book *Establishing a Pure Land on Earth: The Foguang Buddhist Perspectives on Modernization and Globalization* (Honolulu: University of Hawai'i Press, 2004).

11. Tu Wei-ming, "The Search for Roots in Industrial East Asia: The Case of the Confucian Revival," in *Fundamentalisms Observed,* ed. Martin E. Marty and R. Scott Appleby (Chicago: University of Chicago Press, 1991), 742–745.

12. The Dutch planted trading posts along the southwest coast of Ilha Formosa (Beautiful Island) from 1624 to 1662. Their population on the island peaked at twenty-eight hundred, of whom twenty-two hundred were soldiers. The Spanish had settlements in the north from 1626 to 1642; I-shou Wang, "Cultural Contact and the Migration of Taiwan's Aborigines: A Historical Perspective," in *China's Island Frontier: Studies in the Historical Geography of Taiwan,* ed. Ronald G. Knapp (Honolulu: University of Hawai'i Press, 1980), 36. Before this time, only a smattering of Chinese came to the island to fish or conduct trade, with virtually none establishing permanent homes there with their families. Chinese began to settle and farm Taiwan's eastern coastal region under the protection of the Dutch and Spanish forts. Significant numbers, however, began to arrive only when Zheng Chenggong established his renegade anti-Qing regime there in 1661. The island became part of the Chinese imperial state for the first time two decades later, when a Qing fleet forced the Zheng leadership to abdicate their power. John E. Wills, Jr., "The Seventeenth-Century Transformation: Taiwan under the Dutch and the Cheng Regime," in *Taiwan: A New History,* ed. Murray A. Rubinstein (Armonk, N.Y.: M. E. Sharpe, 1999), 84–103.

13. Holmes Welch, *The Practice of Chinese Buddhism 1900–1950* (Cambridge, Mass.: Harvard University Press, 1967), 306–310.

14. Shi, Xingyun (general editor), *Foguang Da Cidian* [Foguang encyclopedia] (Kaohsiung, Taiwan: Foguang Press, 1988), 5190.

15. Ibid., 6665.

16. According to Master Xingyun's diary, when it turned out that he would not be able to attend President Bush's inauguration, there was talk of arranging for him to go to the White House at another time to meet him. The master then goes on to say that the newly elected

president had an interest in coming to Hsi Lai to visit. Shi Xingyun, *Xingyun Riji*, vol. 2, entry for October 19, 1989.

17. These donations are listed in "The United States of America v. Maria Hsia A/K/A Hsia Ling, Defendant," United States Court for the District of Columbia, docket CR.98–0057(PLF). This document is found under the district court opinions category of http://www.westlaw.com.

18. Shi Xingyun, *Xingyun Riji*, vol. 2, entry for October 14, 1989. As the number of American political officials visiting Hsi Lai Temple mounted, Master Xingyun told his disciples, "For us Buddhists to come to America and be able to receive the positive acceptance by the United States government is our greatest vow and hope!" Shi Xingyun, *Xingyun Riji*, vol. 3, entry for January 23, 1990.

19. Stuart Chandler, "Placing Palms Together: Religious and Cultural Dimensions of the Hsi Lai Temple Political Donations Controversy," in *American Buddhism: Methods and Findings in Recent Scholarship*, ed. Duncan Ryuken Williams and Christopher Queen (Surrey, Eng.: Curzon, 1999), 36–56.

20. The Venerable Xinding interview with Jodie Duffy of Prime Television (Wollongong, Australia), Foguang Shan, May 2, 1997. Master Xingyun retired as the abbot of Foguang Shan in 1985, passing on the day-to-day administration of temple affairs to one of his disciples.

21. The Venerable Huijin, one of the first Africans to tonsure under Master Xingyun, told me of these difficulties for monastics in Africa. Because of the dangerous associations with the color black, the African novices were early on granted permission to wear instead the gray-colored work robes or, for special occasions, the mustard-colored robes (normally, only fully ordained graduates of the Buddhist college are permitted to wear these latter).

22. It is important to note that in Tanabe's metaphor the trunk of the tree represents Japanese Shin ancestral religion, whereas I am using the trunk to represent an idealized, universal Buddha Dharma as opposed to a distinctive, local Buddhism.

23. Unfortunately, because of visa regulations, the five young men from the Congo soon had to return to their country, where, due to escalating civil war, it was felt to be too dangerous for them to continue a monastic lifestyle. Several had voiced the hope of returning to Nan Hua Temple and resuming their career as clerics, but little was ever heard of them after their repatriation. It was because of the degenerating political situation in the Congo that Nan Hua shifted its base of recruitment to Tanzania and Malawi.

24. Edward Conze, ed. and trans., *Buddhist Scriptures* (New York: Penguin Books, 1979), 79.

8 The Compassion Relief Diaspora

C. Julia Huang

This chapter presents a multiple-sited case study of the worldwide development of a Taiwanese grassroots lay Buddhist movement. Thirty years after its establishment in Taiwan, the Buddhist Compassion Relief Tzu-Chi Foundation (Fojiao Ciji Jijinghui, commonly known as Ciji Gongde Hui, Compassion Relief Merit Society, in Taiwan, hereafter, Compassion Relief) is currently the largest formal association in Taiwan, and over the past decade has formed branches in about thirty countries. Compassion Relief is the first modern Buddhist organization in any Chinese society to carry out humanitarian missions on a large, international scale that includes delivery of relief on every continent. Such accomplishments have won its leader, a Buddhist nun named the Venerable Zhengyan (or Cheng-Yen), the 1991 Philippine Magsaysay Award and the 1993 nomination for the Nobel Peace Prize.[1] In the year 2000, a textbook for high-school students in Canada devoted one page to Compassion Relief and its leader, both of whom they characterized as exemplary,[2] and *Business Week* recognized Zhengyan as the only Taiwanese among the fourteen—mostly entrepreneurs—"stars of Asia."[3]

This essay examines the characteristics of this example of a global Buddhist movement. More specifically, it seeks to describe the forms and content of the movement's globalism and to examine the ways in which the worldwide spread of a Taiwanese Buddhist movement may represent both the importance of diaspora communities in the globalization process and the desire to move beyond ethnic confines, a two-edged strategy that may or may not succeed in the long run.[4] First, I shall describe the brief history of Compassion Relief by highlighting the external and indigenous sources that have blended in the Venerable Zhengyan's creation of the movement. Second, I shall give an overview of the structure of Compassion Relief's expansion worldwide, which consists of two overlapping parts: mission and missionaries and, more specifically, their global outreach programs and their overseas branches of devotees. The closing section is an attempt to summarize the characteristics of Compassion Relief's route of global development and the possible implications this example has for the interplay between religion and ethnicity in the global context.

Compassion Relief is distinct from traditional religious practice among overseas Chinese. Despite the mistaken common label of "Buddhism," the most widely practiced religion among overseas Chinese has been Chinese popular religion—that is, a combination of Buddhism, Confucianism, and Daoism.[5] "Canonical religions, in particular Christianity and Buddhism," did not significantly rise until the 1990s, when a majority of overseas Chinese communities were comprised of well-educated people instead of the earlier laborers and sojourners.[6]

From the outset Compassion Relief has retained its Buddhist identity—symbolically and legally.[7] However, unlike most Chinese (Mahayana) Buddhists who focus on sutra chanting, Compassion Relief emphasizes building a "pure land" in this world through secular action—namely, making concrete contributions to humanity. Perhaps more important, Compassion Relief is a formal association compared to, although not completely separate from, informal social ties such as personal connections (guanxi), and it operates under a new form of transnational organization in contrast to, although again not completely separate from, familism. To be a Compassion Relief person (Cijiren) is to identify oneself as a "deployable agent" of Buddha's universal compassion for all the living by contributing to the Compassion Relief mission.[8] By thus contributing, one becomes a member of the group and involved in its "religious community." Such engagement in Compassion Relief, as the present case study will show, helps to "retain a sense of plausibility" of one's new religious identity[9] and, at the same time, offers a vision of Buddhist global community among the Chinese and particularly Taiwanese diaspora.

A BRIEF INTRODUCTION TO COMPASSION RELIEF

Compassion Relief was founded in 1966 on the poor eastern coast of Taiwan.[10] At that time, it consisted of a nun, five disciples, and thirty followers, all housewives. Their goal was to defray medical costs for the poor. The housewives each donated NT$0.50 (buying power of about US$0.025 in current dollars) every day from their grocery money and proselytized among their family and friends. The nuns made handicrafts whose sale supported the monastic order and added to the relief fund. Their monthly charity funds in the first year came to less than US$30.

Compassion Relief developed slowly in its first decade, and then rapidly spread across the island in the late 1980s—the time when Taiwan was moving toward a wealthier economy and a more democratic polity. By 2000, Compassion Relief claimed five million members worldwide, with branches in twenty-eight countries. Presently, it gives away over US$157 million (NT$5.4 billion in 1999) in charity each year,[11] runs a TV channel, a secular four-year university with a standard medical school, and two state-of-the-Western-art 900-bed hospitals. It runs free clinics in California and Hawai'i, a medical institute in Vancouver, and a dialysis center in Penang, Malaysia. It has delivered relief to disaster victims in the People's Republic of China, Rwanda, Chechnya, and Papua New Guinea, among many other places.

Compassion Relief is a lay Buddhist movement under monastic leadership. Its founder and leader is the Venerable Zhengyan, a Buddhist nun with great charisma. Most followers trace their conversion to her immediate personal appeals. While she teaches classic Buddhist texts (e.g., the Lotus Scripture, [Miaofa lianhua jing]; the Thirty-Seven Aids to Enlightenment [Sanshiqi daopin, Skt.: Siksananda]; the Scripture of the Medicine Master [Yaoshi jing]; and the Scripture of Parents' Unrequited Kindness [Fumu enzhong nanbao jing]), Zhengyan's Dharma (fa) is the absolute authority for the whole movement.[12] Under her charismatic leadership, the Compassion Relief umbrella organization now has basically two overlapping divisions: the Compassion Relief Foundation proper (Ciji Jijin Hui) and the volunteer association (Ciji Gongde Hui). The nonprofit foundation alone has about five hundred staff members and controls NT$12 billion (approximately US$342 million) in funds.[13] It gave away over NT$5.4 billion (approximately US$157 million) in 1999 in charity, much of it international.[14] Funds provided by the volunteer organization support all Compassion Relief missions and the foundation.[15] The organization has over ten thousand "commissioners" (weiyuan) worldwide who have no position in the foundation.[16] They are committed to supporting all Compassion Relief missions and generally refer to themselves as followers of the Venerable Zhengyan. About 70 percent of the commissioners are women, although male participation has rapidly increased since total membership skyrocketed in the early 1990s.

The Venerable Zhengyan is the key to understanding Compassion Relief not only because she is charismatic but also because all Compassion Relief missions are very largely, if not solely, the result of her vision of Buddhism. She states how and why Compassion Relief is a reform of traditional Chinese Buddhism:

> In the past, Buddhism in this world had sounds but no forms, and was hardly "practical" (shiji). The so-called Buddhism saw only temples and masters speaking of texts. This was the image of Buddhism in the past 2,000 years, and the reason why most people misunderstood Buddhism as only about chanting sutras and worshipping Buddha, a religion of old ladies. . . . I founded Compassion Relief for Buddhism and for all the living,[17] with the hope that Buddhism shall not only exist on [people's] lips,

but also manifest itself—to demonstrate the spirit of Buddha through practical action; to pursue "involvement" *(shi)* (the spirit of Compassion Relief) and "truth" *(li)* (the spirit of Buddha) in tandem.[18]

What Zhengyan meant by "practical action" and what she saw for Compassion Relief engagement, by and large, consisted of contributions to social welfare carried out by both the monastic order and the laity. On the one hand, in contrast with most Chinese Buddhist priests who rely for their livelihood on alms and giving scripture (Skt: *sutra*) chanting services for donations, Zhengyan and her disciples not only completely support themselves independently from donations, but also contribute to the relief funds. On the other hand, the main practice of the lay followers is not chanting scriptures but contributing their time and money to proselytizing, raising funds, and volunteering for the Venerable Zhengyan's mission.

Zhengyan's mission has expanded from uplifting the poor and caring for the needy in the 1960s and 1970s, to building a Compassion Relief hospital on the impoverished eastern side of Taiwan where most aborigines reside in the 1980s, to the "Four Great Compassion Relief Missions" and the four "footprints" *(jiaoyin)*. The Four Great Missions *(si da zhiye)* are charity (i.e., on-site investigation, evaluation, and long-term care); medical care (e.g., building hospitals); education (e.g., building a university and organizing the Compassion Relief teachers' association and youth corps); and culture (e.g., Compassion Relief publications and TV). The additional four "footprints" are international disaster relief; bone-marrow drives (i.e., collecting bone-marrow samples for an international database and transplantation); environmentalism (e.g., sorting garbage for recycling), and community volunteers (e.g., cooperating with public social workers to provide local elders with long-term care). In contrast with the often ad hoc nature or emphatically spiritual practice of Buddhist charity in Chinese societies, Compassion Relief has established a reputation for searching out causes and mobilizing for effective implementation.

The breakthrough Compassion Relief has made in Chinese Buddhism is very much the result of the reformism that Zhengyan developed through her own reflection upon various religious traditions in Taiwan. Compassion Relief literature describes how Zhengyan came to conceive of the organization through a series of events spanning her lay and monastic life. A closer look at these major events reveals clues to the pluralist influences on Compassion Relief of Japanese Buddhism, Taiwanese indigenous Buddhism, reformist Chinese Buddhism, and Catholicism.[19]

At age sixteen (in 1953), Zhengyan prayed to the Bodhisattva Guanyin (the Goddess of Mercy) to take twelve years from her life in exchange for her mother's recovery from an illness. Her mother recovered. As also vowed, Zhengyan became a vegetarian. The significance of this first encounter with Buddhist divinity lies less in linking Zhengyan to Buddhism than in grounding her character in filial piety, since she had yet to receive Buddhist teachings, let alone pursue her monastic vocation, which did not occur until five years later when her father passed away.[20] Bereaved, Zhengyan sought help in Buddhism and began to frequent Buddhist temples in her hometown in central Taiwan, where one of the nuns told her that she could no longer agree with the dependency of Chinese priesthood after she had studied Buddhism in Japan. Zhengyan said to herself, "I shall change the circumstances and build the dignity of Buddhist priests if I become a nun one day."[21] Ever since she embarked on the journey toward becoming a nun Zhengyan has been abiding by the Chan Master Baizhang's teaching "A day without working is a day without eating."[22] Zhengyan further established three "no's" for her monastic order: no scripture chanting for a fee, no Dharma ceremony for a fee, and no begging.

Japanese Buddhism inspired Zhengyan to establish an economically independent priesthood. In addition to Japanese Buddhist influence, Taiwanese indigenous Buddhism played a role in her early years as a priest. After she left home at the age of twenty-four to become a nun, Zhengyan wandered to different temples. Eventually she took refuge with a lay Buddhist in Hualian on the eastern coast. Zhengyan shaved her head by herself and meditated on and studied the Lotus Scripture alone in a humble house.[23] Li argues that both her following a lay teacher and her solitary meditation without formal ordination accord with the tradition of Taiwanese indigenous vegetarian sect Buddhism (zhaijiao), the most prevalent form of Buddhist practice in Taiwan until the Japanese colonization (1895–1945).[24]

A link to a reformist Chinese Buddhism came when a well-known secularizing and reformist monk, the Venerable Yinshun, agreed to be Zhengyan's tonsure master for her ordination in 1963. Yinshun has made his mark in the contemporary religious-political arena. Inspired by the Venerable Taixu in mainland China during his early years as a monk, Yinshun fled to Taiwan after the Communists took over there in 1949 and has long advocated Buddhism of the Human Realm (renjian fojiao; also referred to as Humanistic Buddhism in Chandler's essay).[25] Because his this-worldly approach challenged the then Buddhist authority's otherworldly approach, Yinshun was silenced in the 1950s, when they suggested that his position constituted Communist agitation.[26] Yinshun was later vindicated and is currently one of the most respected masters in Taiwan. Compassion Relief and other large Buddhist groups (e.g., Foguang Shan [see Chandler, Chap. 7] and Fagu Shan) have adopted his reformist notions since the late 1960s.[27]

Catholicism, among other things, compelled Zhengyan to think of a lay organization as the way to save the lives of those too poor to receive medical treatment. Two major events in 1966 led her to conceive of Compassion Relief in this way. The first was the sight of blood on a hospital floor—the remnant of the miscarriage of an unconscious aboriginal woman who was refused admittance to the hospital because her family lacked the deposit money. The second was a visit from three missionizing Catholic nuns, who criticized Buddhism for looking only to self-fulfillment while ignoring the larger problems of society.[28] Though she responded to the criticism by arguing that Buddhists usually contribute anonymously, Zhengyan nevertheless began to contemplate the possibility of *organizing* the widespread "anonymous" Buddhists.[29]

Compassion Relief is therefore a creation that draws inspiration from the religious pluralism in Taiwan. In his historical analysis, Li argued that Compassion Relief is a religious transformation of postcolonialism. It resonates with Taiwanese indigenous Buddhism, which barely survived the repression of Japanese colonization and the coercion of the Chinese Nationalist regime, and incorporates elements from foreign traditions—Japanese Buddhism, Chinese Buddhism, and Catholicism, which experienced significant growth under the above two foreign regimes. Li's analysis grounds Compassion Relief in Taiwan's history of Buddhism and shows that it is not a mere reflection of Taiwan's political history. Rather, it is a new religion that organically combines elements of different religious traditions and that is distinct from, and cannot be attributed to, any of its indigenous and external sources alone.[30]

Yet Li does not explain why Compassion Relief's distinctive appeal received such a tremendous response from women and why it did not achieve a massive following until the economic and political changes of late-1980s Taiwan. In spite of its monastic leadership, Compassion Relief is essentially a lay movement. A comparison of Compassion Relief women and the charitable women in the nineteenth-century West shows the cross-cultural similarities between the two cases. It points to the powerful, shared effects of modernity, the new opportunities women may achieve from rapid structural change, and, in turn, the social ramifications brought about by women's activism. The equally important differences between Compassion Relief and the Western case show that the significance of Compassion Relief lies in its unique expression of Buddhism among people,[31] in the emerging role of women in the public sphere worldwide, and in the development of civic associations in post-martial law Taiwan.[32]

Compassion Relief is therefore significant in Taiwan's historical context as well as modernization. On the one hand, it cuts through the religious pluralism in Taiwan and reveals a dialogue between indigenous and external sources. On the other hand, it opens a space in the public sphere for Buddhism among people, for women's activism, and for the formation of civil society in Taiwan. Moreover, placing it in the larger context of the global arena, Weller points out that the particular timing of Compassion Relief's rapid growth also coincides with significant change in the global context, especially in communications, including both the media and transportation.[33] The significance of Compassion Relief in the global context lies in its breakthrough in manifesting the active role of religion—Buddhism, in particular—in this era of movements. The following section will show the two sides of Compassion Relief's global activism: one is to adopt a global vision for its service-oriented mission resulting in international outreach programs; and the other is to tap its overseas growth among the Chinese, especially Taiwanese, diaspora leading to a mobilization of overseas Chinese that will center on Taiwan as a new religious pilgrimage.

GLOBAL OUTREACH AND TRANSNATIONAL DEVELOPMENT

Concomitant to its rapid growth in Taiwan in the 1980s, by 1990 Compassion Relief had broadened its vistas in the following three ways: dedication to international, as well as domestic, relief projects; the organization of worldwide bone-marrow donation drives; and the development of overseas chapters. Both international relief and bone-marrow donation drives are usually initiated by the headquarters in Taiwan, receiving support from overseas chapters through their fund-raising publicity in host societies.

Four overarching motifs seem to emerge from Compassion Relief's global efforts. One is the vision of a global community, in which peoples of different parts of the world are seen to be possible prospects for becoming Compassion Relief followers, who will then join together to build a better world through their collective good work. In Compassion Relief's words, "[We] invite all benevolent people under heaven to the land of merit; with hearts pure, like ten-thousand lotus buds, we will create a world of compassion relief (*futian yifang yao tianxia shanshi, xinlian wanrui zao ciji shijie*)."[34]

The second motif, especially for international relief projects and worldwide bone-marrow donation drives, is based on the Buddhist notion of the universal connection of, and empathy with, all the living, regardless of any mundane category such as race, ethnicity, and nationality. In Compassion Relief's words, "Great compassion for those who are known and unknown, boundless mercy for all beings (*wuyuan daci, tongti dabei*)."

Overlapping with the first and second motif is the pursuit of "making be-nevolent connections" with people around the world, especially the charity recipi-ents of different races, ethnicities, and nationalities. This motif, akin to Master Xingyun's emphasis on links of affinity described by Chandler in this volume, is highlighted by the priority of direct contacts in its practice of global outreach. It is one of Compassion Relief's principles for international relief that it tries in every possible way to deliver the relief directly, themselves, rather than through other international or local organizations.

Finally, yet perhaps the most crucial motif, is the leader's charismatic appeal. The Venerable Zhengyan, like a lightning rod, finds herself at "ground zero" for international projects, giving the personal push for the urgency of these missions. "When other people are hurt, I feel their pain; when other people suffer, I feel their sorrow" (renshang wotong, renku wobei).[35] Zhengyan embodies the suffering of disaster victims, and in her spellbinding speech evokes the followers' response. As will also be shown in the third section, the Venerable Zhengyan's personal appeal has also played a crucial role in inspiring new converts to start proselytizing, which later resulted in the founding of overseas branches.

INTERNATIONAL RELIEF

The first international relief that Compassion Relief delivered was to flood victims in the People's Republic of China (PRC) in the summer of 1991. In four months, Compassion Relief raised more than NT$400 million (approximately US$13 mil-lion).[36] Zhengyan set up the principles for all their international relief efforts with this first project: on-site investigation and delivery without delegating to or going through mediating organizations or institutions, so as to "make benevolent con-nections" (jie shan yuan) with the victims; giving priority to the most seriously af-fected locations; and respect for local people and culture by not discriminating among recipients.[37] Zhengyan later added another three principles: no wastage of contributions, timely delivery, and gratitude expressed to the victims for the op-portunity to help.[38]

From the Taiwanese perspective, the issues involved in relief to the PRC and other countries are different. The relief to the PRC is more frequent than to other countries, and Compassion Relief literature presents their PRC project distinct from other overseas outreach projects. For example, by 1998 Compassion Relief had delivered relief to major disasters in the PRC at least once a year, building houses, schools, and elders' nursing homes. These are inscribed with the name of

Compassion Relief. The result has impressed people in the PRC,[39] although it does not translate into influences on the government's religious policy.[40]

In addition to the PRC, since 1992 Compassion Relief has provided aid to the victims of natural disasters and warfare and other artificial disasters in over thirty countries.[41]

BONE-MARROW DONATIONS

In order to embody the bodhisattva's ideal of "giving one's head, eyes, marrow, and brain for the benefit of others," Compassion Relief has also channeled its organizational, medical, and manpower resources into bone-marrow donation projects.

In response to a request by the Taiwan government's Department of Health, Compassion Relief founded its Marrow Donor Registry in October 1993. To combat a common misunderstanding of alleged ill effects on marrow donors, Compassion Relief followers held promotional events and gave blood tests across Taiwan. The drive collected data on over 140,000 volunteer donors between 1993 and 1997 and increased the number to 242,039 in 2003. The registry is currently the largest databank in Asia and the third largest in the world. Compassion Relief has helped to carry out 559 cases of non-relative transplants. Among these cases, there were over three hundred international donations to countries such as the United States, Australia, Japan, and Germany.[42] Likewise, almost every overseas branch has held promotions and marrow donation drives in their local community.

OVERSEAS BRANCHES

The first overseas branch, Compassion Relief Foundation–USA (Fojiao Ciji Jijinhui Meiguo Fenhui), obtained legal status in California in 1985 and was formally founded at the turn of 1990 in conjunction with the opening of its chapter house, the Still Thoughts Hall, named after Zhengyan's monastery, the Still Thoughts Abode. In the ensuing ten years, Compassion Relief devotees in other countries opened their own branches. Among the over one hundred countries where there are Compassion Relief members, twenty-eight had formed local chapters by January 2000 (see Table 8.1).

Most chapters have only one congregation in the country, but the scale of local development varies considerably. Local membership ranges from less than a hundred to several tens of thousands. Compassion Relief–USA is the largest branch and had fifty offices in 2003. As of the year 2000, it had 50,000 of the total

TABLE 8.1
Compassion Relief Foundation Overseas Branches

YEAR	NUMBER OF NEW BRANCHES	AFRICA	ASIA	OCEANIA	EUROPE	MIDDLE EAST	LATIN AMERICA	NORTH AMERICA
1990	2				U.K.			U.S.A.
1991	2		Japan; Singapore					
1992	7	South Africa	Hong Kong; Malaysia	Australia; New Zealand	Austria		Argentina; Brazil	Canada
1993	2		Indonesia; Philippines					
1994	2							
1995	1	Lesotho						
1996	1						Paraguay	
1997	5		Thailand; Vietnam		Germany; Spain		Mexico	
1998	2				Netherlands	Jordan		
1999	3		Brunei		France		Dominican Republic	
2000	1					Turkey		
TOTAL	28	2	9	2	6	2	5	2

SOURCE: This table is based on the directory of Compassion Relief Foundation branches in *Ciji yuekan* (Compassion relief monthly), no. 398 (2000).

of 90,000 overseas members, and nearly 400 commissioners among the overseas total of 552.

All Compassion Relief branches are located in the major cities of their host countries. According to Huang Sixian, the head of the Department of Religion as well as one of the highest lay representatives of Compassion Relief, participants in all the branches consist primarily of overseas Taiwanese, secondarily of overseas Chinese. Compassion Relief does not, at any rate, prevent non-Chinese from joining. Rather, as I try to make it clear throughout this chapter, especially later in this section, Compassion Relief makes efforts to go beyond ethnic boundaries. However, there are hardly any non-Chinese among Compassion Relief overseas followers. During our interview in 2000, Huang Sixian listed three exceptions. The coordinator of the Orlando chapter is a Caucasian; but his wife is Taiwanese, and he himself also speaks Chinese. One of the volunteer doctors in the Phoenix chapter is a Caucasian; but this does not necessarily mean that he is a Buddhist or a Compassion Relief follower. And one Caucasian volunteer in the Hawai'i chapter, a hospital administrator by profession, has been a Compassion Relief devotee to the extent that he proselytizes for the organization and received his Compassion Relief commissioner title in 2000. Recently, Compassion Relief Monthly devoted two pages to a profile of a Christian Zulu woman of Compassion Relief–Durban, South Africa. She was a Compassion Relief charity recipient for seven years and in 2002 became an active Compassion Relief volunteer, wearing the uniform and delivering speeches about her experience of Compassion Relief as well as her pilgrimage to the headquarters in Taiwan.[43] The same literature also reports that four hundred out of the fourteen thousand Zulu trainees at the Compassion Relief–Durban career center have begun to participate as volunteers in the local branch's AIDS relief programs.[44] The special attention given to these exemplars suggests that they are still somewhat exceptional. The majority of Compassion Relief devotees worldwide are Chinese or, more specifically, Han Chinese according to my fieldwork up to 2000 and my research so far.

Ideally, all overseas branches work toward the model of the headquarters, that is, the "Four Great Missions" plus the four "footprints." In practice, the scope of the overseas branches varies and may be generally divided into three levels: basic, intermediate, and the most active. The interplay between participants' Chinese ethnicity and their practice varies at each level. Practice in the least active level consists of the initiates' proselytizing efforts, volunteering at local social service institutions and/or hospitals, and providing emergency help to Taiwanese and Chinese immigrants and travelers. There is significant overlap in Compassion Relief overseas branches at the basic level between ethnic boundaries and the scope of practice; they function pretty much as ad hoc ethnic associations based on a shared belief in the Compassion Relief path of Buddhism.

At the intermediate level, services extend beyond ethnic boundaries, even while there is increasing attention to shared cultural heritage. A chapter at this level has a regular schedule of recruitment meetings, with teas and vegetarian buffets, specific volunteer services, intragroup activities, and special events such as bone-marrow drives, free on-site clinics, fund-raising for the headquarters' international relief projects and for local projects. Regular volunteer services reach out to the local community and include visits to local institutions (e.g., seniors' houses), support for other charitable organizations (e.g., homeless shelters), street cleaning, and a system for the provision of care to individual charity recipients. Intragroup activities include regular weekend (usually Sunday) scripture chanting and meetings on the branch's affairs; a study group on the Venerable Zhengyan's teachings; retreats; and community activities such as chorus, sign language (Chinese) for the deaf, and Chinese (Mandarin) language classes for the locally born second generation. Branches at the intermediate level also have chapters of the Compassion Relief Youth Corps among Taiwanese students at local colleges. The corps functions as an auxiliary to local chapters. In sum, intermediate-level branches are ethnic Buddhist associations that reach out to the wider community across ethnic boundaries while creating social ties and establishing secondary socialization among participants based on a shared cultural heritage.

Branches at the most active level tend to institutionalize their efforts both in reaching out to a variety of ethnicities and in preserving the Chinese cultural heritage. On the one hand, large branches take further steps toward transcending ethnic boundaries. They not only establish medical institutions and charitable systems for serving the local poor of all ethnicities, but also initiate the delivery of disaster relief to neighboring countries. For example, Compassion Relief–USA runs a free clinic in Alhambra, California, which provides most of its services to local Hispanic communities. At the same time, Compassion Relief–USA provides substantial relief to Mexico and other countries in Latin America, whereas Compassion Relief–Australia and Malaysia play leading roles in relief to countries in Southeast Asia.

On the other hand, large branches establish secondary socialization institutions that preserve Chinese cultural heritage and spread Compassion Relief teachings. These institutions consist of Chinese schools for second-generation immigrants and the Youth Corps for Taiwanese college students. Large branches in Western societies—the United States, Canada, and the United Kingdom—have founded seventeen "Compassion Relief Humanities Schools" (ciji renwen xuexiao)[45] and currently have a total of over two thousand pupils, whose parents do not necessarily participate in Compassion Relief. Every weekend, youngsters up to the twelfth grade learn Chinese characters through the official textbooks of the Taiwan-based Committee for Overseas Chinese Affairs, as well as the Venerable Zhengyan's "Still Thoughts" teachings, using the pedagogical methods formulated by the Compassion Relief Teachers' Association in Taiwan.

The Compassion Relief Youth Corps is important to the education mission, for it brings students outside of Compassion Relief institutions into contact with the Venerable Zhengyan's teachings. The Compassion Relief Youth Corps of some chapters in the United States (e.g., Berkeley and Boston) have their own separate pages on the Compassion Relief web site, and also organize activities and function as a distinct group in cooperation with local Compassion Relief followers. In comparison, the Compassion Relief Youth Corps of Malacca, consisting of local-born Chinese rather than Taiwanese college students, has become the branch's focal source of mobilization.

In addition to the obvious importance of socializing the younger generation to Compassion Relief values and practices, the Chinese schools and youth corps are felt to be important because of their potential for bringing Compassion Relief to people who do not have a Chinese ethnic background. When asked if Compassion Relief has a particular plan to draw in non-Chinese, Mr. Huang immediately replied: "Compassion Relief youth are our future, because they study [abroad] and have their cross-ethnic social connections. When they are out of school and start working, they may draw in their classmates, colleagues, and friends."

Meanwhile, Compassion Relief is not waiting for the future to come with the next generation. Recently it has significantly increased its use of a variety of languages and the media. In addition to holding special meetings completely in English for local non-Chinese,[46] it has been distributing an English quarterly since 1993 and including English pages in its monthly newsletter, along with publishing a series of English translations of the Zhengyan's teachings and children's books. In addition, it has been publishing a monthly journal in Japanese since 1997. A Compassion Relief web page, in both Chinese (traditional and simplified) and English, not only covers its daily news and each branch's profile around the world, but also airs the programs of its Taiwan-based TV channel. English subtitles have been added to each of the Venerable Zhengyan's televised sermons since 2000.

While extending communication beyond the Chinese language and excelling in the use of global media, Compassion Relief has been knitting together its dispersed congregations into a transnational system since 1995. Every January, core members from North and South America and Southeast Asia participate in a "Compassion Relief Spirit" retreat in Houston, Texas. In addition to horizontal ties between branches, the headquarters maintains direct ties to overseas branches. On the one hand, Huang Sixian, sometimes accompanied by one or two of Zhengyan's disciples, represents the headquarters and presides at every important ceremony of each major branch, such as the end-of-the-year thanksgiving party. On the other hand, overseas members (including mainland Chinese) visit the headquarters as part of the "homecoming" ceremonies. Moreover, overseas followers take individual trips to the headquarters in the name of "finding one's roots" (*xungen*), often obtaining a special audience with the Venerable Zhengyan and priority in the long waiting line for volunteer opportunities at the Compassion Relief hospital in Hualian. In addition to these occasional individual links to their religious "roots," every year representatives of each branch join in a retreat in conjunction with the anniversary ceremony at the headquarters; the headquarters also has vacation camps exclusively for the overseas youth and followers' school-age children. A system of transnational itineraries centering on Taiwan has therefore emerged in Compassion Relief worldwide.

In sum, Compassion Relief's overseas development is an ongoing process of transforming an ethnic religious association into both localized community service and an international nongovernmental organization not limited by ethnic boundaries. At the same time, the linkage among Compassion Relief congregations has created not only itineraries bringing dispersed overseas Taiwanese, as well as Chinese, under the "sacred canopy" of Compassion Relief Buddhism,[47] but has also strengthened ties to Taiwan as a pilgrimage center for overseas Chinese. To some extent, like Foguang Shan (see Chap. 7), Compassion Relief has created a new "homeland" of religious identity in Taiwan in lieu of the traditional cultural homeland in mainland China. It is in this sense that Compassion Relief worldwide development can be seen as a compassion relief diaspora.[48]

RELIGIOUS TRANSNATIONALISM

A good example of how Compassion Relief emphasizes global development was the ceremony for its thirty-third anniversary, held in May 1999. One week prior to the anniversary ceremony, seven hundred representatives of various overseas branches arrived at the headquarters and joined an additional three hundred local followers to begin the core members' training retreat being held at the Still Thoughts Memorial Hall. The retreat consisted of various programs, including speeches delivered by, and questions and answers with, the Venerable Zhengyan and lay leaders of each of the Compassion Relief missions, intensive small group discussions, and a celebration concert of performances presented by each branch. The corridors to the auditorium in the Still Thoughts Hall were converted into a photo gallery for a "global tour" of overseas branches. Several hundred additional overseas core members arrived on the day of the anniversary ceremony, for the event and a retreat over the following week.

The televised anniversary ceremony in the evening of Sunday, May 9, 1999, began with overseas followers entering the auditorium via the central aisle. All were dressed in the Compassion Relief volunteer uniform of blue polo shirts and white pants, with the first one of each national branch holding the flag of their host country. Each branch sat in a column, with the branch leader in the second row, holding the flag. Meanwhile, the local followers entered the hall through the rear corridors and sat in the balconies. When the second row formed an array of flags and the hall was filled with blue-and-white uniforms, about forty monastic disciples of the Venerable Zhengyan entered by the central aisle in two columns and sat down in the first row.[49] The Venerable Zhengyan entered by the central aisle, followed by two columns of male corps in uniform suits, each holding a lighted candle. Zhengyan sat among her disciples. The emcee called for all to rise, face the stage, and bow three times (san wenxun) to the Buddha. The stage backdrop was a six-story-high portrait of Shakyamuni Buddha compassionately looking at, and laying his hand above, the globe. A ten-foot-high panel of the world map stood in front of the backdrop on the stage.

The program included the three essential parts of all Compassion Relief rituals: sign-language song performance, a sermon by the Venerable Zhengyan, and candle lighting. Sign-language song preceded the sermon. When the sermon ended, with the lights out, representatives (mostly women) of each branch slowly came to the stage, each holding a candle and her/his respective national flag. They formed a row and fell on their knees at the Venerable Zhengyan's feet. Zhengyan lit each representative's candle. One by one, each representative approached the world map panel, placed the candle and the flag below the map in a row, turned on one sparkling light on the map to indicate the location of her/his branch's host country, bowed to Zhengyan, and exited the stage. One after one followed, until the world map shone with sparkling lights of all the Compassion Relief overseas branches.

This anniversary ceremony symbolizes Compassion Relief's perception of its future as a global Buddhist movement. The vision is portrayed in the grand backdrop of Shakyamuni Buddha overlooking the globe. The ritual of candles and lights on the world map embodies how this vision will be realized: the lay followers who approach the Venerable Zhengyan for teaching shall carry those teachings to the world. Clearly, overseas followers are central to the Compassion Relief future. Yet, these central carriers of Compassion Relief's future, as present at the anniversary ceremony and the Compassion Relief official description, are primarily Taiwanese and secondarily Chinese. Why are overseas Chinese so interested in Compassion Relief Buddhism? How may such an ethnic constituency contribute to the globalization of Buddhism?

Based on my ethnographic research of Compassion Relief overseas branches in New York, Boston, Tokyo, and Malacca,[50] and supplemented with Compassion Relief literature, the four case studies share the following aspects. First, overseas Compassion Relief is a rather recent phenomenon. Its first branch in the United States began in 1989 and all the four mentioned above were not founded until the 1990s. Second, Compassion Relief overseas development, at least from the four cases, stemmed from the support of overseas Taiwanese and Chinese from societies other than Taiwan (e.g., Compassion Relief–Malacca consisted mainly of locally born Chinese; and Compassion Relief–Boston began with the support of Chinese immigrants from Vietnam), and the participants in overseas Compassion Relief have so far remained within this ethnic group. Third, they have always extended charity beyond ethnic Chinese. Fourth, the founders were already pious Buddhists prior to taking up Compassion Relief practice. Fifth, all the four cases began with women's efforts in response to the appeals of the Venerable Zhengyan's charisma and her emphasis on social service. Women continue to play an active role in overseas Compassion Relief. No overseas branch is created, led, or staffed by Compassion Relief monastic disciples. Women's pivotal role in the organization's development is similar to that in the Japan-originated, grassroots lay Buddhist organization Soka Gakkai (see Clarke and Learman, Chap. 5 and Introduction, for a comparison between the two cases).

Compassion Relief overseas development not only reveals but also contributes to change in the associations of overseas Chinese. First, its significance for Chinese transnationalism lies in its contribution to the role of Buddhist women in overseas Chinese formal organizations, in which, until recently, women have been underrepresented.[51] Compared to charitable women's groups such as the "redemptive" societies and "salvationist" halls among overseas Chinese in the first half of the twentieth century, overseas Compassion Relief has distinctive formal Buddhist identity and enjoys international prestige, whereas the predecessors were primarily charitable and spiritual, and were often deemed inferior to Buddhism by the intellectuals because of their image as "women's religions."[52] The fact that all four cases discussed here began with women's efforts confirms the fact that Chinese women are not socially inept but have the informal ties that enable mobilization for civic associations.[53] Moreover, women's initiatives in their host societies are a direct response to Compassion Relief's appeal for Buddhists to contribute to this world through secular action: in each of the four cases we see women taking action—proselytizing and finding a local niche for Compassion Relief practice—immediately after being exposed to Zhengyan's appeal. Although the formal establishment often was brought about by a push from other than the pioneer women, the formation of each branch would have been unlikely without the women's enthusiasm and early mobilization outside their homeland. Like their sisters in Taiwan, who in the last three decades have developed a small local group into an island-wide movement,[54] overseas Chinese women were the carriers for the ongoing worldwide growth of Compassion Relief Buddhism.

The second significance of Compassion Relief in the context of Chinese transnationalism lies in its contribution to the emerging study of Taiwanese immigrants and Taiwan. Taiwanese immigrants in each host society have been indispensable in the formation of local Compassion Relief branches. The four cases either received their first Compassion Relief information from Taiwanese immigrants or were founded by Taiwanese. Indeed, the timing of Compassion Relief overseas development is not only linked to its headquarters' growth on a massive scale in Taiwan but is also grounded in the phenomenon of Taiwanese emigration during the period of the 1990s. According to the Ministry of the Interior, from 1990 to 1996, the number of emigrants from Taiwan increased more than fourfold, from 25.5 thousand to 119.1 thousand. As Wang points out, the majority of emigrants consisted of "middle-class businesspersons, investors, and professionals," and "no matter where they settle, a majority of them continue to be integral members of the society from which they originated."[55]

The spread of Compassion Relief during the Chinese and especially Taiwanese diaspora demonstrates the interplay between Chinese transnationalism and Buddhism. On the one hand, increasing Taiwanese transnationalism—in terms of number of people and intensity of mobility—provides the resources for the overseas development of a Taiwan-based Buddhist organization. On the other hand, the differential appeal of a Buddhist nun's charisma and her mission of social service to overseas Taiwanese reveals a changing aspect of the Chinese diaspora: overseas Chinese from Taiwan, rather than the PRC or the host society, are demonstrating their influence in their local communities, both in the associative life among Chinese communities and in the contributions that reach beyond ethnicity.

Moreover, transnational as they can be, the emerging pilgrimage route between Compassion Relief overseas followers and the headquarters more or less promotes Taiwan as a new "homeland" of religious identity for the Chinese diaspora. In contrast to other Taiwanese transnational Buddhist organizations, Compassion Relief overseas adherents focus on Taiwan as embodying an idea of "home" by first identifying with its Buddhist charismatic center, rather than as a "bridge to cultural heritage" as in the case of Foguang Shan (see Chandler, Chap. 7). Whether overseas Chinese, defined as "Chinese not residing in China," ever constituted what Maurice Freedman calls "a residual China," or, as Nonini and Ong rephrase it, "an imperfect replication" of "real 'Chinese culture' in China,"[56] overseas Compassion Relief reveals not only the diversity of Chinese descendents living outside any Chinese society, but also the Buddhist influence on the changing identities among "the" overseas Chinese. In the context of Chinese transnationalism, the Compassion Relief diaspora therefore shows an alternative face of diasporan community among Chinese descendents in the global context.

CONCLUSION

In this chapter I have tried to describe and analyze the respects in which the Compassion Relief movement may be termed "global": first, the creation of the movement was a synthesis of external and indigenous sources, and the timing of its rapid domestic growth was both brought about by intensive social change and by a breakthrough in the interplay of women, religion, and civil society; and second, the global vision of its mission was an adaptation to, and a manifestation of, the role of religion in intensified global communications. The result of Compassion Relief's global mission has been to put Buddhism on the world map of border crossings in the fields of international relief and bone-marrow donation drives. Another outcome of its global mission has been to organize and highlight the resources of the Chinese, especially the Taiwanese, diaspora in such a way as to channel it into an active religious movement that is universal in terms of its causes but particularistic in terms of its ethnic constituency, as it focuses on Taiwan as a new religious pilgrimage center for Chinese transnationalism.

Compassion Relief is international yet ethnically specific. The Compassion Relief case shows (1) the importance of culture, in terms of both the unique context of the movement's origins and the salience of ethnic identity; and (2) the power of world-affirming religious charisma. First, the trajectory of Compassion Relief's development—from a grassroots women's group to an island-wide mass movement to an international nongovernmental organization—is closely related to Taiwan's cultural context. Taiwan is a postcolonial society that is culturally hybrid. It is also a newly developed and democratized society that has ample space for social change. And finally, it is, as an ambiguous nation-state, endowed with wealth and a pool of transnational people. Second, inasmuch as Compassion Relief's trajectory can be attributed to the cultural context of Taiwan, the fact that its overseas development has drawn upon the Chinese-speaking people from societies other than Taiwan suggests strongly that ethnicity is a salient cultural boundary. Yet it is not enough to point out that Compassion Relief appeals to the Chinese diaspora. The question remains: just why are overseas Chinese so interested in Compassion Relief's particular path of Buddhism?

The answer perhaps lies in the power of the Venerable Zhengyan's world-affirming charisma: her personal appeal serves as a catalyst for a practice that emphasizes concrete contributions to human welfare; that appeal is unique in the context of Chinese Buddhism yet is still embedded in the Buddhist canon of universal compassion. Her charisma has led overseas followers to take the initiative to start local missions; and it has also moved people in Taiwan to contribute to relief projects on the mainland despite cross-Strait political tensions. Yet, at the same time, the fact that Compassion Relief's overseas development has heretofore remained within the Chinese diaspora seems to suggest a limit to Zhengyan's transcultural appeal.[57]

Is it, then, precisely Compassion Relief's appeal to the Chinese diaspora that limits its appeal to the Chinese people? Is its characteristic diaspora a result of the Compassion Relief approach or of Chinese ethnicity? Or, is it a common issue of ethnicity and religion in globalization? In some way, Compassion Relief's distinctive charismatic model of a practical approach to Buddhism appeals to the Chinese diaspora and, as it turns out, characterizes its global development within that diaspora. In the Introduction to this volume, Learman suggests that Compassion Relief's social-service approach is perhaps too familiar or too secular to appeal to Western people, and Chandler (Chap. 7) indicates that the lack of overseas temples and monastics has resulted in the overseas Compassion Relief's low profile outside of Chinese communities. These are explanations from the "native point of view." Yet, in some way, the attribute of Chinese constituency shared by Compassion Relief's and Foguang Shan's global development seems to suggest that religious diaspora may be in tension with religious ecumenism. The fact is, despite their different emphases, Compassion Relief and Foguang Shan both show a strong commitment to transcending ethnic, racial, national, and cultural boundaries; and, at the same time, both have heretofore succeeded in being global mainly by means of developing within the Chinese diaspora. Such tension may not be intrinsically Chinese, but an issue of negotiation between the mobilization of particularistic resources and the pursuit of universalistic spirit—a problem that has been broached in studies of religion and globalization.[58] Further research should explore the complex interplay between ethnicity and ideals of universality in the shared circumstances of change in the global context.[59]

Notes

I am grateful to all the Compassion Relief followers and staff, especially Mr. Huang Sixian and the coordinators and core members of the four branches where I conducted field research, in New York, Boston, Japan, and Malaysia. I also thank Robert P. Weller, Charles Lindholm, Christopher Queen, Peter Gregory, Stuart Chandler, and Pal Nyiri for their comments. Linda Learman read different versions of this essay in detail. I am very grateful for her insightful suggestions and helpful editing. I have also benefited from the suggestions of the two anonymous readers at the University of Hawai'i Press. All shortcomings are mine.

1. According to Compassion Relief literature, the Philippine Magsaysay Award is "the Asian Nobel Peace Prize."

2. Barry Corbin, John Trites, and James Taylor, *Global Connections: Geography for the 21st Century* (Don Mills, Ont., Canada: Oxford University Press, 1999), 408.

3. *Business Week*, July 24, 2000, 72.

4. I thank the first anonymous reader for his or her helpful suggestion for clarifying this point.

5. Vivienne Wee and Gloria Davies, "Religion," in *The Encyclopedia of the Chinese Overseas*, ed. Lynn Pan (Cambridge, Mass.: Harvard University Press, 1999), 80.

6. Ibid., 82.

7. This distinctive Buddhist identity distinguishes Compassion Relief from the Buddhism-inspired charitable associations among overseas Chinese in the first half of the twentieth century; see Prasenjit Duara, "Transnationalism and the Predicament of Sovereignty: China, 1900–1945," *American Historical Review* 102, no. 4 (1997): 1030–1051, and Maurice Freedman and Marjorie Topley, "Religion and Social Realignment among the Chinese in Singapore," *Journal of Asian Studies* 21, no. 1 (1961): 3–23.

8. This term originally appeared in John Lofland and Rodney Stark, "Becoming a World-Saver: A Theory of Conversion to a Deviant Perspective," *American Sociological Review*, no. 30 (1965): 862–875. I borrow it to refer to a committed member who not only contributes significantly but also draws others in. However, I do not share Lofland and Stark's view on religious cults as "deviant." Their original "deviant" connotation is later modified in Rodney Stark and William Sims Bainbridge, *A Theory of Religion* (New York: Peter Lang, 1987).

9. Peter L. Berger and Thomas Luckmann, *The Social Construction of Reality: A Treatise in the Sociology of Knowledge* (New York: Doubleday, 1967 [1966]), 158.

10. For a detailed introduction to Compassion Relief, see Chien-yu Julia Huang and Robert P. Weller, "Merit and Mothering: Women and Social Welfare in Taiwanese Buddhism," *Journal of Asian Studies* 57, no. 2 (1998): 379–396.

11. Himalaya Foundation, *Directory of 300 Major Foundations in Taiwan* (Taipei: Himalaya Foundation, 2002), 28.

12. *Fa* literally means "law." In Buddhism, *fa* means "Dharma," Buddha's truth.

13. Himalaya Foundation, *Directory*, 28. The endowment decreased from NT$18.6 billion (approximately US$0.6 billion) in 1997 (Himalaya Foundation, *Jijinghui zai Taiwan* [Foundations in Taiwan]) (Taipei: Zhonghua Zhengxin She, 1997), 10.

14. Himalaya Foundation, *Directory*, 28.

15. Compassion Relief has a total of eight missions. It has long claimed its goal to be the original "Four Great Missions." More recently, particularly in the 1990s, Compassion Relief developed four additional missions—international relief, bone-marrow drives, community service, and garbage recycling—which, together with the original four, make the "Eight Footprints."

16. A *weiyuan* is a devoted follower and volunteer who has recruited forty or more households and has vowed to abide by the Compassion Relief spirit and Buddhist disciplines, and to devote her- or himself to all Compassion Relief missions. Compassion Relief English literature uses "commissioner" as the translation of *weiyuan*.

17. "For Buddhism and for all the living" (*wei fojiao wei zhongsheng*). This was the maxim Zhengyan received upon her ordination from the Venerable Yinshun.

18. Quoted in Li Dingzan, "*Zongjiao yu zhimin: taiwan fojiao de bianqian yu zhuanxing, 1895–1995*" [Religion and colonial discourse: The historical transformation of Buddhism in Taiwan, 1895–1995], *Bulletin of the Institute of Ethnology, Academia Sinica*, no. 81 (1996): 43.

19. Li, "*Zongjiao yu zhimin.*"

20. Huang and Weller, "Merit and Mothering," 381. Compassion Relief literature emphasizes that her change of diet is an act of filial piety rather than a result of Buddhist teaching, see Chen Huijian, *Zhengyan fashi de Ciji shijie* [The Venerable Zhengyan's world of Compassion Relief] (Taipei: Ciji Wenhua Zhiye Zhongxin, 1993 [1983]), 6.

21. Chen, *Zhengyan*, 10–11.

22. Compassion Relief Foundation, *Let Ten Thousand Lotuses of Heart Blossom in This World: Dharma Master Cheng Yen [Zhengyan] and the Buddhist Compassion Relief Tzu Chi [Ciji] Foundation* (Taipei: Fojiao Ciji Jijin Hui, 1994), 5.

23. Chen, *Zhengyan*, 11–20.

24. Li, "*Zongjiao yu zhimin,*" 37.

25. The Venerable Yinshun developed his notion of Buddhism of the Human Realm from

the Venerable Taixu's notion of the "Buddhism of Human Life" (C: *rensheng fojiao*). For a comparison between Yinshun's and Taixu's thoughts, see Yang Huinan, *Dangdai fojiao sixiang zhanwang* [A survey of modern Buddhist thought] (Taipei: Dongda Tushu Gongsi, 1991), 109–125. Most of Yang's argument is elaborated in Charles Brewer Jones, *Buddhism in Taiwan: Religion and the State 1660–1990* (Honolulu: University of Hawai'i Press, 1999), 133–135. I use Buddhism of the Human Realm instead of Humanistic Buddhism as the translation of *renjian de fojiao* because it is more faithful to Yinshun's original phrase. Yinshun explicates his notion in relation to Taixu's that "the true Buddhism is of the human realm. . . . we should inherit the true meaning of 'Buddhism of Human Life' to manifest the Buddhism of the human realm" [C: *zhenzheng de fojiao, shi renjian de. . . . women ying jicheng 'rensheng fojiao' de zhenyi, lai fayang renjian de fojiao*] (quoted in Yang, A Survey, 113, my translation).

26. See Yang Huinan, "*Taiwan fojiao de chushi xingge yu paixi douzheng*" [The characteristics of other worldly and the factional conflict in Buddhism in Taiwan], *Dangdai*, no. 31 (1988): 68–81; and Jones, *Buddhism in Taiwan*, 131–133.

27. For the linkage of Foguang Shan and Compassion Relief to Yinshun's Buddhism of the Human Realm, and hence to Taixu's Buddhism of Human Life, see Jones, *Buddhism in Taiwan*, 205; and Lu Hwei-syin, "*Fojiao ciji gongde hui 'feisimiao zhongxin' de xiandai fojiao texing*" [The Buddhist Compassion Relief Society's 'non-temple-centered' approach and its characteristics of modern Buddhism], in *Simiao yu minjian wenhua yantaohui lunwenji* [Proceedings of the Conference on Temples and Popular Culture] (Taipei: Committee of the Development of Culture, Executive Yuan, Taiwan Government, 1995), 745–746. I agree with Lu's point in her explication of the Venerable Zhengyan's approach that it takes a step further from her predecessors in emphasizing social actions or the practice of Dharma among people.

28. Huang and Weller, "Merit and Mothering," 382.

29. Interview with a Zhengyan's monastic disciple in 1998.

30. Li, "*Zongjiao yu zhimin.*"

31. I use "Buddhism among people" here to convey to English readers Zhengyan's emphasis on social practice—a practice that distinguishes her approach from that of Yinshun and Taixu; see Lu, "The Compassion Relief Society," 745–746.

32. Huang and Weller, "Merit and Mothering," 392–395.

33. Robert P. Weller, "Living at the Edge: Religion, Capitalism, and the End of the Nation-State in Taiwan," *Public Culture* 12, no. 2 (2000): 496.

34. Linda Learman helped me with this translation, and I thank her for it.

35. I am grateful to Linda Learman for pointing out to me the charismatic nature of this appeal. Although the first-person pronoun *wo* can be singular for "I" and plural for "we," ethnographic data show that Zhengyan's personal appeal was crucial to Compassion Relief's

successful mobilization for its mission. For a detailed analysis of Zhengyan's charisma, see chapter 2 in Chien-yu Julia Huang, "Recapturing Charisma: Emotion and Rationalization in a Globalizing Buddhist Movement from Taiwan" (Ph.D. diss., Boston University, 2001).

36. Duanzheng Wang, ed., *Zainan, wuyian de dengdai: Ciji Jijinhui dalu jiuyuan jianjie* [Disasters, waiting in silence: Introduction to relief to China, the Compassion Relief Foundation] (Taipei: Fojiao Ciji Jijin Hui, 1998), 6. Although the first relief outside Taiwan that Compassion Relief supported was to the flood victims in Bangladesh a few months before the need in the PRC, its role was limited to fund-raising for the Red Cross to deliver the relief to Bangladesh; see Gan Shanjun, in *Ciji Nianjian 1966–1992* [Compassion Relief yearbook 1966–1992], ed. Shi Zhengyan (Taipei: Ciji Wenhua Chuban She, 1993), 397. The relief to the PRC was the first "overseas" relief work that Compassion Relief initiated, funded, and delivered. Compassion Relief publications often refer to the delivery to the PRC as the "beginning of [its] international relief work"; see The Compassion Relief Foundation, *Love Transcends Borders* (Hualian, Taiwan: Fojiao Ciji Jijin Hui, 2000 [1999]), 12.

37. Douglas Shaw, ed., *Lotus Flower of the Heart: Thirty Years of Tzu Chi Photographs* (Taipei: Jinxsi Wenhua Zhiye, 1997), 25.

38. Duanzheng Wang, ed., *Da'ai wuyuan fojie: Ciji jijinhui guoji jiuyuan jianjie* [Boundless great love: Introduction to international relief, the Compassion Relief Foundation] (Taipei: Fojiao Ciji Jijin Hui, 1998), 2–4.

39. C. Julia Huang, "Sacred or Profane? The Compassion Relief Movement's Transnationalism," *European Journal of East Asian Studies* 2, no. 2 (2003): 217–241.

40. André Laliberté, "'Love Transcends Border' or 'Blood Is Thicker than Water'? The Charity Work of the Compassion Relief in the People's Republic of China," *European Journal of East Asian Studies* 2, no. 2 (2003): 243–261.

41. These include, in chronological order: Mongolia, Nepal, the refugee camps in northern Thailand, Cambodia, Azerbaijan, Ethiopia, Rwanda, Chechnya, Ivory Coast, Afghanistan, Lesotho, Swaziland, South Africa, North Korea, Liberia, Gambia, the Philippines, Vietnam, Peru, Papua New Guinea, Senegal, the Dominican Republic, Haiti, Honduras, El Salvador, Nicaragua, Guatemala, Colombia, the Kosovo refugees in Albania, earthquake victims in Turkey, and Venezuela; see Wang, "Boundless Great Love," and The Compassion Relief Foundation, *Buddhist Compassion Relief Tzu Chi [Ciji] Foundation* (Taipei: Fojiao Ciji Jijin Hui, 1999).

42. http://www2.tzuchi.org.tw/focus/index.html, accessed on August 24, 2003; Duanzheng Wang, ed., *Ciji ninajian 1998* [Compassion Relief yearbook 1998] (Taipei: Ciji Wenhua, 1999), 510.

43. Ou Junping, "*Diyiwei feizhouyi ciji zhigong: geleidisi*" [The first African Compassion Relief volunteer: Gladys], *Ciji yuekan* [Compassion Relief Monthly], no. 435 (2003): 22–23.

44. Ou Junping, *"Xuehui ziligengsheng, ye xuehui ai"* [Learning to be independent and to love], *Ciji yuekan* [Compassion Relief monthly], no. 435 (2003): 20.

45. This term highlights the fact that its curriculum goes beyond that of a language-learning institute.

46. For example, in December 1998 the Canada branch held a meeting to introduce Compassion Relief to English speakers. Audiences were staff of the institutions where Compassion Relief followers regularly volunteer (e.g., a children's hospital, an AIDS association, and a seniors' house); see Duangzheng Wang, ed., *Ciji Nianjian 1998*.

47. Peter L. Berger's term.

48. Cf. Steven Vertovec, *The Hindu Diaspora: Comparative Pattern* (London: Routledge, 2000), 3.

49. As of 1999, the Venerable Zhengyan had about eighty disciples, all women. The number has increased to around two hundred in 2003.

50. I participated in the New York branch in the spring of 1992, conducted major fieldwork in the Boston branch between 1996 and 1997, and did follow-up research in 1999. I visited the Japan branch in December 1997 and the two Malaysia branches in April 1999.

51. Edgar Wickberg, "Overseas Chinese Organizations," in *The Encyclopedia of the Chinese Overseas,* ed. Lynn Pan (Cambridge, Mass.: Harvard University Press, 1999), 83–91.

52. For the "redemptive" societies, see Duara, "Transnationalism and the Predicament of Sovereignty." For the "salvationist" sects, see Freedman and Topley, "Religion and Social Realignment among the Chinese in Singapore"; and for the inferior status of the salvationist groups, ibid., 22.

53. Robert P. Weller, *Alternate Civilities: Democracy and Culture in China and Taiwan* (Boulder, Colo.: Westview Press, 1999).

54. Huang and Weller, "Merit and Mothering."

55. Horng-luen Wang, "In Want of a Nation: State, Institutions and Globalization in Taiwan" (Ph.D. diss., University of Chicago, 1999), 214.

56. Donald Nonini and Aihwa Ong, "Introduction: Chinese Transnationalism as an Alternative Modernity," in *Ungrounded Empires: The Cultural Politics of Modern Chinese Transnationalism,* ed. Aihwa Ong and Donald Nonini (London: Routledge, 1997), 7.

57. For a detailed ethnographic analysis of Master Zhengyan's charisma, see chapter 2 in Huang, "Recapturing Charisma."

58. See, for example, James A. Beckford, "Religious Movement and Globalization," in *Global Social Movements,* ed. Robin Cohen and Shirin M. Rai (London and New Brunswick, N.J.: Athlone, 2000), 178–181; Peter Beyer, *Religion and Globalisation* (Thousand Oaks,

Calif.: Sage, 1994), 28. For a comparative example in which a diaspora community turns a proselytizing world religion into a transnational bridge between host and home countries, see Peggy Levitt, *The Transnational Villagers* (Berkeley and Los Angeles: University of California Press, 2001): 159–179.

59. See Robert P. Weller, "Afterword: On Global Nation-States and Rooted Universalisms," *European Journal of East Asian Studies* 2, no. 2 (2003): 321–328.

9 Uniting Religion and Politics in a Bid for Autonomy: Lamas in Exile in China and America

Gray Tuttle

An examination of the activities of Tibetan lamas in China in the early decades of this century reveals the repetition of centuries-old traditions as well as innovations associated with modernity. Most interesting for those who are familiar only with the current interest in Tibetan Buddhism in America is the fact that many of the strategies for propagating Buddhism to a non-Tibetan audience and seeking support for an autonomous Tibetan polity have earlier antecedents. The spread of Tibetan Buddhism in China, and later in the West, has been intimately linked to the political status of exiled Tibetan lamas. For this reason, this chapter discusses the connection between certain prominent Tibetan lamas' search for political patronage and the Tibetan Buddhist mission. The host of other Tibetan Buddhists with little interest or involvement in politics who helped to disseminate their religion in China and in America must unfortunately be neglected here. However, I should add that, both in China and America, ethnic Tibetan and Mongol lamas who focused more exclusively on teaching religion were important forerunners, preparing the ground, so to speak, for the later political activities of the lamas who are the subject of this chapter.

Viewing the activities of Tibetans in China in the early twentieth century allows us to discern patterns that provide significant parallels to the current place of Tibetan Buddhism in contemporary America. The assertion that these lamas were merely the pawns of Chinese politicians is a commonplace, while few Americans have a historically informed perspective on the current Dalai Lama's relations with the American government. I contend that all of these lamas, past and present, have exercised an agency that elevates their roles above that of pawns in someone else's game. At the same time, I recognize the very real context of events (or, in Buddhist terms, the nexus of causes and conditions) that serves to limit these actors' choices. Among the issues I will discuss are the enduring role of nationalism in prompting Tibetan "missions" abroad, the initial religious nature of such missions, their gradual politicization, and finally a combination of religious and political activities that has been a characteristic feature of Tibetan Buddhism for centuries.[1]

In the study of the cross-cultural transfer of Buddhism and globalization, the Tibetan Buddhist example holds a special place. Even before the Mongol successors of Genghis Khan became patrons of Tibetan Buddhism from the Middle East to China, this religion had been linked with prominent political leaders. The origins of some Tibetan Buddhists' orientation toward patrons from outside Tibetan regions date back to the time of the Western Xia state (1038–1227). Lamas from a branch of the Kagyu school became spiritual preceptors to the ethnically Tangut rulers of the Western Xia state and were still serving in this role when Genghis Khan eliminated the state and the dynastic family to whom the Tibetan Buddhists had been ministering. Within a few short decades, branches of the Kagyu school and the Sakya school had all come under the sway and received the patronage of various descendents of Genghis Khan.[2] This relationship—the Genghissid patronage of various Tibetan Buddhist religious schools and the claim on their associated properties—led to a vast dispersal of Tibetan Buddhism over much of East Asia, and even parts of the Middle East.

This first wave of Tibetan Buddhism's "global" dispersal was less the result of a mission undertaken by Tibetans than a requirement of their relationship with the rulers of the Mongol empire. Qubilai Khan (1260–1294) must be given the greatest credit for ensuring the enduring relationship between the Chinese empire and Tibetan Buddhism. Through the relationship between Phagpa lama Lo drö gyal tshan (1235–1280) and Qubilai Khan, a close bond between China and Tibet and between the religious and political functions of Tibetan lamas in the service of the state was established. Certain elements of this "contract" remained prominent in Sino-Tibetan relations into the twentieth century, though there was rarely direct continuity; these instances represent an enduring, rather than an unbroken, tradition. In his *Tibetan Nationalism: The Role of Patronage in the Accomplishment of a National Identity*, Christiaan Klieger described this Tibetan tradition as follows: "Tibetan culture provides a mechanism whereby forces and personnel from the 'outside' can be utilized . . . to economically and ideologically support the perceived continuation of Tibetan cultural patterns."[3] Instead of focusing on the reception of Tibetan Buddhism in China and America, as discussed by Richard Payne (Chap. 4), I explore how certain lamas engaged with "outside" resources, spreading their religion while simultaneously pursuing political goals.

On the one hand, disciples of Tibetan Buddhism in China and America shared an interest in potent ritual activity and the prestige associated with being the patron (and student) of prominent religious figures. On the other hand, teachers shared the desire to propagate their religion and receive patronage. Elsewhere I have explored why Tibetan Buddhism was so popular in the early twentieth century among Chinese Buddhists, and also the link between Angarika Dharmapala and Master Taixu (Tai Hsü). A key figure in supporting Tibetan Buddhism in China, Taixu embraced the Tibetan tradition of uniting religious and secular concerns. His brief education in a Buddhist mission school inspired by Dharmapala is a thread that links several of these chapters together, as Taixu's "this-worldly" reforms of Chinese Buddhism influenced both Foguang Shan's Master Xingyun and, through Master Yinshun, Ciji's Master Zhengyan.[4] In this essay, therefore, I will focus on a scarcely explored connection between Tibetan Buddhist mission activity and the political goals of exiled lamas. As these varied interests make obvious, a union of religious and secular matters was involved in forging the modern relations between Tibetans and their Chinese and American disciples.

The Tibetan understanding of the proper relation between religion and politics can be traced back to the end of the Tibetan empire in the eighth century, but was set in place most firmly in the time of 'Phagpa and Qubilai. Far from a conception of the separation of church and state, the Tibetan idea of the inextricable connection between religion and politics (chos srid zung 'grel) implies that these are not two opposing fields of activity which are meant to be kept separate. Rather, the linking of these two arenas is seen as perfectly appropriate in Tibet. As the current Dalai Lama stated in his autobiography, "religion and politics do mix."[5]

Tibetan society, since at least the time of the fifth Dalai Lama in the seventeenth century, had been accustomed to the notion of a joint religious and secular rule.[6] When the global wave of nationalism closed in on Tibet from British India and Han China, the thirteenth Dalai Lama tried to centralize these two aspects of leadership under his personal control more effectively than had any Tibetan leader in the past. With his success in this endeavor, other lamas found their positions—which shared similar features of joint religious and political rule, but on a local level—challenged. Unable to resist the Dalai Lama's military and political power, some Tibetan Buddhist hierarchs fled to China. Although modern Chinese may have shared some of the Western beliefs in the separation of the "church" and state, Tibetan Buddhists certainly did not.

As discussed in Julia Huang's essay (Chap. 8), globalization was largely a product of the spread of nationalism. The appearance of first a British, then a Chinese army bent on redefining the relations of power in the very heartland of Tibet forced the Tibetans to take a more active role in the world of nations. The thirteenth Dalai Lama, Thub ten gya tsho (1876–1933), was able to elevate his role to what is commonly perceived today to be an ideal model for Tibetan leadership: a truly unified secular and religious head of state. His innovation was actually taking into his hands all the secular power that had so often been associated *in principle* with religious leadership. By tightening his control over Tibet and modernizing, as much as possible, the Tibetan administration, the Dalai Lama hoped to assert Tibet's independence. Nevertheless, his efforts to create a compact national territory caused tensions in the larger Tibetan cultural world, parts of which did not necessarily recognize the supreme authority of a central Tibetan government. Just as Tibet had broken with China when the Chinese attempted to administer Tibet directly, so the leaders of heretofore self-governing Tibetan regions resisted the authority of the centralizing policies of the Tibetan government in Lhasa. Some of these leaders turned to their enemy's enemy, China, in order to counter these efforts at nation building.

At least partially, the Chinese aggression toward Tibet throughout the twentieth century has involved a similar contestation of power. Whereas the thirteenth Dalai Lama felt that he should exercise dominion over all culturally Tibetan regions, the Chinese believe that they have rightful dominion over all of the former Qing frontier dependencies, which included Tibet. The real source of the Tibetans' current claim to independence is that the central Tibetans succeeded in driving out the Chinese forces at the end of the Qing dynasty. On the other hand, the monastic polities that resisted the centralization of Tibet under the rule of the thirteenth Dalai Lama were not successful in resisting central Tibetan aggression. Therefore, they—like the current (fourteenth) Dalai Lama—were forced to seek support outside of Tibet proper. The impetus of nationalism that drove the Tibetans to consolidate a Tibetan nation in the first half of this century is not entirely different from the forces of nationalism that impelled the Chinese to exert control over Tibet in the second half of the century. In both cases, smaller polities, which wished to be separate and independent (but were not recognized as such by the international community), were forcibly incorporated into a larger community on the basis of nationalistic motivations.

Within a decade of his return from exile, the thirteenth Dalai Lama's efforts to centralize and militarily maintain a Tibetan nation-state resulted in the alienation of one of the most important figures in the Tibetan Buddhist world, the Panchen Lama. The Chinese were happy to receive the lama when he arrived in Chinese territory and provided for his basic needs for many years.[7] Similarly, India and the United States would later support the fourteenth Dalai Lama against the "communist menace" of the PRC.[8] Although the circumstances of these two lamas' going into exile are not identical, the parallels are striking. Neither was forcibly ejected from his home territory. Rather, in each case the stronger power tried to coerce the weaker but legitimate authority to adjust to a reduction of autonomy.

When both lamas felt that their lack of cooperation would soon lead to their imprisonment, they fled into exile. Another example of a lama driven into exile did not share this common fate. The Nor lha Hutukhtu (1865–1936), the spiritual and political leader of territory in Khams, was actually imprisoned by the Tibetan government and only went into exile after he escaped his captors.[9] He arrived in Beijing late in 1924,[10] just as the Panchen Lama himself was making his way to the Chinese capital overland.

TEACHING RELIGION TO FOREIGNERS

Rather than playing prominent roles in the politics of a fragmented China, during their early years in China, the Panchen Lama and the Nor lha Hutukhtu were involved almost exclusively in spreading Tibetan Buddhist teachings. The Panchen Lama was careful to maintain a low political profile at first. Part of the tension between the Dalai Lama and the Panchen Lama had been over the latter's relations with the Qing state and the British in India. During his early years in China, while the Panchen Lama was still hoping to quickly return to Tibet, he did not want to add to the accusations that could be leveled against him. The fourteenth Dalai Lama was to face a similar dilemma in both 1951 and 1957. At these times, his acceptance of proffered American aid would only have confirmed the Chinese condemnation of imperialist intrigue in Tibet, while he still held out hope for a working relationship with the Chinese. The Dalai Lama was also careful not to meet directly with these foreign agents.[11] Likewise, in his early years in China, the Panchen Lama only sent representatives to deal with political officials, while he propagated religion.

The Panchen Lama's first teachings were directed at Mongolian, Tibetan, and Chinese adherents of Tibetan Buddhism at the sites of the old imperially supported Tibetan Buddhist temples in and around the capital, Beijing. However, he quickly moved into contexts that were purely Chinese, both ethnically and in terms of the form of Buddhism practiced. In these communities, the Panchen Lama largely focused on teaching about Buddhist figures that were shared with his Chinese Buddhist brethren. At the same time, he infused his teachings with elements unique to Tibetan Buddhism, especially emphasizing the esoteric aspects of the Buddhist figures. Once he had won a substantial following and the government's recognition of his religious status, the Panchen Lama sought to create a bureaucratic administration to support his interests.

Meanwhile, the Nor lha Hutukhtu pursued Chinese government assistance in claiming his domains but failed to secure it. At best, he was given permission to try, but without resources this was an impossible task. As there was no way to return to the combined political and religious position that had formerly been his, the Nor lha Hutukhtu was also limited temporarily to religious activities among the Chinese. Unlike the Panchen Lama, however, he seems to have focused on presiding over rituals whose precedents were of long standing in imperial China. As the Qing elite were no longer a viable audience, he adapted these traditions by making them available to the Chinese Buddhist laity. Although a prominent local politician aided him, his actual support appears to have come from a very broad base of the Chinese Buddhist community in Sichuan province. In these early years in China, then, these two prominent Tibetan Buddhist hierarchs focused their attention primarily on spreading Tibetan Buddhism among the Chinese, without ever losing sight of their longer-term goals.

When the Dalai Lama first came to America, he was allowed entry only as a religious leader and not as the leader of the Tibetan government-in-exile. Even in this capacity, his entry into the United States was blocked until 1979. As early as 1977 a student of Tibetan Buddhism in the Carter administration had secured official permission for the Dalai Lama to come to America, but it was two years before all obstacles were cleared.[12] Like the two lamas in China, the Dalai Lama initially spent his time abroad in religious contexts, offering Buddhist teachings to relatively small crowds from 1979 to 1985. In 1981, he brought esoteric Tibetan Buddhism to America in the form of an elaborate ceremony and practice known as the Kalachakra Tantra. The first group to attend this ritual numbered only twelve hundred, but this number nearly doubled each time the event reoccurred over the next decade.[13] As will become clear, the Dalai Lama was not the first to share this esoteric ritual with a foreign culture in modern times; in this, too, he followed a precedent. Thus, the Dalai Lama—like the lamas in exile in China—was only able to participate directly in American politics after he had built up a religious base of support abroad.

The Panchen Lama's first activities in China were perfectly consonant with his being a prominent religious leader. Seeing the death and destruction caused by the ravages of warlord battles, he offered prayers for those killed. Shortly thereafter he sent an open telegram to all the warlords, requesting that they cease fighting one another so that peace and prosperity might return to China.[14] He favored no side but made only vague statements about his support of the central government based in Beijing. Moreover, when the government invited the Panchen Lama to the National Reconstruction Meeting in 1925—which brought together the rulers of northern China with the "father" of Republican China, Sun Yat-sen—he studiously avoided becoming too involved in Chinese politics. He sent a representative to the conference while he stopped at the sacred Buddhist pilgrimage site of Mount Wutai and gave Buddhist teachings there until the conference ended.[15]

This instance of first contact with the central Chinese government set the pattern that the Panchen Lama was to follow for several years: sending representatives to deal with political matters while he frequented temples and expounded on Buddhist topics, thus eschewing direct involvement in politics. Aside from considering how the Tibetan government would respond to his having dealings with that of China, the Panchen Lama also might have been aware of the Chinese condemnation of monks who involved themselves in political affairs. Unlike Tibetan society, Chinese culture had little tolerance for religious figures who were active in politics.[16] For instance, Taixu was pejoratively labeled a "political monk."

At least at first, the expectations governing the behavior of the fourteenth Dalai Lama in America largely mirrored this Chinese attitude. The Dalai Lama was limited to traveling abroad only as a religious figure with restrictions placed on what he could say and do.[17] For example, in 1987 he was reprimanded by the U.S. State Department for addressing the U.S. Congressional Human Rights Caucus. Somehow this activity was deemed "inconsistent with his status as a respected religious leader" and a violation of the terms of his visa.[18] This has certainly changed in recent years, as it did for the Panchen Lama in his later years in China. Yet, despite the fact that the fourteenth Dalai Lama has obviously embraced a very political role in America, emphasizing this fact—as this essay consistently does—will no doubt be perceived by some as insulting to Tibetan Buddhism in general and the current Dalai Lama in particular. Yet he himself has said that "I find no contradiction at all between politics and religion."[19] In any case, the pattern followed by the Dalai Lama for many years was very similar to that of the Panchen Lama upon his arrival in China: he acted as a religious figure, visiting local political leaders wherever he went but taking no direct role in politics.

When the Panchen Lama first arrived in Beijing, he taught at Yonghe Gong, which had served as the main imperial Tibetan Buddhist temple under the Qing dynasty. Though some ethnic Chinese were pursuing the study of Tibetan Buddhism at Yonghe Gong at that time, the audience would have been primarily ethnic Mongolian Tibetan Buddhists, as this group comprised the principal monastic population of the temple. This instance demonstrates the subtle yet significant role Mongols continued to play in "globalizing" Tibetan Buddhism. Just as the earliest Chinese scholar of Tibetan Buddhism (Yu Daoquan) studied at the ethnically Mongol Tibetan Buddhist monastery of Yonghe Gong, so the first American scholars of Tibetan Buddhism (Robert Thurman and Jeffrey Hopkins) studied in an ethnically Mongol Tibetan Buddhist monastery in New Jersey. This monastery, by far the earliest one in America, catered to and was supported by an immigrant Kalmyck Mongolian community.[20]

The Panchen Lama's first contact with a purely ethnic Chinese audience seems to have taken place in the first few months of 1925. His two-and-a-half-month-long southern tour into the heartland of Chinese culture in Jiangnan, south of the Yangtze River, marked the first instance of a Tibetan Buddhist reaching large ethnically Chinese audiences. This visit to Jiangsu and Zhejiang was especially significant because the region was the heart of active Chinese Buddhist education and training. Holmes Welch has described how these two provinces represented the best and the brightest of Chinese Buddhism. In fact, according to his figures, the number of Buddhist monks and laity in these two provinces outnumbered those in most of the other provinces combined.[21]

In April of 1925, the Panchen Lama transmitted the long-life (Amitayus) Buddha's mantra according to the esoteric tradition. The long-life Buddha cycle of teachings was especially significant coming from him, as he was understood to be an emanation of Amitabha, who is closely associated with Amitayus. This transmission linked the recipients to the Panchen Lama through a powerful set of religious beliefs; he was the master and they the disciples. The Panchen Lama clearly built a religious following oriented toward Tibetan Buddhist practice, though initially he did this through Buddhist teachings and deities shared by Tibetan and Chinese Buddhism.

The Panchen Lama also traveled to a second of the four Buddhist sacred mountains in China, the island Mount Putuo. The island was home to a very concentrated Chinese Buddhist monastic population that was well known for the intensity of its study and practice.[22] He blessed with the touch of his hand the fourteen hundred monks who had gathered to see him; to each he also gave two silver dollars. This was a significant financial contribution at the time, especially for a refugee who had fled home due to lack of funds.[23] On the next day, he lectured to two thousand monks on the Buddhist theories of birth, old age, sickness, and death, as well as on the three trainings in ethics, meditation, and wisdom. He also transmitted the esoteric mantras of Tara and Avalokitesvara. This gathering was a historic occasion, marking as it does the first time in the history of Sino-Tibetan relations that a Tibetan Buddhist taught so many Chinese monks.

In late July 1925, the provisional chief executive of China and temporarily the dominant warlord of north China, Duan Qirui, invited the Panchen Lama to the capital to receive the government's official recognition. Duan's recognition of the Panchen Lama was based on earlier models dating back as far as the Yuan dynasty. The tradition since the Mongol rule of China had been that rulers of China —whether Mongol, Han, or Manchu—would award respected Tibetan Buddhist hierarchs eloquent religious titles and accompanying symbols of respect.[24] The most recent example, which Duan followed fairly closely, was the Qing court's treatment of the thirteenth Dalai Lama: "the Qing court, by imperial decree, conferred on him an additional title, inscribed in a gold leaf album, of 'The Loyally Submissive Viceregent, Great, Good, Self-Existent Buddha of Heaven.'"[25] On August 1, Duan bestowed the title "Propagator of Honesty, Savior of the World" on the Panchen Lama and gave him a certificate printed on plates of gold and a golden seal as symbols of his new honor.[26] Thus, Duan demonstrated no new ability to "utilize" the Panchen Lama's presence in China in the service of the struggling Chinese nation-state. Though aware of the need to preserve the integrity of the former Qing dynasty's borders, he was unable to conceive of any modern methods of employing Tibet's second most famous hierarch to this end. In fact, the only innovation that came about as a result of the Panchen Lama's interaction with this conservative leader of China was undertaken at the Panchen Lama's request. After receiving these honors, the Panchen Lama requested that he be permitted to set up his own offices within China.

The Nor lha Hutukhtu, on the other hand, had little success either gaining assistance from the government or teaching the Chinese in his early years in the north. His lack of a common language seems to have hindered his ability to communicate, especially in north China. He was from the eastern Tibetan region of Khams, which had its own dialects. In addition, the Nor lha Hutukhtu was trained in the Nyingma school of Tibetan Buddhism, whereas most of the Tibetans living in China proper at that time were adherents of the Geluk school. These differences may well have made it difficult for the Nor lha Hutukhtu to find disciples or venues in which to teach.

The Nor lha Hutukhtu's one successful contact with a Chinese politician while living in Beijing is described in two separate biographical accounts printed in a single volume. One account tells how he reached the president of China, Duan Qirui, through the practice of a great "dharma" which was "in response to a need (*ganying dafa*)."[27] Duan was said to be very surprised by this, and the event apparently increased his respect for the Nor lha Hutukhtu. The biography also implied that Duan studied the Buddha Dharma with the lama, though it does not state this directly and no other source confirms it.

In addition, Duan apparently "gave the Nor lha Hutukhtu permission to return to Khams to try to retake his lost territory" (fol. 4v). The language of the biography suggests that the Nor lha Hutukhtu was seeking support for his former rule, rather than that the Chinese were seeking to utilize his good services to retake the area. The northern Chinese had their own problems at the time, and Tibet was far away and far from a priority. Another version of the Nor lha Hutukhtu's biography adds that Duan gave him one thousand Chinese *yuan* in cash (fol. 8v). Be that as it may, by the autumn of 1925, Duan was already losing the support of the warlords who had placed him in control of the Beijing government.[28] When Duan resigned his office in April 1926, the Nor lha Hutukhtu was left without even this weak patronage.

This problem was solved when a warlord leader of Sichuan province, named Liu Xiang, heard about the Nor lha Hutukhtu.[29] His career as a teacher to Chinese Buddhists blossomed in the next three years, during which time he built up a huge following in Chongqing. We are told that after the Nor lha Hutukhtu transmitted the esoteric teachings, his disciples numbered over ten thousand. In the words of his biographer, "the Guru went from none to an abundance [of students]." The one English-language biography I have found of the Nor lha Hutukhtu simply states that he "was invited to Szechuan by Gen. Liu Hsiang to preach Buddhism [in] 1926 and won many converts to the faith,"[30] It is doubtful whether the Nor lha Hutukhtu would have considered his disciples "converts," as most were probably already Buddhists, but Tibetan Buddhism and Chinese Buddhism probably appeared different enough to the Western observer to merit this term.

The Nor lha Hutukhtu's ritual activities were marked by a combination of tradition and modernity that is remarkably similar to Tibetan Buddhist practices in the West today. For example, in the spring of 1927, he held a "Dharma assembly for peace *(heping fa hui)*" that lasted forty-nine days. The event was held on the second floor of a Chinese company's office in Chongqing. Common laypeople were permitted to attend the esoteric ceremony.[31] Both of these conditions were new in the realm of Sino-Tibetan relations. Under the auspices of the Qing dynasty, such rituals were performed at court-supported temples dedicated to the practice of Tibetan Buddhism. Only the Buddhist elite and the imperial family would have taken part in such ceremonies, though they too had been for the benefit of both the dynasty (and by extension, the country) and the people.

In other respects this situation also anticipated the modern, and soon to be global, diffusion of Tibetan Buddhism. Instead of being initiated by the state, these ceremonies were privately sponsored by common people with business connections. At the same time, they were public events, open to anyone, rather being restricted to an imperial elite. Westerners accept as normal the events of 1991, when the Dalai Lama taught in New York's Madison Square Garden and a sand mandala was displayed at the IBM office building, but the Nor lha Hutukhtu was the pioneer in this move into nonreligious space. Even the Panchen Lama continued to teach in temples or imperial palaces until the 1930s.

The next spring, in 1928, the Nor lha Hutukhtu held a one-hundred-day "great Dharma assembly for prayers *(qidao da fa hui)*" (fol. 4v). At this assembly, a vajra-mandala was constructed. Though such mandalas had previously been constructed in imperially sponsored temples or within the imperial palace, this new public construction of a mandala again anticipated exiled Tibetan Buddhist activities on the global stage. In introducing this phenomenon's appearance in America, Jensine Andresen noted that the first public display of a sand mandala took place in China, and this particular occurrence predates the one she noted by four years. As in the United States, where some fifty mandalas were constructed between 1988 and 1997, this became somewhat of a regular practice in China.[32] Moreover, this activity did not merely draw an anonymous fringe of Chinese Buddhists; many officials sent either telegrams or representatives to attend such ceremonies.

If the Nor lha Hutukhtu's main goal in coming to China had been to regain power in his native region of Khams, he had made little direct progress in his first five years of exile. He gained permission to make the attempt and secured limited financial support, but far from the contested region and from a warlord on his way out of power. Nevertheless, his time was not entirely wasted, as he built up a large following among the Chinese in Sichuan. In the end, the Nor lha Hutukhtu's efforts at cultivating Chinese Buddhists as his disciples had the positive result of bringing him to the attention of the central government. As was the case for the Panchen Lama, only after all of China united under the Nationalist government was the Nor lha Hutukhtu's influence actually brought to bear on political questions.

Sometime after the Panchen Lama had received his title and honors from the government, he requested the right to set up offices to handle his affairs. The first such office was apparently located in a temple in Beijing with government approval. However, at that time, the government neither funded nor otherwise oversaw the offices. Far from being part of a government ploy to enlist the services of this prominent Tibetan Buddhist in Chinese schemes, the offices were the result of Tibetan initiative. On the basis of linguistic evidence, the Panchen Lama appears to have adapted an old Qing institution to his own purposes.[33] I suspect that their principal reason for existence was to handle the business affairs that accompanied the massive donations made by the Panchen Lama's Buddhist followers. For most of 1926, the Panchen Lama was teaching in Chinese Buddhist temples around the capital. In mid-September he gave an initiation into the tantric practice of the Amitabha Buddha to lay and monastic Buddhists. One feature of tantric initiation is the often substantial donations made to the teacher of such liberating techniques. It seems likely that these initiates' donations provided both the reason and the funding for creating offices that would handle the Panchen Lama's affairs.

From late 1926 until early 1929, the Panchen Lama lived among the Mongol adherents of Tibetan Buddhism in Inner Mongolia. During this period, he started to perform initiations into the Kalachakra Tantra. The ceremonies that conferred these initiations attracted enormous crowds (eighty thousand Mongols were said to have attended each of the first three initiations into this tantra) and brought the Panchen Lama much prestige and many rich donations. As Andresen noted in researching the Kalachakra tantra in America, "economically, western patronage of Kalachakra provides an important source of financial support for exiled Tibetans."[34] The growth of the number and the institutional development of the Panchen Lama's offices were no doubt given great impetus by similar donations.

THE POLITICIZATION OF THE TIBETAN BUDDHIST MISSIONS ABROAD

The real politicization of the Tibetan Buddhist leaders in China did not occur until 1929, after the success of Chiang Kai-shek's Northern Expedition had suppressed the warlords of north China and opened the way for a truly centralized government. The new Nationalist government was much more willing to involve these Tibetan Buddhist lamas in the politics of China. The Panchen Lama had sent his envoys to offer his congratulations to the new regime in Nanjing in the spring of 1928. By January 11 of the following year, the "Office of the Panchen's resident in [the capital] Nanjing to handle official affairs (Banchan zhu [Nan]jing bangong chu)" was officially established. For the first time in the history of modern China, the government had created a special office for a Tibetan Buddhist hierarch. To mark the establishment of this office, the government issued a proclamation of its opening, a chart of the organization of the office, and detailed rules and regulations to guide how affairs were to be managed there.[35] In the meantime, the Panchen Lama established additional offices, one in Taiyuan (located on the main road between Inner Mongolia and Nanjing) and one in Khams.[36] In this way, the previously religious nature of the Panchen Lama's role in exile was transformed into an official one, with a political administration.

After having established these offices, the Panchen Lama remained in Inner Mongolia for two more years. During this period, he communicated with Chiang Kai-shek, the leader of China. Judging from the content of the letters exchanged between the two men, it seems that the Panchen Lama was trying to see what sort of political support he could gain from Chiang Kai-shek. Specifically, in April 1930, he requested military supplies—five thousand rifles, a quarter of a million rounds of ammunition, five thousand uniforms, and funds to pay soldiers—to be used against a bogus Nepalese "invasion" of Tibet.[37] The Nationalists, who probably understood this request as the attempt to create a private army that it was, shrewdly linked the supplying of these items to the Panchen Lama's agreement to provisions that would have eliminated Tibetan autonomy entirely, at least in principle. So he refused these conditions and received no military aid. Despite the official cooperation and ongoing communication between these two men, neither the Nationalist government nor the Panchen Lama was to have their wishes fulfilled at that time. The similarity between this situation and the negotiations that arose between the Tibetan government and the CIA in 1951 is remarkable and will be discussed later.

In 1929, just months after having established the Panchen Lama's office in the capital, the central government summoned the Nor lha Hutukhtu from Sichuan province to the capital in Nanjing. Once there, he was made a member of the Mongolian and Tibetan Affairs Commission. An office similar to the Panchen Lama's, called the "Office of the Hutukhtu's resident in [the capital] Nanjing to handle affairs (Hutuketu zhu [Nan]jing banshi chu),"[38] was then established, while three branch offices were eventually set up in Chongqing, Chengdu, and Kangding. The concentration of these three offices in the single province of Sichuan demonstrates the more limited scope of the Nor lha Hutukhtu's influence compared to that of the Panchen Lama.[39] Because his influence was most important for securing the loyalty of the Tibetans in Khams, he was also made a member of the commission to establish the province of Xikang.

The Nor lha Hutukhtu's presence in the capital was also important for the foreign community. The Nationalist government could counter Tibetan claims that the contested Tibetan region of Khams belonged to Tibet if they had a spokesman from that region within their own government. In the 1933 supplement to *Who's Who in China*, the compilers gullibly reported that the Nor lha Hutukhtu was the "former secular and religious ruler of Hsikang [Khams]."[40] This was an obvious error in fact, as the Nor lha Hutukhtu had only ruled a small portion of Khams. Nevertheless, the ignorance of westerners living in China and the prestige conferred on this individual by the Chinese government were a powerful combination. Not only was the Nor lha Hutukhtu given positions within institutions that dealt with Inner Asia, he was also made a member of the legislature (*lifa weiyuan*). Though this governmental body was actually powerless in the Nationalist party-state, few foreigners were fully aware of this at the time. Thus, after an initial period of avoidance of or exclusion from the political realm, both the Panchen Lama and the Nor lha Hutukhtu had been welcomed into the Chinese government bureaucracy. However, although their influence was brought to bear on the ethnic and territorial problems China faced at that time, these men were pursuing their own interests as well.

While the Panchen Lama and the Nor lha Hutukhtu were being officially recognized in these various capacities by Chiang Kai-shek, the Dalai Lama was also in communication with China's new leader. In 1928 the Nationalist government claimed that it would remain true to Sun Yat-sen's policy of "equality for all nationalities of the country." Encouraged by this stance, the Dalai Lama sent his resident representative to Nanjing. This exchange, which was heralded as "the beginning of contact between Tibet and the KMT [Nationalist] government," followed the initiative of the Panchen Lama by almost half a year, giving the impression that the central Tibetans were trying to keep up with the Panchen Lama's efforts.[41]

Given the presence of the Panchen Lama's office in the capital since early 1929, the central Tibetan government must have begun to worry about the possibility that he could undermine its de facto independence by cooperating too closely with the Chinese. Later that year, the abbot of the Yonghe Gong monastery in Beijing, who had been appointed to the post by the Dalai Lama, went to Nanjing and conveyed to Chiang Kai-shek that the Tibetan government was friendly to China and welcomed the Panchen Lama's return. The abbot, Kön chok jung nay, continued on to Tibet, carrying Chiang's message to the Dalai Lama. When he returned to China in 1931, he was made the Dalai Lama's chief resident representative in Nanjing. Adapting a former Qing religiopolitical institution to the modern context of overtly political offices, the Dalai Lama transferred an abbot at what had been the primary imperial Tibetan Buddhist temple in the old capital in Beijing to serve as his representative to the Chinese government at the new capital. Thus, in 1931 an "Office of Tibet" was set up in Nanjing.[42] Originally, the Chinese had wanted the office to be called merely the "Dalai Lama's Representative Office" (Tib. Tâ la'i don gcod khang), which would have put it on par with the Panchen Lama's office. However, his representatives insisted that the office represented Tibet and not merely the Dalai Lama.[43]

The creation of this office in China was a significant precedent for the later globalization of such offices. At present, the Dalai Lama's government-in-exile has Offices of Tibet in New York, Geneva, London, New Delhi, Paris, Zürich, Budapest, Moscow, Tokyo, Taipei, Washington, D.C., and Kathmandu, as well as in South Africa and Australia.[44] The first of these overseas offices were CIA-sponsored centers for the coordination of a National Security Agency (NSA) Special Group program built "around the Dalai Lama to heighten a sense of nation among his refugee constituency and to keep his cause before the international community." This 1.7-million-dollar program was funded by the NSA. An annual budget of US$150,000 was given to the fourteenth Dalai Lama's older brother, Gya lo don drub, to run the first two offices set up in New York and Geneva.[45] Ken Knaus, the former CIA officer in charge of Tibetan operations, reported that in 1963 the U.S. State Department was willing to allow a New York office as an "unofficial embassy" for Tibet and informed India of this permission (Knaus 1999:283, 310). Unlike the Panchen Lama and the Nor lha Hutukhtu's offices, these new Offices of Tibet are similar to the Dalai Lama's office in China, having served political purposes from the start.

Knaus credited an American adviser to the Tibetans with the idea of creating these offices, though he acknowledged that Gya lo don drub "readily recognized that they would provide the Dalai Lama with unofficial representation" (ibid:282). Given that Gya lo don drub had been intimately familiar with the offices in China, I suspect that he played a significant role in the creation of these CIA-funded offices.[46] In any case, the Dalai Lama's offices in China, and initially in the United States and elsewhere, were very different from those of the Panchen Lama and the Nor lha Hutukhtu in China in that they did not provide for a religious mission. They were purely political offices, functioning principally as unofficial embassies. Since 1974, when the United States eliminated such aid to the Tibetans as part of its renewed relations with China (ibid.:310), the various Offices of Tibet have come to coordinate both the religious and political roles of the Dalai Lama. In this respect they now resemble those of his fellow Tibetans in China earlier in the century.

UNITING RELIGION AND POLITICS

Although I have been able to periodize the Tibetan Buddhist mission to China into neatly divided "religious" and "political" sections, the men examined here would certainly not have compartmentalized their lives in the same way. I suspect that they would have felt neither that they were using religion to achieve political ends nor that their involvement in politics was merely some "expedient means" to be employed in the spread of religion. Rather, they likely felt that the political and religious concerns were linked in a most natural way. They were Buddhist leaders and had been ousted from their rightful place in the cultural context in which they were raised. Given these circumstances, they did whatever was necessary and appropriate within the confines of the situation and their worldview to restore themselves to power. In the meantime, spreading Tibetan Buddhism allowed them both to practice the religion so central to their world and to build up the political power that accompanies being a celebrity in the modern world.

From 1931 to 1935, the Nor lha Hutukhtu's popularity grew immensely. His biography states that he had disciples from all provinces of China.[47] He traveled and taught in Beijing, Tianjin, Chongqing, Shanghai, Hangzhou, Guangzhou, Nanchang, Wuhan, and Changsha, while being based in the capital, Nanjing (fol. 9r). He taught an impressive array of Tibetan tantric cycles over the six years when he was based in the capital. These included cycles of teachings dedicated to Amitabha Buddha, the Medicine Buddha, the bodhisattvas Avalokitesvara and Green Tara, Padmasambhava, and a host of tantric deities previously unknown to the Chinese. His disciples set up the the Nor lha Students' Society to provide funds to support his living and travel expenses, as well as for the publication of his teachings.[48] We are told that he initiated twenty thousand disciples into the esoteric teachings of Tibetan Buddhism. Although no gender ratio can be determined, the Nor lha Hutukhtu's biography, unlike those of other figures in China at that time, does mention that he had women disciples.[49] His experience anticipated that of dozens of teachers who have come to America: without the status of the Panchen or Dalai Lamas, such men have relied on a devoted following of students. Devotees' supporting their lama was certainly nothing new to the Tibetan Buddhist tradition; however, the formation of particular societies dedicated to this purpose appears to be a modern phenomenon that has reached new heights in America.[50]

Prior to 1929, the Nor lha Hutukhtu had had a decidedly local influence tied closely to his home region, as it was nominally controlled from the very provincial capital in which he lived. After 1929, the Nor lha Hutukhtu became a national figure for the Chinese. He represented the interests of the nation and not just the local concerns of an exiled Tibetan Buddhist leader. By embracing this role, he both gave the Chinese Nationalists his religious and political support and earned for himself their trust. The differences between the current Dalai Lama's relationship to foreign governments and the Nor lha Hutukhtu's relationship with the Chinese government are most pronounced in this respect. Although the Dalai Lama has become an international figure, he has never been offered or accepted a position or title from any other government body.

For the Nor lha Hutukhtu, the culmination of this trust was the Nationalist government's conferral of the title Pacification Commissioner of Xikang. This abrupt assignment to an officially political role was occasioned by the Communist Long March through the Nor lha Hutukhtu's native Tibetan region of Khams. In August 1935, the Nor lha Hutukhtu went to Kangding and assembled the important religious and political figures of the region to explain the position of the Nationalist government and the threat of the Communists.[51] Nevertheless, he failed to prevent the Communist advance, or even to return to his homeland before his death in 1936. In the end, although the Nor lha Hutukhtu was able to use the influence gained over all his years of missionizing in China to secure the support of the Chinese government in returning to his homeland, he failed to retake his former domains.

Meanwhile, the differences between the Panchen Lama and Chiang Kai-shek had been resolved by February 1931, when the Nationalists invited the Panchen Lama to the National Conference to be held later that year. He accepted and on May 4 was welcomed to Nanjing by a huge crowd of people—official representatives from all government ministries, councils, and commissions, as well as "several tens of thousands of citizens and students."[52] The next day the Panchen Lama met with Chiang Kai-shek and throughout the period was housed in his headquarters. From that time, the Panchen Lama took a stand in support of Chinese policy toward Tibet while the Chinese government solidly backed the Panchen Lama. No doubt this open and public acknowledgment of the position that China had consistently maintained toward Tibet was the deciding factor in the close relations the Chinese government now adopted toward the Panchen Lama. A similar situation governed the United States' support for the Dalai Lama. In 1951, when the fourteenth Dalai Lama was in India trying to decide whether to return to an occupied Tibet, the State Department conditioned support for Tibetan autonomy upon the Dalai Lama's disavowal of the Seventeen Point Agreement made with the Chinese, as well as a promise to resist the Communist regime. At that time, the Dalai Lama refused to agree to such externally imposed conditions and was refused overt aid by the Americans.

By late 1932, the Nationalist government rewarded the Panchen Lama for his support of China's titular sovereignty over Tibet. They publicly granted him a title that suggested a more political orientation while preserving the religious elements of its precedents, Protector of the Nation, Propagator of Transformation, Great Master of Infinite Wisdom. With such government recognition, he enjoyed an enormous surge in popularity. The Chinese government also committed itself to supplying an annual subsidy of 120,000 *yuan* to the Panchen Lama.[53] Likewise, when the Dalai Lama repudiated the Seventeen Point Agreement in 1959, the U.S. government agreed to support him and his government-in-exile with a yearly subsidy of US$175,000.[54]

As with the Nor lha Hutukhtu, the conferral of official recognition brought with it a whole new level of missionizing activity. The most important were Kalachakra rituals. Although the Panchen Lama had given the Kalachakra initiation to enormous crowds in Tibetan Buddhist Inner Mongolia, the practice of this ritual among the Chinese was unprecedented. The first ceremony, held in the Forbidden City in Beijing, accommodated as many as one hundred thousand people by some estimates. The second, held in 1934 in Hangzhou, was said to have been attended by some seventy thousand.[55] Admittedly, these numbers represent a tiny proportion of the Chinese population at that time (roughly 500 million), nevertheless, it represents over 150 times the proportion of Americans who have attended the Dalai Lama's Kalachakra ceremonies in the United States. Few Americans or Tibetans are aware that the performance of the Kalachakra for foreign audiences was first popularized in China.

The growth of the Panchen Lama's religious popularity was accompanied by an increasing political importance. At the end of 1932, he was granted a purely political office for the first time. He was to serve as the Western Borderland Publicity Commissioner, whose job it was "to publicize the desires of the central government to the borderland . . . [and] to propagate, with the help of religious belief, the Three People's Principles, teachings of the late Director-General Sun Yat-sen."[56] In this way, the Tibetan Buddhists had brought the Chinese around to their perspective: religion and politics had to go hand in hand when trying to settle relations between China and Tibet. Following a different tradition, in the United States propaganda was handled by a public relations firm hired by the CIA to help the Tibetans make their anti-Communist case in 1959.[57]

In return for his help, throughout 1933 the Chinese government assisted the Panchen Lama in negotiating with the Tibetan government permission for the Panchen Lama's return to Tibet. His last major public appearance in China, just days after the second Kalachakra ceremony, was to be his best attended event. According to Chinese sources, he lectured in Shanghai to a crowd of three hundred thousand on the topic "Mongolia and Tibet are China's important frontiers." By July 1934 he had set off for the western borderlands to carry out his duties and, it was hoped, return to Tibet. Like the Nor lha Hutukhtu, the Panchen Lama had finally secured the support of the Chinese government in his attempt to return to his former domains. Also like the Nor lha Hutukhtu, he was ultimately to die (in 1937, in the borderlands between China and Tibet) unsuccessful in his effort to return to his former position of authority.

CONCLUSION

Despite their cooperation with Chinese politicians, these Tibetan Buddhists were pursuing their own goals. In order to return to their previous positions, they sought the financial and military backing that only the Chinese government could have provided. In fact, as religious figures cooperating with the Chinese government, they established an important pattern for the future of Sino-Tibetan relations. As is still the case today, Chinese politicians were forced to work with the religious leaders of Tibet to try to maintain control over the populace in the region.

At the same time, these men invented and adapted strategies for dealing with the new challenges of a modernized world. They taught religion and gathered disciples when there was no way to enter into the political life, but accepted and often initiated political contacts and institutions when this was possible. Finally, they succeeded in combining religion and politics in an almost seamless fashion, linking their religious activities with their political causes.

For those who are privy to the world of Tibetan Buddhism in America today, this may well sound a familiar note. With regard to nationalism, the current Dalai Lama—whether or not he coordinated his plans with the American government —has fulfilled the 1963 goal of the NSA's Special Group: he continues to serve as the key rallying point for the Tibetan nationalist movement. And, like the lamas in China, he taught religion to foreigners as long as he felt that that was his only option. In his *The Making of Modern Tibet*, Grunfeld cynically (though probably accurately) described this early period as one in which "[Tibetan] Buddhist monasteries, study groups, rural communes, and even an accredited college . . . have converted hundreds, if not thousands, to their religious beliefs—thereby creating a large, receptive audience for their political beliefs."[58] He also prophetically noted, as he completed the writing for the first edition in 1985, that the Dalai Lama's "spiritual role . . . far outweighs his political functions—for the time being" (Grunfeld 1996:210).

This balance of religion and politics did change after 1985. As Grunfeld reported in his second edition, the Dalai Lama has always officially come to the United States only as a religious leader of the Tibetan people. However, since the "Tibet lobby" has enlisted a powerful law firm to serve as its United States agents for the Tibetan government-in-exile, the Dalai Lama has had decidedly more of an international political force.[59] At present, he, like the lamas before him in China, has also succeeded in uniting religion and politics abroad, as anyone who has attended one of his large public events will readily acknowledge. Whatever the different causes that resulted in these diverse missions to China and now to the world, the strategies have remained true to tradition while at the same time evolving in new—but surprisingly parallel—directions.

Notes

1. In this analysis I am indebted to the work of the prominent late Tibetologist, Dung dkar Blo bzang 'phrin las, *The Merging of Religious and Secular Rule in Tibet*, trans. Chen Guansheng (Beijing: Foreign Languages, 1991), and David Ruegg, *Ordre spirituel et ordre temporel dans la pensée Bouddhique de l'Inde et du Tibet*, Publications de l'Institut de Civilisation Indienne (Paris: Collège de France, 1995).

2. Ruegg, *Ordre spirituel*, 34–37.

3. P. Christiaan Klieger, *Tibetan Nationalism: The Role of Patronage in the Accomplishment of a National Identity* (Berkeley, Calif.: Folklore Institute, 1992), 20.

4. Gray Tuttle, *Faith and Nation: Tibetan Buddhists in the Making of Modern China (1902–1958)* (New York: Columbia University Press, in press).

5. Bstan 'dzin rgya mtsho, Dalai Lama XIV, *Freedom in Exile: The Autobiography of the Dalai Lama* (New York: Harper Collins, 1990), 202.

6. Franz Michael, *Rule by Incarnation: Tibetan Buddhism and Its Role in Society and State* (Boulder, Colo.: Westview, 1982), 40-50.

7. Ya Hanzhang, *Biographies of the Tibetan Spiritual Leaders Panchen Erdenis*, trans. Chen Guansheng, Li Peizhu (Beijing: Foreign Languages, 1994), 258-260.

8. Ken Knaus, *Orphans of the Cold War: America and the Tibetan Struggle for Survival* (New York: Public Affairs, 1999), 275.

9. Han Dazai, *Kang-Zang Fojiao yu Xikang Nona Hutuketu yinghua shilüe* [Brief account of Khams-Tibetan Buddhism and the manifestation of the Nor lha Hutukhtu of Khams] (1937), fols. 4r, 8v. I want to thank Professor Lawrence Epstein and Peng Wenbin of the University of Washington for alerting me to the presence of this text.

10. Two conflicting dates are given in Han (*Kang-Zang Fojiao*) for his arrival in Beijing: Mar. 15, 1924 (fol. 4v) and Oct. 15, 1925 (fol. 8v). Other sources, including Holmes Welch, *The Buddhist Revival in China*, Harvard East Asian Series, 33 (Cambridge, Mass.: Harvard University Press, 1968), 175, indicate that he was present in Beijing in 1924, so I have accepted this date.

11. Knaus, *Orphans of the Cold War*, 88–103, 140. Instead, a chain of intermediaries informed him (at least partially) of the negotiations of his older brothers. However, it should be noted that they were not officially the Dalai Lama's representatives and at times followed their own agenda.

12. Roger Hicks and Ngakpa Chogyam, *Great Ocean: An Authorized Biography of the Bud-*

dhist Monk Tenzin Gyatso His Holiness the Fourteenth Dalai Lama (New York: Penguin, 1990 [1984]), 164.

13. Rick Fields, *How the Swans Came to the Lake: A Narrative History of Buddhism in America* (Boulder, Colo.: Shambala, 1981), 378; Jensine Andresen, "Kalacakra: Textual and Ritual Perspectives" (Ph.D. diss., Harvard University, 1997), 15–16.

14. Ya, *Panchen Erdenis*, 261.

15. Fabienne Jaguo, "A Pilgrim's Progress: The Peregrinations of the 6th Panchen Lama," *Lungta* 1, no. 10 (1996): 6, 14.

16. Welch, *The Buddhist Revival in China*, 157.

17. Hicks and Ngakpa Chogyam, *Great Ocean*, 164.

18. Tsering Shakya, *The Dragon in the Land of Snows: A History of Modern Tibet since 1947* (London: Pimlico, 1999), 416.

19. Bstan 'dzin rgya mtsho, *Freedom in Exile*, 203.

20. Fields, *Buddhism in America*, 291–293.

21. Welch, *The Buddhist Revival in China*, 251.

22. Ibid., 239.

23. These were probably Mexican silver dollars.

24. For photographs of Qing examples of a golden certificate, see entry 74, and of a golden seal, entry 71, in *A Collection of the Historical Archives of Tibet* (Beijing: Wenwu chubanshe, 1995).

25. Ya Hanzhang, *The Biographies of the Dalai Lamas*, trans. Wang Wenjiong (Beijing: Foreign Languages, 1991), 263.

26. Ya, *Panchen Erdenis*, 264; Danzhu Angfen, *Liwei Dalai lama yu Banchan erdeni nianpu* [Chronicle of the genealogy of the Dalai Lama and Panchen Erdeni] (Beijing: Zhongyang minzu daxue chubanshe, 1998), 637–638.

27. Han, *Kang-Zang Fojiao*, fol. 4v. What exactly occurred is left to the reader's imagination.

28. Joseph K. H. Cheng, Richard C. Howard, and Howard L. Boorman, eds., *Biographical Dictionary of Republican China*, 3 vols. (1970), 3:335.

29. Han, *Kang-Zang Fojiao*, fols. 4v, 8v–9r.

30. Jerome Cavanaugh and Chinese Materials Center, *Who's Who in China, 1918–1950, with an index*, 1933 supplement ed. (Hong Kong: Chinese Materials Center, 1982 [1933]), 82.

31. Han, *Kang-Zang Fojiao*, fol. 4v.

32. Andresen, "Kalacakra," 238.

33. For details, see Tuttle, "Faith and Nation," 198.

34. Andresen, "Kalacakra," 17.

35. Danzhu Angfen, *Nianpu*, 639.

36. In May 1929 and April 1930, respectively; see Danzhu Angfen, *Nianpu*, 640.

37. Li Pengnian and Fang Qingqiu, eds., *Jiushi Banchan neidi huodong ji fanzang shuoxian dang'an xuanbian* [Selections from the archives concerning the ninth Panchen's activities in China and the restrictions on his return to Tibet] (Beijing: Zhongguo Zangxue chubanshe, 1992), 15–17.

38. In Tibetan, this institution was simply called Norlha's Representative Office (Nor lha don gcod khang); see Thub bstan sangs rgyas, *Rgya nag tu Bod kyi sku tshab*, 44.

39. Han, *Kang-Zang Fojiao*, fols. 5r, 9r; Sichuan sheng difang zhi bianji wciyuanhui, Sheng zhi renwu zhi bianji and Ren Yimin, eds., *Sichuan jin xiandai renwu zhuan* [Biographies of Sichuan's contemporary figures], vol. 1 (Chengdu: Sichuan sheng shehui kexue yuan chubanshe, 1985), 291.

40. Cavanaugh and Chinese Materials Center, *Who's Who in China*, 81.

41. Ya, *Dalai Lamas*, 341; Thub bstan sangs rgyas, *Rgya nag tu Bod kyi sku tshab*, 25–26

42. Ya, *Dalai Lamas*, 342, 345–346; Goldstein, 214, 219; Thub bstan sangs rgyas (*Rgya nag tu Bod kyi sku tshab*, 55) provided an English translation of this office's name in Tibetan transcription, the "Bureau of Tibet" (Tib. Be 'u ru 'u/ Ob/ Kri bi kri).

43. For a full history of the office, see Thub bstan sangs rgyas, *Rgya nag tu Bod kyi sku tshab*.

44. The official web site of the Tibetan Government-in-exile: www.tibet.com

45. Knaus, *Orphans of the Cold War*, 275, 282.

46. Gya lo don drub frequented the Tibet Office while studying in Nanjing from 1947 to 1949. However, his relations with this office and the conservative officials it represented were tense. Knaus, *Orphans of the Cold War*, 48–49; Mary Craig, *Kundun: A Biography of the Family of the Dalai Lama* (Washington, D.C.: Counterpoint, 1997), 134.

47. Han, *Kang-Zang Fojiao*, fol. 5v.

48. Welch, *The Buddhist Revival in China*, 175.

49. Han, *Kang-Zang Fojiao*, fols. 3r, 6v. He also tried to improve the status of women in Khams.

50. Alexander Berzin, *Relating to a Spiritual Teacher* (Ithaca, N.Y.: Snow Lion, 2000), 16.

51. Han, *Kang-Zang Fojiao*, fol. 9r.

52. Ya, *Panchen Erdenis*, 271–272; Danzhu Angfen, *Nianpu*, 641.

53. Danzhu Angfen, *Nianpu*, 642; Jaguo, "A Pilgrim's Progress," 16.

54. Knaus, *Orphans of the Cold War*, 275, 310.

55. Ya, *Panchen Erdenis*, 274, 284.

56. Ibid.; italics added.

57. Knaus, *Orphans of the Cold War*, 204.

58. Thomas A. Grunfeld, *The Making of Modern Tibet*, rev. ed. (New York: M. E. Sharpe, 1996 [1985]), 209.

59. Grunfeld, 230–240; see also Shakya, *The Dragon in the Land of Snows*, 412–416.

List of Contributors

Stuart Chandler is an assistant professor at Indiana University of Pennsylvania, where he teaches about the religions of China and Japan. His dissertation at Harvard University analyzed the modernization and globalization of the Foguang Shan Buddhist order. He has also been very involved with the Pluralism Project, a multiyear enterprise tracking the emergence of Buddhist, Hindu, Sikh, Jain, Islamic, and other religious communities in the United States.

Peter B. Clarke is a professor of the history and sociology of religion at the University of London, King's College. He is founding and present coeditor of the *Journal of Contemporary Religion* and has researched contemporary religions in Africa, Brazil, Japan, and Western Europe. His books include *Japanese New Religions in the West* (ed., 1994), *An Annotated Bibliography of New Religions in the West* (1997), *New Trends and Developments in the World of Islam* (ed., 1998), *An Annotated Bibliography of Japanese New Religions in the West* (1999), and *Japanese New Religions in Global Perspective* (1999).

C. Julia Huang is an assistant professor at the Institute of Anthropology, National Tsing Hua University, Taiwan. She received her Ph.D. in anthropology from Boston University and completed a postdoctoral fellowship at the Institute for Human Sciences, Vienna, and a senior fellowship at the Center for the Study of World Religions, Harvard University. Her research focuses on religion, charisma, and transnationalism. She is currently finishing a book on the topic.

Steven Kemper is a professor of anthropology at Bates College. He is the author of *The Presence of the Past: Chronicles, Politics, and Culture in Sinhala Life* (1991) and *Buying and Believing: Sri Lankan Advertising and Consumers in a Transnational World* (2001). His research interests range from monasticism to transnational forces such as advertising and Western models of education.

Linda Learman received her A.M. from the University of Illinois, Urbana-Champaign, in Asian studies and her Ph.D. in anthropology from Boston University. Her dissertation focused on religion, marriage, and modernity in Taiwan. She organized the conference, The Globalization of Buddhism: Case Studies of Buddhist Missions, on which this book is based.

Sarah LeVine is a research associate in human development and psychology, Harvard Graduate School of Education. Her books include *Mothers and Wives: Gusii Women of East Africa* (1979) and *Dolor Y Alegria: Women and Social Change in Urban Mexico* (1993).

Richard K. Payne is dean of the Institute of Buddhist Studies at the Graduate Theological Union, Berkeley, where he is also a member of the doctoral faculty. He is the author of *Tantric Ritual of Japan* and editor of *Re-Visioning "Kamakura" Buddhism*, as well as being the chair of the editorial board of *Pacific World: Journal of the Institute of Buddhist Studies*. His main area of research is Shingon ritual, and he is currently working on developing a cognitive theory of ritual.

Cristina Rocha received her Ph.D. from the University of Western Sydney, Australia. Her publications include: "Zen Buddhism in Brazil: Japanese or Brazilian?" *Journal of Global Buddhism* 1 (2000); "Catholicism and Zen Buddhism: A Vision of the Religious Field in Brazil," in *The End of Religion? Religion in an Age of Globalisation*, ed. Carole Cusack and Peter Oldmeadow (2001); "The Brazilian Imaginaire on Zen: Global Influences, Rhizomatic Forms," in *Japanese Religions in and beyond the Japanese Diaspora*, ed. Ronan Pereira and Hideaki Matsuoka (forthcoming); "Zen in Brazil: Cannibalizing Orientalist Flows," in *Orientalism and Identity in Latin America*, ed. Eric Camayd-Freixas (forthcoming); and *Zen in Brazil: The Quest for Cosmopolitan Modernity* (forthcoming). She has been the recipient of a Urasenke Foundation scholarship (1992–1993) and a Japan Foundation fellowship (2000).

George J. Tanabe, Jr., is a professor of Japanese religion in the Department of Religion at the University of Hawai'i. He has authored *Myōe the Dreamkeeper: Fantasy and Knowledge in Early Kamakura Buddhism* (1992), coauthored *Practically Religious: Worldly Benefits and the Common Religion of Japan* (1998), edited *Religions of Japan in Practice* (1999), and coedited the second edition of *Sources of Japanese Tradition* (2001).

Gray Tuttle received his Ph.D. from Harvard University and now teaches Asian history and religion at Trinity College. He specializes in the history of Tibetan Buddhist institutions and relations with the Mongol, Chinese, and Manchu rulers of China. The chapter in this volume is drawn from his dissertation, "Faith and Nation: Tibetan Buddhists in the Making of Modern China 1902–1958" (2002).

Index

missionaries, 1. *See also* Coen sensei; colonialism; economic development: and American foreign aid in Nepal and Anglo-American missions; Hunt, Ernest and Dorothy; romanticism

Wilson, Governor Pete, 173

women: and Anglo-American missions, 3; early Chinese Buddhist, 8; Han Buddhist, 186, 187, 190, 200–201, 202; Newar Buddhist, 11, 51, 57–58, 59–60, 67–72; Pentecostal, 4; and Tibetan Buddhism, 225, 231n. 49. See also *bhikkhuni* ordination; Coen sensei; Dhammawati, Venerable; Dharmacari, Venerable; Soka Gakkai: and women; Zhengyan, Venerable

World Fellowship of Buddhists (WFB), 34, 37, 43, 64

World Tathagata Movement (Korea), 37

Xa Loi Temple (Saigon), 36

Xia state, Western (China), 211

Xinding, Venerable, 175, 184n. 20

Xingyun, Venerable (or Hsing Yun): and *bhikkhuni* ordination, 46n. 27; and Boy Scouts, 107; on Buddhist missions, 9, 162, 170, 171; and Chinese diaspora, 163, 170; as founder of Buddha's Light International Association, 164; as founder of Foguang Shan, 162; and globalization, 162; on homeland, 170–171; and homelessness, 179–181; and Humanistic Buddhism, 182n. 5; and localization (*bentuhua*), 176–177; and the media, 175; and monastic disciples, 162, 169–170, 177; and politics, 172–175, 184n. 18; on religion and society, 174–175; retirement, 184n. 20; and Taixu, 212; and universalism, 180–181; and vow to globalize Buddhism, 171. *See also* Buddha's Light International Association; Foguang Shan; links of affinity

Yinshun, Venerable, 182n. 5, 189, 205n. 25, 206n. 31, 212

Yonghe Gong (Beijing), 216, 223

Young Buddhist Association (Y.B.A., Hawai'i), 90

Zen Buddhism, 1, 101, 114; and African-Brazilian religions, 153–154, 157; and conversion, 10, 39, 115, 125, 135, 156; creolization of, 149–158; and ecology, 148; and ethnic conflict, 140–142; as "funeral religion," 142, 150, 158; and healing, 155; and Japanese new religions, 156, 157; and the laity, 144–147, 148; and macrobiotics, 155; and martial arts, 155, 156; and the media, 115, 145–147, 151, 155; and meditation, 142, 143–144, 149, 155, 156; and modernism, 103, 115, 147–149; and New Age religion, 149, 154–155, 157; and psychoanalysis and psychotherapy, 146, 149, 155; and "reflexive syncretism," 135, 152; Sōtō Zen missionaries and congregations, 19n. 30, 96–97, 140–142, 157; and Spiritualism (including Kardecism and Umbanda), 151–154, 155, 157; and vegetarianism, 146, 155–156

Zen Center of Los Angeles (ZCLA), 140

Zengenji (Moji das Cruzes, Brazil), 143

Zhengyan (or Cheng-Yen), Venerable, 12, 16; biography of, 188–190; on Buddhist missions, 9; charismatic leadership of, 187, 192, 201, 203, 206n. 35; and filial piety, 188–189, 205n. 20; "Four Great Compassion Relief Missions" and "four footprints," 188, 195, 205n. 15; and Humanistic Buddhism, 182n. 5, 189; monastic disciples of, 198, 199, 208n. 49; and 1991 Philippine Magsaysay Award, 185; and nomination for Nobel Peace Prize, 185; and reform of Buddhism, 187–188, 203; Still Thoughts Abode (in Hualian, Taiwan), 193; and Taixu, 212; and universalism, 203. *See also* Buddhist Compassion Relief Tzu-Chi Foundation

Zurcher, Erik, 6

Production Notes for Learman/*Buddhist Missionaries in the Era of Globalization*
Cover and text design by Elsa Carl. Text in Goudy Old Style with display in Hiroshige
Composition by Tseng Information Systems, Inc.
Printing and binding by The Maple-Vail Book Manufacturing Group
Printed on 60 lb. Sebago Eggshell, 420 ppi